FORGED IN IRON

A Minnesota Rusyn Immigrant's Tale

Mary P. Soroko

HERITAGE BOOKS
2025

HERITAGE BOOKS

AN IMPRINT OF HERITAGE BOOKS, INC.

Books, CDs, and more—Worldwide

For our listing of thousands of titles see our website
at
www.HeritageBooks.com

Published 2025 by
HERITAGE BOOKS, INC.
Publishing Division
5810 Ruatan Street
Berwyn Heights, MD 20740

Copyright © 2025 Mary P. Soroko

Dedication: To my parents, grandparents, and all Iron Range immigrant families who quietly and courageously forged better lives for themselves and their children, inspiring their descendants with perseverance and strength.

To Emma and Andy for their unwavering love and support.

Cover photo from the Iron Range Research Center, Chisholm, Minnesota.

International Standard Book Number
Paperbound: 978-0-7884-5097-6

Preface

My paternal grandfather lived with my family when I was a young girl. At the time, I didn't see our living arrangement as an opportunity to learn about my heritage. I remember he pronounced his th's as d's and always had a prayer book in his pocket—but it never occurred to me that his childhood could have been any different from mine.

As the youngest grandchild, I was born after everyone had heard my grandfather's old country stories. He took pride in being a U.S. citizen and saw little reason to dwell on the past. Like most 20th-century immigrants, he believed his early life experiences would be of little interest to his American-born grandchildren. Nevertheless, he occasionally shared cherished memories from his earlier life—how he tended sheep, picked berries and mushrooms in the nearby mountains, and how his father enjoyed chasing him through the woods. He especially enjoyed retelling the story of the fiddle he won in a music contest; his entire face lit up as he hummed the prize-winning tune. Although entirely self-taught, Rusyn immigrants were highly esteemed for their musical talent. I, too, learned to play the violin by ear and had a gift for the performing arts.

My grandmother, Mary Syvak Soroka, passed away a year before I was born, but my dad often remarked on how much I embodied her spirit. We were both talented cooks and shared fiery tempers. As a teenager, my grandmother faced a life-altering decision: enter a convent or immigrate to the United States. She couldn't remember a time when she wasn't hungry. Many women chose the nunnery to escape starvation, the hardships of farming, the dangers of childbirth, or the unfortunate realities of marrying an abusive spouse. Mary wanted a family, so she decided to move to the United States. Her mother had little to offer, and her father had died years before. When I found the Ellis Island manifest that said she was destined for Chisholm, I felt like we shared a moment her death had long denied.

This book is my gift to them. Had they remained in Europe, I might never have been born. Despite having few resources, limited education, and minimal English-speaking skills, my grandparents completely transformed the trajectory of their lives. They did so with extraordinary courage, strong religious faith, and a determination to make something of their lives. Immigrants like my grandparents deserve the same recognition as the industrial titans of the Gilded Age, who shamelessly pocketed the fruits of their labor while remaining remarkably indifferent to their fates. Sadly, the millions of stories of those who sacrificed everything to make others rich are typically forgotten. While never amassing great wealth themselves, my grandparents and others like them achieved something no less extraordinary. They built America and defended democracy against tyranny in two world wars. According to the Minnesota Discovery Center, the Iron Range supplied 70% of the iron ore used by the United States during World War II, totaling over 333 million tons.

In authoring this book, I carry on the legacy of my late aunt, who shared my passion for genealogy, education, and my first and last name. Fate chose me to complete what she began fifty years ago. I am grateful to her for giving me a starting point for my research. I only hope she looks favorably upon my efforts from her heavenly vantage point.

Findings

Over the last decade, I discovered our family legends are only partially true. For example, my grandparents identified as Ukrainians but were, in fact, members of a Slavic minority known as Rusyns. Despite the cultural pride of the Rusyn people, our ethnicity remained a closely guarded secret, presumably to avoid being confused with Russians during the anticommunist era of my youth. In Europe, political elites condemned generations of Rusyns to relentless persecution. Seeking the isolation and protection of the Carpathian Mountains, Rusyns developed a distinct ethnic identity rooted in Eastern and Western European traditions, an awe-inspiring spiritual faith, a deep love of nature, and an unassuming way of life. Theirs was a multicultural world situated at the very crossroads of Europe. For centuries, my ancestors lived peaceably in a multilingual society, tilling substandard soil in an unforgiving terrain. Their governments labeled them as inferior for refusing to renounce their language, culture, and traditions—the only things they could truly call their own.

My great-grandfather, remembered by family members as a *Cossack*, urged my grandfather to leave the country before social instability could destroy him. I mistakenly assumed he meant a *Russian* Cossack and the *Russian* Revolution. However, at the time of his departure, all of Central and Eastern Europe was engulfed in demands for more egalitarian forms of government. Western nations, however, enjoyed unprecedented peace, prosperity, and freedom, seemingly making war seem like a relic of the past. Tragically, my great-grandfather's prophecy came true. World War I claimed the lives of an estimated 22 million people and resulted in the collapse of the Russian, Austro-Hungarian, and Ottoman Empires. An additional three million souls would fall victim to the Spanish flu. Twenty years later, the Nazis destroyed the remaining Rusyn communities, and the Poles forcibly deported many of the survivors to Soviet Ukraine.

Other Discoveries

Family members have long believed that the Sorokas descended from Vikings. My great-grandfather's flowing red hair, along with my fair complexion, supposedly supported this genetic association. Our ancestral homeland, situated on the western edge of Viking territory, was reputedly named after the Norseman who invaded the region centuries ago. However, recent archaeological findings suggest a different narrative that neither history nor genetics can fully explain.

There were also surprising revelations. My grandmother was one of three siblings who emigrated to the United States, yet we were completely unaware of their existence. Immigration permanently separated families, and economic burdens left them with little time to maintain family bonds. Fictional portrayals of immigrant households masked the harsh reality. I witnessed the tragic outcomes but could not identify the cause.

My grandfather was the eldest of nine children and the only member of his immediate family to move to the United States. Out of guilt, love, and loyalty, he sent whatever money he had to Europe until shortly before he died. His sister immigrated to Canada thirty years later, and one of his brothers was rumored to have gone to South America. While my grandfather never confessed to feeling homesick, his actions conveyed a different story. He spent countless hours recreating his boyhood village through an almost obsessive involvement with the Greek Catholic Church—time that family members often claimed would have been better spent at home. He settled in Chisholm, in a Rusyn community he helped establish, where he and other families struggled to uphold their faith and maintain connections with those they had left behind.

As children, we gathered wild berries in the old mining "locations." We picked mushrooms on the ore dumps outside Chisholm—but didn't realize these activities held cultural significance or fully understood that family members had once called the locations their home. Where I saw undergrowth, weeds, and ore-stained mud, they saw familiar streets and gardens.

Despite immense suffering, immediate family members who remained in Europe managed to survive. However, my grandparents gained personal freedoms, rights, and equal citizenship, which they had been denied for centuries. They escaped the near-constant turmoil that plagued their homeland well into the twentieth century. Had they stayed in Europe, my father would have been born in the Austro-Hungarian Empire, raised in Poland, resisted Nazi and Russian invasions, been deported to the USSR, lived under communist oppression, and ended his life in an independent Ukraine, where his Rusyn heritage would have been systematically erased.

Although their immediate living situation in the U.S. was not significantly better than in Europe, my grandparents' choices enabled future generations to build lives based on choice rather than desperation. Their story exemplifies the resilience of the human spirit. At times, I sensed their presence, guiding my research and even helping me think of an original title for this book.

As a young adult, I was often embarrassed about my modest origins. Today, I feel a deep sense of pride and am honored to say I am a part of their legacy.

Illustration .10: Photo of the Soroka Glenn location residence at the Minnesota Discovery Center in Chisholm, Minnesota.

Table of Contents

Photos, Illustrations, and Maps

How are Rusyns Different from Ukrainians?

1. **Ethnic Identity**
   - Rusyns identify as a distinct ethnic group with a unique cultural and historical identity. Several countries, including Slovakia, Poland, Hungary, and Serbia, recognize them as an ethnic minority.
   - Ukrainians identify as part of the larger Ukrainian nation, with a national identity tied to the modern state of Ukraine.

2. **Language**
   - Rusyns speak Rusyn, which some consider a distinct language and others a Ukrainian dialect. The Rusyn language has several regional variations or dialects.
   - Ukrainians speak Ukrainian, Ukraine's official language, in a standardized form.

3. **Geographical Distribution**
   - Rusyns predominantly inhabit the Carpathian Mountains, including parts of Slovakia, Poland, Hungary, Romania, and Serbia.
   - Ukrainians predominantly live in Ukraine, but there are also significant communities in Russia.

4. **Historical Context**
   - Rusyns have a history of being part of several states, including the Austro-Hungarian Empire, Poland, the Czech Republic, and Russia.

     Their identity has been suppressed or assimilated by neighboring cultures.

   - Ukrainians have a long history of striving for national independence, culminating in the establishment of the modern Ukrainian state in 1991.

5. **Cultural Practices**
   - Rusyns maintain distinct cultural traditions, including folk music, dance, and religious practices. Many Rusyns adhere to the Greek Catholic or Byzantine faith.

o   Ukrainians have a rich cultural heritage,
     including traditional music, dance, literature,
     and art. Most Ukrainians are Orthodox
     Christians. A minority adheres to the Greek
     Catholic Church.

Ukrainians share many words with other East Slavic
languages, such as Russian and Belarusian, as well as
influences from neighboring states. Rusyn contains
vocabulary distinct from Ukrainian and has influences from
Slovak, Hungarian, and other Central European languages.

Sources

Blanco, Cindy, Hope Wilson, and Mykhalo Zakryzhevskyy. "Language Matters: What Learners Need to Know about Ukrainian." Duolingo Blog. March 22, 2022. https://blog.duolingo.com/ukraine-language/.

Goodman, J., Caines, A., & Foley, R. (2023). Shibboleth: An agent-based model of signaling mimicry. Plos One, 18 (7), e0289333.

Magocsi, P. Robert. "Rusyn." *Encyclopedia Britannica*, February 1, 2022. https://www.britannica.com/topic/Rusyn-people.

Moser, M. (2016). Rusyn: A New-Old Language In-between Nations and States. In: Kamusella, T., Nomachi, M., Gibson, C. (eds) The Palgrave Handbook of Slavic Languages, Identities and Borders. Palgrave Macmillan, London. https://doi.org/10.1007/978-1-137-34839-5_

Introduction

My grandfather, Nicholas, was an artist who made his living mining iron and coal. He played his violin while sharing cultural anecdotes that celebrated humanity's virtues and poked fun at its flaws. Neighbors admired his talents, especially during the harsh winter months when ice and snow left them with little to do. His gray eyes sparkled as he performed Rusyn folk tunes, evoking warm memories of his youth. Hailing from a region bordering some of Europe's most vulnerable frontiers, Rusyns were accustomed to having little control over their lives. To cope, they balanced a fatalistic wit with an unwavering faith that all would be well as long as they heeded God's word.

Nicholas was a man of profound spirituality. I believe he would have studied to be a priest had he been the youngest child. (1) He carried a prayer book neatly marked with paper icons of revered saints. His faith was a constant source of strength and inspiration. He once shared the story of a young girl traveling through the Carpathian Mountains when, suddenly, a giant bear appeared, causing her to fear for her life. The terrified girl knelt and asked for God's protection, and the bear miraculously went on his way. In his broken English, he would say, *"Remember dis— because it is de power of God."*

My grandfather was deeply indebted to the United States for granting him freedom and citizenship. He often said that in the old country, people lived in constant fear. He asked his grandchildren to refrain from criticizing the United States, because its government provided them with protection and jobs, and the possibility of a better tomorrow. He loved his native village but was extremely thankful to have escaped communist rule. My sister remembers long conversations about how the Bolsheviks

---

(1) In traditional Rusyn families, older siblings often pursued the same occupations as their fathers, while younger children received an education. The older siblings earned their keep, while the younger ones nurtured their family's souls.

destabilized Europe. As communism spread, Greek Catholic churches were shuttered, and Rusyns were forced to adapt to the culture of the ethnic majority in the nation-state to which they belonged. Governments confiscated property owned by the "kulaks," or peasant landowners, and involuntarily resettled them on collective farms.

Nicholas had large, bruised hands, which he explained were the result of mining underground. "The ore is very sharp," he explained. He urged his fellow miners to negotiate for reciprocal benefits, such as insurance, medical coverage, and improved working conditions. He was troubled by the ongoing conflict between management and miners because he wanted them to develop a relationship based on shared interests and goals.

Like all immigrants, my grandfather embraced the American Dream, succumbing to schemes that promised great wealth. However, while his peers engaged in activities that could land them in jail, he prudently invested $100 in a California gold mine. At that time, this was a substantial sum. His ability to save so much while earning a dollar a day highlighted his determination to create a better life for his family.

So, what forces shaped him into the man he would ultimately become? Join me as I explore my family history.

Illustration .11: Nick Soroka with his favorite rum. (Personal Photo)

Illustration .12: Mary and Nick at my parents' wedding. (Personal Photo)

Chapter 1
Beginnings In The Old Country

Nicholas Soroka was born in November 1886 in a small village in the foothills of the Carpathian Mountains. His parents named him after the Greek Catholic Church's patron saint, which came to represent the generosity and kindness that defined his life. His birthplace is now located in the southeastern region of Poland, but was then part of the Austro-Hungarian province of Galicia and Lodomeria. Before the rise of politically defined nation-states, an individual's ethnic identity was shaped by their community's evolving religious, linguistic, and cultural traditions.

The Sorokas were Rusyns, a lesser-known but distinctive ethnic minority. For generations, their uniqueness was ignored in discussions of Central and Eastern European culture. The result was that many U.S.-born Rusyns identified as Russians, Slovaks, Poles, Czechs, Hungarians, or Ukrainians, unaware of their Rusyn origins. Immigrants from my grandparents' villages, including my grandparents, seldom spoke about their Rusyn heritage.

To distinguish them from Russians, Rusyns in Eastern Galicia (Krosno, Sanok, and Lesko) were commonly referred to as Ruthenians or Ukrainians. Conversely, Rusyns in Western Galicia (Jasło, Grybów, Gorlice, and Nowy Sącz) suffered less ethnic ambiguity. In the 20th century, Rusyns were also known as Lemkos, Hutsuls, or Boykos, reflecting the geographic and cultural variations among the Rusyn people throughout Central and Eastern Europe.

Illustration 1.00: Kingdom of Galicia. Note the locations of the Sanok, Lesko, and Krosno districts. My grandparents were from the Lesko region (2).

Nicholas was the firstborn son of Michal Soroka and Tekla (Theodora) Fecycz, later translated to Fescnik or Fesnick. At the time of Nicholas's birth, his father was 43 years old, and his mother was 27 years old. Consistent with the European Marriage Pattern, the couple married later in life. Only wealthy peasants could afford to marry young, while most postponed marriages for practical reasons. Late marriage served as a form of birth control. Couples also needed money and property to establish a new household. Therefore, men worked as farmhands, on lumber rafts, and served in the military. Women worked to increase their dowries to expand their marriage prospects and provide some means of support in the event of their spouse's premature death or abandonment. Widows were prohibited from inheriting property unless they had underage children.

(2) Wikipedia. 2024. "Subdivisions of the Kingdom of Galicia and Lodomeria." Wikimedia Foundation. Last modified October 16, 2024.

Otherwise, marital property passed to the eldest son. Regardless, the law required that heirs be married, so weddings were often arranged on short notice. Without the means to support themselves, widows were compelled to accept anyone willing to marry them. If a couple were childless, a widow risked losing her home.

Chastity before marriage was essential for the noble class, whose lives were based on inheritance, succession, and royal privileges. In aristocratic circles, a woman's virginity determined her value. (3) For peasants, a woman's ability to bear children was of greater importance. According to author and historian Lucy Worsley, *"Premarital sex was not seen as disastrous, and pre-marital pregnancy, welcome proof of fertility."*(4) Procreation was critically important in agricultural communities where infant mortality rates were 50% and life expectancies were often cut short.

Couples, therefore, participated in two ceremonies: the betrothal ceremony (5) and the marriage ceremony, the latter occurring after the bride discovered she was pregnant. Illegitimacy was therefore quite common, especially because it was so broadly defined. Children born within seven months of a marriage ceremony were regarded as

---

(3) This is not to say that bearing children was not important for the upper class, but virginal marriages ensured the purity of bloodlines. Ironically, aristocratic women faced a higher mortality rate from childbirth because they were married at a shockingly young age. Because breastfeeding was discouraged, noble women were nearly always pregnant, and medieval medical procedures often caused infections, resulting in death.

(4) Worsley, Lucy. 2013. *If Walls Could Talk: An Intimate History of the Home.* New York: Bloomsbury, USA, page 67.

(5) During the betrothal ceremony, the couple exchanged rings and were blessed by a priest.

illegitimate. Children of common-law couples, "untimely" children (born more than 10 months after the father died), and the offspring of those who married outside the church were also deemed illegitimate. Unmarried mothers were labeled as immoral and faced harsh societal and economic repercussions, while the father's role varied but was entirely driven by choice. Some acknowledged and supported their children, while others allowed their mothers to bear the financial and societal burden in shame.

Illegitimate children had limited rights to inheritance and benefits available to other children. This changed with Emperor Joseph's *General Civil Code of 1786*, which aimed to reverse the stigma and legal disadvantages faced by illegitimate children. Joseph's reforms allowed illegitimate offspring to hold public office, enter trades and guilds, inherit property, and pursue an education or a vocation within the church. (Village clergy positions were often hereditary, however, passing from father to son, while other ecclesiastical roles were reserved for those of noble birth.)

While many of Joseph's reforms were widely unpopular and repealed after his death, his successor reinstated most of the rights previously granted to the illegitimately born. Nevertheless, most peasants remained in the same social class throughout their lives. If a peasant managed to rise above his or her station, their humble beginnings would not be entirely forgotten. Peasants rarely left the village where they were born. All social classes considered commoners having power over others as an affront to the natural order.

Michal and Tekla's first child was born in 1884 and died in infancy. Consistent with the statistical averages of the time, four of Nicholas's eight siblings died before reaching the age of five. (6) According to church records, Nicholas, his father, and his grandfather were born at residence number 42, indicating that the family lived in the same home for most of the 19th century. Following the Habsburgs' acquisition of Galicia in 1772, Austrian authorities assigned numbers to village homes based on their completion dates or their distance from a church, school, or government building.

Homes reflected the social hierarchy of the time. Noble homes, often grand and fortified, were designed to display wealth and power while also ensuring protection and security. Their properties were constructed from durable materials, such as stone or brick. In contrast, peasant homes were simpler and more functional, typically built with locally sourced materials such as timber and thatch. Peasant dwellings were small, dark, and cramped. Generally, the more prominent families lived near the village center.

Before the Austrian mandate, houses were named after their first inhabitants. These names remained permanently associated with a dwelling, even after the original inhabitants had gone. (7) In addition to house numbers, church records documented the social rank of marriage partners, births, and deaths. However, a family's prestige was based on its reputation, which in turn was based on its decency, self-sufficiency, common sense, and property ownership. Church records identified Nicholas's parents as Greek Catholic peasants; his father was born in Wola Michowa, and his mother in a neighboring village known as

---

(6) Roser, Max. "Mortality in the Past: Every Second Child Died." https://Ourworldindata.Org/Child-mortality-in-the-past. April 11, 2023.

(7) Lenius, Brian. "House Numbers and House Names in the Austrian Empire." *Eastern Genealogical Newsletter* (2016).

Maniow. The numbering system allowed me to trace the district's church records back to my third great-grandparents.

Illustration 1.01: East Lemko Map, now part of Poland. My grandparents' villages are on the lower right. (8)

More than a Name

According to the Ancestry website, family surnames offer a valuable starting point for ethnogenetic research. Thus, I initiated my investigation by looking into our family surname to determine if it provided any insights into my ancestors' occupations, origins, or family lineage. From this, I determined that *Soroka* is an Eastern European (and Jewish) surname and one of the more common names in

---

(8) Kozak, Roman. "Folk Costume and Embroidery." Folkcostume.Blogspot.Com. May 11, 2019. https://folkcostume.blogspot.com/2019/05/overview-of-folk-costumes-of-poland_11.html.

what is now called *Lemkovyna* (9) It originated in regions of Poland, Ukraine, and Belarus. (10)

For centuries, surnames served as a means of identification for social elites, while peasants were identified by their first name or an established nickname. (11) Nobles could lose their assets and social status without legal documentation. (12) Surnames ending with "ski," "cki," and "dzki" were exclusively associated with the nobility. (13) Peasants generally did not own any inheritable assets or reasons to abandon their local village, so a surname was unnecessary. However, surnames were common in rural locations among peasant *landowners* as early as the 14th and 15th centuries.

---

(9) Maksimovich, Walter , and Ivan Krasowskii . "A Dictionary of Lemko Surnames." L.V. Productions Limited, March 27, 2020. https://www.lemko.org/genealogy/krasowskii/.

(10) "Soroka last name popularity, history, and meaning." *NameCensus.com. Accessed on December 9, 2024. http://namecensus.com/last-names/soroka-surname-popularity/*

(11) Interview with Thomas Prymak, Historian, Writer, and Scholar." SoundCloud. February 11, 2020. Video: https://soundcloud.com/krynytsya/thomasprymak.

(12) Stankiewicz, Janusz , and Magdalena Znamirowska. "How Surnames Came Into Being in Poland." November 28, 2017. olishorigins.com/blog/how-surnames-came-into-being-in-Poland/.

(13) Wikipedia. 2017. "Polish Names." Wikimedia Foundation. Last modified: November 28, 2017. https://en.wikipedia.org/wiki/Polish_name.

Illustration 1.02 Soroka Surname Origins. (14) In the 16th century, the SOROKA name was documented in the Polish-Lithuanian Commonwealth, particularly in the regions of Galicia and Volhynia.

In 1787, however, the Austrian Emperor ordered his constituents to adopt hereditary surnames, regardless of their wealth or status. While the mandate explicitly targeted Jews, it led to standardized surnames throughout the Empire. (15) Jews adopted common first names as their surnames to comply with local naming laws and to assimilate into their communities. This practice was widespread in Eastern Europe during the 18th and 19th centuries. Some peasants chose aristocratic names to signify a connection to a noble family, even crafting oral histories to strengthen their claims. Some tenants adopted the name of the estate where they lived. In everyday interactions, however, peasants continued

---

(14) Spatial Planning at the National Level: Comparison of Legal and Strategic Instruments in a Case Study of Belarus, Ukraine, and Poland" *Land* 12, no. 7: 1364. https://doi.org/10.3390/land1207136414

(15) Most peasant surnames were written phonetically, and this, combined with various language influences, resulted in inconsistent spelling.

to use the same identifiers as they always had, with only the village priest to know otherwise.

Even before the Austrian mandate, Rusyns had two identities: their given name and the name of the farmstead where they lived. The latter helped distinguish individuals in small, close-knit communities where many shared the same first name. Family and friends favored the farmstead name. (16) According to Dr. Stephen Rapawy:

> *A Lemko's identity was tied to the land, specifically to a particular farm. The region did not typically see many land sales; it was not the norm. Farms were passed down from one generation to the next. If a particular family had no sons and the farmstead was passed on to a married daughter, the farmstead would retain its original name, and even a married daughter's husband would be known by the farmstead's name.*

Church documents indicate that my third great-grandfather, Lucas Soroka, was born in 1757, before the Austrian decree, which suggests that his parents were peasant landowners.

Surnames were often based on their fathers, grandfathers, or other male ancestors' given name, place of birth, physical traits, occupation, or the names of animals, birds, plants, or even months of the year. While I cannot be certain about the origins of our surname, my research identified several compelling possibilities.

---

(16) Caudill, Corinna W. "Lemko Project: The Lemko Villager's Dual Identity: Surnames and Household Names." The Lemko Project. November 12, 2012. https://lemkoproject.blogspot.com/2012/11/the-dual-identity-of-village-lemko.html.

The Meaning of Soroka

According to the Ancestry website, "soroka" is a Slavic term for magpie. Birds were mystical creatures in Slavic folklore and Norse mythology. The god Odin had two ravens, Huginn and Muninn, tasked with reporting on mortal activities. Birds also held religious significance, similar to that of angels, as they were believed to be conduits of spiritual messages from above. Galicia's coat of arms also featured a crow. People have long been fascinated by corvids (crows, ravens, and magpies) because of their eerily human-like mannerisms. They employ advanced communication methods, learn from each other's mistakes, mate for life, maintain lifelong family ties, and even conduct funerals for their loved ones. They are also curious and highly intelligent.

Illustration 1.03: Galicia Lodomeria Coat of Arms (1804-1914) features a jackdaw, a crow noted for its inquisitive nature. (17)

(17) Kovalska, Areta. "The Coats of Arms of the Kingdom of Galicia and Lodomeria." Forgotten Galicia. May 9, 2020.

A literary reference to a magpie, however, carries negative connotations, portraying someone who hoards items of little value, talks excessively, or is prone to thievery. (18) Several Soroka descendants, including my father, collected items of little value. One was downright miserly! Thus, one possible origin of our family surname may have been a disparaging personal attribute.

Illustration 1.04: Magpie.

A second explanation is also possible. In Russian, a *soroka* is part of a woman's headdress. (19) In the old country, women, especially married women, always covered their hair to avoid attracting evil spirits. A soroka is a scarf worn over a *kichka*, or a married woman's cap. A soroka consists of an embroidered front, side flaps with laces for tying, and a back. Before the advent of commercial textile mills, women's skills in embroidery, weaving, and sewing were highly valued. In medieval times, cloth served as a

(18) "Soroka Name Meaning & Soroka Family History." Ancestry. May 9, 2020. Soroka Name Meaning & Soroka Family History at Ancestry.com®.

(19) "Soroka Name Meaning & Soroka Family History." The Free Dictionary. The Free Dictionary, https:/encyclopedia2.thefreedictionary.com/Soroka.

form of currency, enabling women to supplement their income by weaving and embroidering fabric. Though seldom acknowledged, women played an active role in medieval economies, including those beyond conventionally defined "women's work." In addition to operating bakeries, laundries, and dairies, women worked alongside their husbands as carpenters, stone masons, and blacksmiths. Perhaps our surname was based on a talented family *matriarch*. However, most European societies viewed women as inferior, and expert Thomas Prymak asserts that only 6% of family surnames were based on women. The Ancestry website also described Soroka as a gender-neutral surname.

Illustration 1.05: A soroka headscarf. Image from hatguide.co.uk.

A third source of our family surname requires a deeper historical understanding. My grandparents' villages were situated in what was once known as Red Ruthenia, a principality of the Kievan Rus. It later became part of the independent Kingdom of Galicia and Volhynia, after which its name was forgotten, and its lands were incorporated into the Polish-Lithuanian Commonwealth. (20) In 1772, the region was annexed to the Austrian Empire, where it remained until the end of World War I. Today, Rusyn lands are divided among Poland, Ukraine, Slovakia, and Hungary.

During the 16th century, when many Carpathian communities were first established, the Polish monarch granted land and tax breaks to settlers in the underpopulated regions of his empire in return for their protection of vital trade routes to help secure his royal claim. Peasants settled in these newly constructed royal communities, fleeing the destruction caused by the Tartars and Mongols, as well as the expanding influence of the Polish elite. These settlements were generally the first to suffer from foreign invasion and, therefore, were of little interest to aristocrats. (21)

The early inhabitants of the Beskid Mountains (22) would eventually become known as Lemkos, Boykos, and Hutsuls. (23) Lemkos settled in the western lowlands, while Boykos and Hutsuls (the latter based on the Romanian term for robbers) resided in the eastern highlands. The Polish Army also settled prisoners of war in communities near Wola Michowa to construct roads and bridges and provide military defense. According to Spuscizna, a Polish heritage

---

(20) Wikipedia. 2024. "Red Ruthenia." Wikimedia Foundation. Last modified: May 7, 2024. https://en.wikipedia.org/wiki/Red_Ruthenia.

(21) During the 12th and 13th centuries, Kievan Rus' and Galician princes also constructed fortified villages to protect the local lucrative salt trade and the borders with the Kingdoms of Poland and Hungary.

(22) The Beskid Mountains are a series of mountain ranges in the Carpathians, extending from the Czech Republic in the west along the Polish border with Slovakia to Ukraine in the east.

(23) Wikipedia. 2024. "Galicia (Eastern Europe)." Wikimedia Foundation. Last modified: June 22, 2024. https://en.wikipedia.org/wiki/Galicia_(Eastern_Europe).

research group, Cossack and Tartar POWs were forcibly resettled in Blizianka, Gwozdzianka, Bonarowka, Oparowka, Wola Pietrusza, and other villages within a sixty-mile radius of my grandfather's village.

The region's history, therefore, suggests that Carpathian settlers largely originated from somewhere else — but where? According to Paul Magocsi, Rusyns descended from early Slavic people who migrated from the Danubian Basin, White Croats from regions north of the Carpathian Mountains, and Vlach shepherds from southeastern Europe.

Illustration 1.06: Rusyn migration. The Rusyns are descendants of the ancient Rus people and share connections with other tribes living at the crossroads between ancient Rus and Europe, including Poland, Bohemia, Moravia, Slovakia, and Bukovina. Source: Carpatho Rusyn Association.

Two communities within the former Commonwealth bore the Soroka name: a village in the Ternopil Oblast on the Ukrainian steppes, approximately 250 miles east of Wola Michowa, and a second community in Moldova, southeast of my grandfather's village. The Moldovan community was once part of a Cossack hetmanate, a military state. The Mongols and Ottomans ravaged the Soroka villages before they came under Polish rule, but their origins remain unknown.

Illustration 1.07: Soroka Settlements. Image from Mapquest.com.

This discovery raised two intriguing possibilities. The first is that the family adopted the name of their ancestral village. Just as Leonardo da Vinci was from Vinci, perhaps the Sorokas were from Soroka. Alternatively, the town may have gotten its name *from* the Soroka family. It was common in Eastern Europe for villages to be named after prominent families. If the Soroka family settled or owned land in the region, the village may have taken their name, particularly if they were a noble family. Is it possible that the Sorokas were once a noble family?

Background on Noble Families

The Commonwealth had two types of noble families—those with state recognition and those without. Recognized nobles, known as the *szlachta*, played a significant role in the nation's history. Unlike aristocrats in other parts of Europe, the szlachta (regardless of their wealth and social influence) were regarded as equal to their king.

An individual could become a member of the Polish nobility in several ways. (24) The most common method was by birth or inheritance (though female szlachta did not have the right to vote in the parliament and were never granted any official titles or roles). A monarch could also bestow noble status for significant contributions to the state. Ennoblements from the king typically included land and other privileges, such as exemption from military service or tax obligations.

Noble status could also be granted through adoption. If a noble couple were unable to have children, they might adopt a non-noble relative to carry on the family name. The permanence of this status varied. Sometimes, the adopted individual's noble status depended on specific factors, such as the family's continuing favor or meeting certain obligations. Marrying into a noble family could also elevate a person's status, though this distinction was more common for women than for men. The male line granted noble status, meaning that children of noblewomen who married commoners lost their privileges. When mixed marriages occurred, they typically involved a wealthy peasant and an impoverished noble.

Certain professionals, like military officers and high-ranking officials, could also be ennobled for their lifetime. Even today, knighthood is a title granted for services rendered to the king and country, regardless of a person's birthplace or social standing. Their titles and privileges ended when the individual fell from favor or the exulted person died.

---

(24) "The Polish and Lithuanian Nobility." Nobility Titles. December 13, 2017. https://nobilitytitles.net/polish-and-lithuanian-nobility/.

A noble Soroka family resided in the Galician community of Dobra Szlachecka, approximately 250 miles west of Wola Michowa. As recognized members of the Polish nobility, this family likely assimilated into the local culture. According to present-day descendants of this village:

> *Dobra is a village situated on the right bank of the San River, 11 miles north of Sanok, in the Galician region of Poland. The village's original inhabitants were Ruthenians. In 1339, Casimir the Great, King of Poland, annexed the Ruthenian principality of Halych. On June 28, 1402, the Ruthenian residents of Dobra received a grant of privileges from Jagiello, King of Poland and Grand Duke of Lithuania, who needed warriors for the conflict with the German Teutonic Knights. (25)*

A second type of noble, Ukrainian or Ruthenian noble (26), was neither acknowledged nor recognized by the Polish parliament or king. Ruthenian nobles lived almost exclusively in the newly acquired territories of the Commonwealth, which today are part of Ukraine. Many unrecognized nobles assimilated into Polish culture to maintain or expand their privileged status. However, those who lacked the interest or the means became nearly indistinguishable from other peasants. Unrecognized nobles

(25) Popiel, Jan. "History of Dobra Szlachecka." The Dobra Szlachecka Society. The Dobra Szlachecka Society, Accessed May 25, 2023. https://www.dobra.org/history/history.html.

(26) Rusyns were often referred to as Ruthenians in the historical context. Wikipedia. 2024. "Ruthenians." Wikimedia Foundation. Last modified October 24, 2024. https://en.wikipedia.org/wiki/Ruthenians.

owned property and were governed by a separate judicial system but were prohibited from owning serfs. (27)

Ruthenian nobles often chose village names as their surname. If the Sorokas had been Ruthenian nobles, they might have enjoyed elite status at one time. However, when serfdom was abolished in 1848, all Ruthenian nobles lost whatever privileges they had once had. Their status may also have been lost before 1848 if the family had been arbitrarily reduced to serfs. As one source explained:

> *Their relative poverty was a barrier to assimilation with the wealthy Polish landowners, helping them retain their East Slavic identity. Poor boyars, whose military service to the Polish crown had confirmed their noble status, quickly lost this status when they were reduced to serfs. Some regions had large concentrations, most notably southern Galicia, north of the Carpathian Mountains, and to the east in what is now the Ternopil oblast. A number of them went east to join the Zaporizhian Cossacks. (28)*

Regardless of their status, ancestral home, or reasons for migrating, the Sorokas settled in a royal village in the Carpathian Mountains. The mountains provided them with land, freedom from serfdom, and a degree of protection from encroaching profiteers. The ongoing threat of military invasion, loss of social standing and property, fear of conscription, and the availability of free land would have all been convincing reasons to move west. According to Spuscizna and other sources, most Rusyns who settled in the Carpathian Mountains came from the east.

---

(27) Wikipedia. 2024. "Ukrainian Nobility of Galicia." Wikimedia Foundation. Last modified: April 8, 2024.
https://en.wikipedia.org/wiki/Ukrainian_nobility_of_Galicia.

(28) Wikipedia. 2024. "Ukrainian Nobility in Galicia." Wikimedia Foundation.

The community near Ternopil most closely aligns with our family's oral history and ancestral claims, especially since the Moldovan community has no record of ever having Rusyn inhabitants. The community was also within reach of the influence of the Cossack Hetmanate. In 1546, just eight years before the Mongol invasion of Ternopil, the Polish king established Wola Michowa as a royal town. The laws governing this region (Vlach or Wallachian law) liberated its inhabitants from feudal bondage, including serfdom and taxes, for more than two decades in exchange for developing the land for agriculture and protecting the Commonwealth's profitable trade routes from thieves and foreign conquest. Peasants in other parts of Poland were required to work for their landlords for 180 days or more each year (an obligation that could be shared among family members), leading one scholar to describe the flight to the Carpathians as *a call to freedom.* (29)

(29) Magocsi, Paul R. 2015. *With Their Backs to the Mountains: A History of the Carpatho-Rus and Carpatho-Rusyns.* Budapest-New York: Central European University Press. Page 70.

Illustration 1.08: The Polish and Lithuanian Commonwealth (30)

While the origins of our surname remain uncertain, this discussion provides insight into the Soroka family, as well as the traditions and customs of their region.

DNA Analysis

When faced with limited historical documentation, contemporary genealogists turn to DNA. In this section, I will present the results of my DNA investigation, beginning with a discussion of our supposed Viking ancestry.

---

(30) Wikipedia. 2024. "The Polish-Lithuanian Commonwealth, 1466–1667; Https://Commons.Wikimedia.Org/." Wikimedia Foundation. Last modified: July 14, 2024. https://commons.wikimedia.org/.

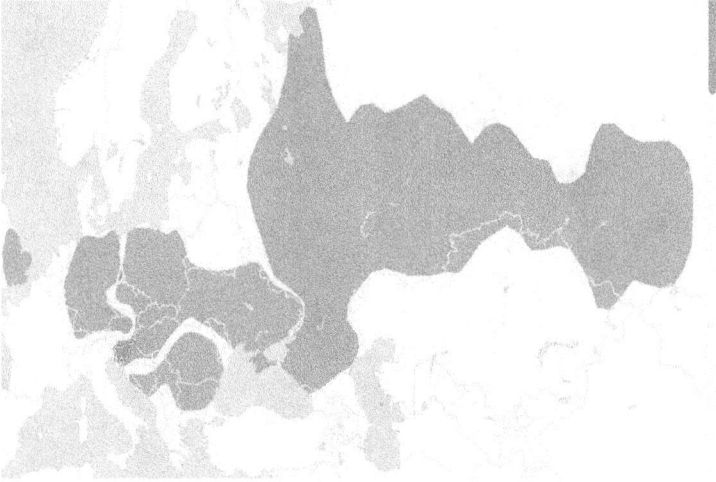

Illustration 1.09: Author's DNA results identified her as Rusyn, showing 85% Central/Eastern European ancestry, 5% Germanic, 4% Russian, 4% Balkan, and 2% Northwest European ancestry, which may suggest a potential Viking heritage. Image from Ancestry.com.

The Vikings

There is little doubt that the Vikings had a significant impact on Europe. However, their role in founding the first Russian state (Muscovy), Kievan Rus, and their genetic influence on the people in the regions they traveled remain unclear.

Illustration 1.10: The Rus and Red Ruthenia. My grandparents' villages were located on the extreme western edge of the Red Rus. (31)

      Historians have two theoretical explanations for the origins of the Rus. Western scholars, known as ***Normanists***, suggest that the people who inhabited the Kievan Rus descended from the Norsemen, who raided, traded, and ultimately settled along the Russian river system connecting Europe to the Islamic trade network. Eastern scholars, or ***Anti-Normanists***, contend that the Vikings played a minor role in both the settlement and development of Kievan Rus.

      Both agree, however, that the Vikings entered the European continent through the Gulf of Finland around the eighth century, traveled down the Neva River to Lake Ladoga, and then proceeded overland to the Volga River and the Caspian Sea. There, they exchanged furs, amber, honey, beeswax, weapons, and any enslaved people they collected along the way for luxury goods, including precious metals,

---

(31) Editorial Commentary. "Who Are the Rus?" Veritas Journal. March 7, 2022. https://veritasjournal.org/2022/03/07/who-are-the-rus/.

gems, and silk. (32) The Islamic State controlled the region, so trade was permitted only with the consent of the Khan.

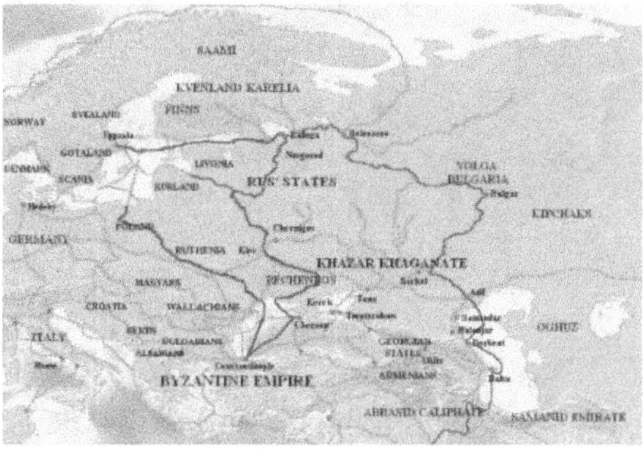

Illustration 1.11: Viking Trade Routes of the Black Sea region, 8th–11th centuries. (33)

After the Vikings determined it was more profitable to trade directly with Constantinople, they shifted their trade route west, south of Novgorod, toward the Dnieper River and across the Black Sea. The western trade route had limited oversight but also passed through an area controlled by a ruthless, semi-nomadic Turkic people called the *Pechenegs,* whose battle tactics made them particularly deadly opponents. The Pechenegs mercilessly attacked the advancing Vikings as they portaged their trade goods around the falls at the mouth of the Dnieper River. They were skilled horsemen and experts with the composite bow, gaining advantage through speed and surprise.

---

(32) Wikipedia. 2024. "Anti-Normanism." Wikimedia Foundation. Last modified: June 10, 2024. https://en.wikipedia.org/wiki/Anti-Normanism.

(33) *Illustration* from Wikipedia Commons in the public domain.https://en.wikipedia.org/wiki/Khazars#/media/File:Varangian_ro utes.png

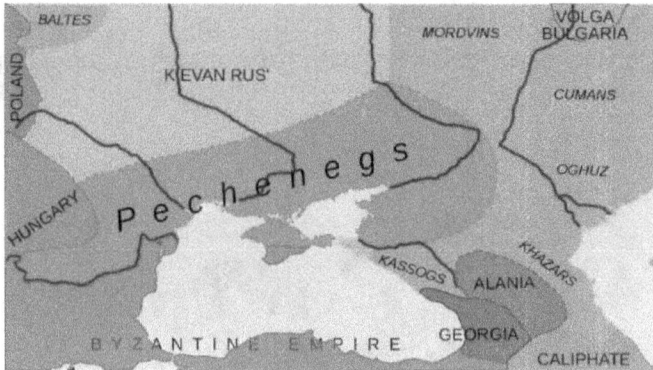
Illustration 1.12: Pecheneg Territory c 1030. (34)

In response, the Vikings installed fortified market towns along the western trade route and assimilated into Slavic culture. With its capital in Constantinople, the Byzantine Empire encouraged the Norsemen to convert from paganism to Orthodox Christianity. Byzantine policies strengthened the Rus's ties to the East while distancing them from the cultural and religious traditions of Western Europe. The Vikings used a runic alphabet to memorialize their dead and communicate with their gods. But lacking a standard literary language, Viking lore was passed down through a rich tradition of oral history, sagas, and legends.

Despite failing to document their history in more conventional ways, the Vikings left an indelible mark wherever they traveled. The Danish Vikings are credited with unifying England and colonizing the Frankish region of Normandy. The Norwegian Vikings discovered Iceland, Greenland, and parts of North America. The Swedish

(34) *Illustration* from Wikipedia Commons in the public domain https://en.wikipedia.org/wiki/Pechenegs.

Vikings reestablished the global trade network, thereby reviving the European economy centuries after the Roman Empire collapsed. Rapid population growth prompted the Danes to seek new settlements in England and France. Harold Finehair's unified government and conversion to Christianity encouraged the Norwegian Vikings to venture west. The reasons behind the Swedish Vikings' eastward migration remain unclear, but leading scholars have proposed several plausible explanations.

Sweden had a less imposing geographical presence during the Viking Age. (see Illustration 1.13) Impenetrable forests, along with the Keel Mountains, the Gotars, the Lapps, the Saami, and the Baltic Sea, contained the inhabitants, forcing them to cling to a coastline characterized by a shortage of arable farmland, especially for those other than the eldest son. This, combined with a declining number of marriage partners (due to their culture's polygamous norms), is thought to have driven the Swedish Vikings east.

Illustration 1.13: Map of Uppland. Observe the size of Uppland on this map. Source: Worldhistorymaps.info.

Because they relied on the sea, the Scandinavians were exceptionally skilled shipbuilders and navigators. Long, narrow, and flat, longships were fast, durable, and capable of navigating both open seas and shallow inland riverways, and could land anywhere to resupply or launch surprise attacks. Their flexible green timber frames could withstand violent storms, and their retractable masts allowed passage under tight spaces. Even a gentle breeze could propel their 40-foot sails. Their ships were also light enough to be carried over land. The Vikings' military strength stemmed from their mental and physical endurance, which was developed by living in close proximity for months at a time, rowing against the current, and navigating treacherous seas.

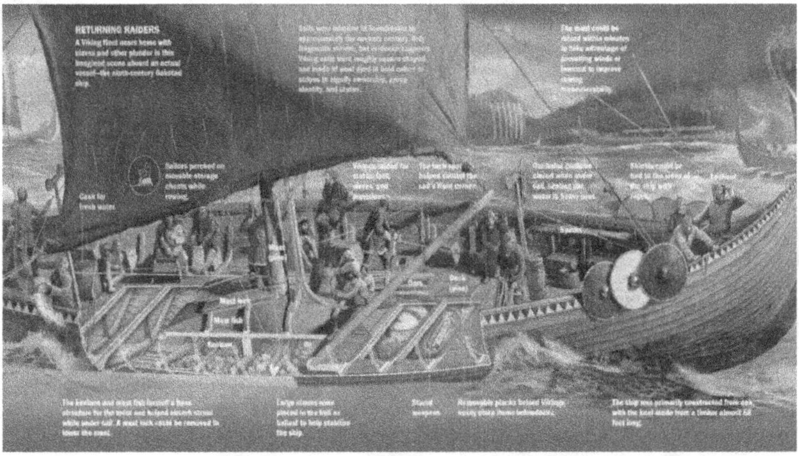

Illustration 1.14: Viking Ship. (35) Note its shallow draft and removable mast.

To avoid unnecessary loss of life, Vikings preferred exacting tribute over military confrontation, tribute which almost always included slaves. Human trafficking was their most profitable enterprise, especially since disease-ridden Islamic cities were always in need of replacement laborers. Arab markets sold their human tribute, along with other goods that the enslaved individuals carried from the North.

(35) *Illustration* from nationalgeographic.com/specialprojects/interactive-assets/nggraphics/vikingsettlements-graphic/build-2017-03-27_16-28-31/

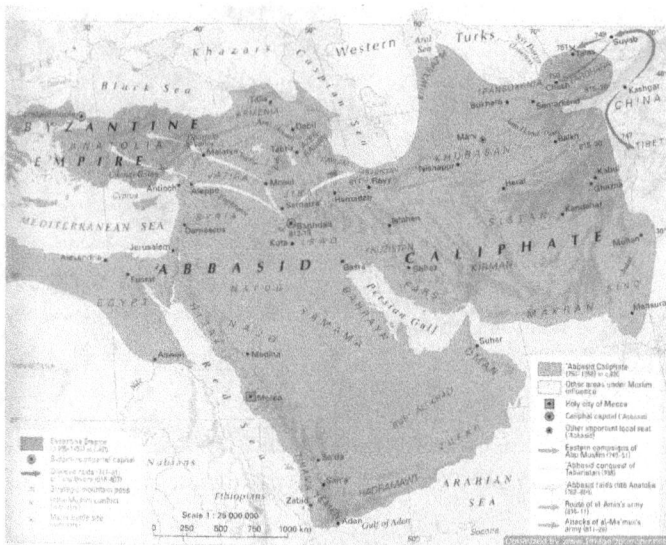

Illustration 1.15: Abbasid Caliphate in the 9th century. (36)

In the ninth century, their fortified market towns along the Volga and Dnieper Rivers united to form a political confederation known as *Kievan Rus*. (37) Normanists believe the Vikings played a key role in shaping Rus culture, law, and language. Its first Viking leader, Rurik the Great, established his dynastic capital in Novgorod. Its capital was later moved to Kyiv after his kinsman Oleg killed local rulers Askold and Dir and defeated the Ottoman Turks. Oleg is credited with being the founder of Kievan Rus. In Old Norse, "Rus" means *men who row*. Rus is also a Finnish term for Sweden. Swedish DNA has been identified in the remains of the

---

(36) Image from: *Abbasid Caliphate in the 9th Century. Encyclopedia Britannica.*

(37) "The Rus of Kiev and the Varangians." Sons of Norway. March 18, 2013. https://sonsofvikings.com/blogs/history/vikings-in-the- Rus-of-Kiev-and-the-Varangians.

Rurik dynasty and those of Russian princes. Some genetic researchers suggest that a typical Rusyn's DNA contains elements of Slavic, Germanic, Scandinavian, and Baltic ancestry. (Magocsi) According to Genome, the portion of my DNA attributed to Northwest Europe is Viking DNA.

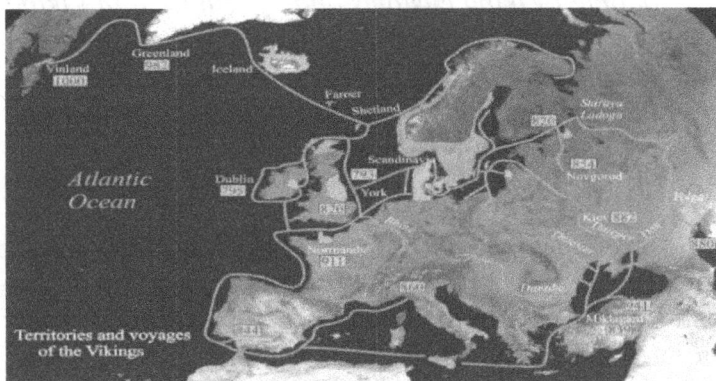

Illustration 1.16: Viking territories and trade routes. Note the frequent use of rivers as transportation routes. Image credit: Wikipedia, CC BY-SA 3.0.

Does DNA Prove Anything?

The Smithsonian Institute recently uncovered a surprising diversity of DNA in Swedish Viking burial sites. Some remains lacked any evidence of Scandinavian DNA, suggesting that genetics alone might be an unreliable marker of Viking ancestry. In fact, some remains were of genetic Slavs. (38) During the Viking Age, all Scandinavians were called Vikings, but only a few could be explicitly defined as such. Researchers at the University of Cambridge and

(38) Wu, Tara. "Sweeping DNA Survey Highlights Vikings' Surprising Genetic Diversity." Smithsonian Magazine. Smithsonian, September 18, 2020. Sweeping DNA Survey Highlights Vikings' Surprising Genetic Diversity.

Copenhagen concluded that Viking communities were characterized by a shared way of life, rather than a specific ethnic identity.

> *"Viking" was often more of a social role than a genetic or ethnic identity, as non-Scandinavians adopted Viking customs and were buried in Viking-style graves. Despite their extensive travels, genetic mixing within Scandinavia remained limited, with inland populations staying genetically distinct for centuries.* (39)

Scandinavian DNA among Rusyns may have originated from the 17th-century Swedish Invasion of the Polish-Lithuanian Commonwealth. Western Galicia was devastated during the *Great Northern War*, a twenty-year conflict between Russia and Sweden that involved Polish armies on both sides. Villages were destroyed as Swedish forces ravaged the countryside, resulting in widespread famine and hardship.

A Second Theory

A second theoretical explanation, based on a slightly different interpretation of historical events, suggests that the Vikings did not play a significant role in the formation of Kievan Rus. *Anti-Normanists* assert that two ethnic communities settled in what would become the Rus. The Northern or Great Russians formed early Russian society and descended from Vikings, while the southern population, known as Little Russians, descended from Slavic tribes.

---

(39) Eske Willerslev of the University of Cambridge and the University of Copenhagen

Anti-Normanists trace the origins of the Rus to the Balkans and the Black Sea. They assert that Slavic people established a thriving market economy long before the Vikings arrived and argue that Rusyns with Viking ancestry would have a larger portion of their DNA—10% to 25%-- from present-day Norway, Sweden, and Denmark. They believe that the Byzantine Emperor hired Viking mercenaries for protection, but beyond that, Viking conquest was limited to trade. (40) In contrast to Western Europeans, who sought to expel or convert the pagan Vikings, the Byzantine Empire demonstrated remarkable religious tolerance toward people of all faiths. Thus, anti-Normanists believe that Slavic tribes were the original inhabitants of Kievan Rus. The Vikings were mere opportunists seeking land and commercial opportunities, as well as a means to escape the political turmoil and economic challenges in their homelands.

Anti-Normanists claim that "Rus" refers to the River Ros, a tributary of the Dnieper River flowing through present-day Ukraine. Over time, this river became synonymous with the region's inhabitants and territory. Despite the differences between Old Norse and Slavic languages, anti-Normanists concede that a shared vernacular emerged from trade, conflict, and cross-cultural interaction. At least one credible eyewitness supports the anti-Normanists viewpoint, highlighting the importance of considering multiple perspectives when conducting historical or genealogical research:

> *The only occupation of Rus is the trade with sable, squirrel, and other furs. They harry the Slavs, using ships to reach them; they carry them off as enslaved people and sell them. They have no fields but live on*

---

(40) Magocsi, Paul R. 2015. *With Their Backs to the Mountains: A History of the Carpatho-Rusyns.* Budapest-New York: Central European University Press. Page 50.

*what they get from the Slavs' lands. When a son is
born, the father will go up to the newborn baby,
sword in hand; throwing it down, he says, 'I shall not
leave you with any property: You have only what you
can provide with this weapon.* Ibn Rustah (41)

Western scholars assert that the recent discovery of
Viking remains in Bereg County, Western Ukraine, supports
the Normanists' view. But, for purposes of this story, it
remains unclear if the Sorokas had any Viking ancestors.

Rusyns with German Ancestry?

Over the centuries, Polish, Prussian, Russian, and
Austrian monarchs actively promoted German colonization
within their expanding empires by offering land grants,
livestock, military exemptions, religious freedom, and tax
benefits. (42) Lands designated for German settlement
included royal estates, frontiers, and former monastic
institutions.

Despite their largely unfulfilled promises, German
industriousness, tidiness, organizational skills, record-
keeping, urban planning, and economic expertise
transformed living conditions and increased tax revenues
wherever they settled. Germans employed sophisticated
farming and crop management techniques and supported
education to expand community literacy. Several German
communities were established near my grandparents'
villages, including Baligrad, a few miles north of Wola
Michowa. Many Galicians sought seasonal work in German

---

(41) "The Rus of Kyiv and the Varangians." Sons of Norway

(42) Dakiniewicz, Iwona. "German Colonization in Galicia." Forgotten
Galicia. July 16, 2018. https://forgottengalicia.com/german-colonization-
in-galicia/.

settlements across Europe. Those in German-occupied areas fared significantly better than those in other parts of Poland.

German aristocrats were also favored by elite society. Russian aristocrats preferred to marry German princesses because, unlike their Catholic counterparts in the West, they were more willing to convert to the Orthodox faith. Before unification, German principalities had little political influence, so marital alliances posed minimal threat to the continent's balance of power. Still, these marriages provided the Russian court with valuable political connections to the German sphere, making Peter the Great the last entirely *Russian* Tsar.

The first wave of German immigrants settled in western Galicia and quickly assimilated into Polish culture. The second wave settled in eastern Galicia, retaining their language and cultural traditions. Fluency in German was associated with social mobility in the Austro-Hungarian Empire. The Habsburgs believed that a common language would unite their multicultural empire.

Given my ancestors' proximity to German communities and my great-grandfather's military role as a Germanized Slav, it is understandable why so many Rusyns have inherited German ancestry and other cultural influences.

Chapter 1 References

Wikipedia. 2024. "Anti-Normanism." Wikimedia Foundation. Last modified: June 10, 2024. https://en.wikipedia.org/wiki/Anti-Normanism.

Caudill, Corinna W. "Lemko Project: The Lemko Villager's Dual Identity: Surnames and Household Names." The Lemko Project. November 12, 2012. https://lemkoproject.blogspot.com/2012/11/the-dual-identity-of-village-lemko.html.

Dakiniewicz, Iwona. "German Colonization in Galicia." Forgotten Galicia. July 16, 2018. https://forgottengalicia.com/german-colonization-in-galicia/.

Editorial Commentary. "Who Are the Rus?" Veritas Journal. March 7, 2022. https://veritasjournal.org/2022/03/07/who-are-the-rus/.

Wikipedia. 2024. "Galicia (Eastern Europe)." Wikimedia Foundation. Last modified: June 22, 2024. https://en.wikipedia.org/wiki/Galicia_(Eastern_Europe).

Gawell, Donna. 2024. *Our Galician Ancestors: The History and Culture of the People from Poland and Ukraine from the Middle Ages to WWI.* Independently Published.

Interview with Thomas Prymak, Historian, Writer, and Scholar." SoundCloud. February 11, 2020. Video: https://soundcloud.com/krynytsya/thomasprymak.

Kovalska, Areta. "The Coats of Arms of the Kingdom of Galicia and Lodomeria." Forgotten Galicia. May 9, 2020.

Kotlarchik, Carl. https://Ahmilitary.Blogspot.Com/.

Kovalska, Areta. "The Coats of Arms of the Kingdom of Galicia and Lodomeria." Forgotten Galicia. May 9, 2020.

Kozak, Roman. "Folk Costume and Embroidery." Folkcostume.Blogspot.Com. May 11, 2019. https://folkcostume.blogspot.com/2019/05/overview-of-folk-costumes-of-poland_11.html.

Wikipedia. 2024. "Kievan Rus People." Wikimedia Foundation. Last modified: June 11, 2024. https://en.wikipedia.org/wiki/Kievan Rus%27_people.

Lenius, Brian. "House Numbers and House Names in the Austrian Empire." *Eastern Genealogical Newsletter* (2016).

Levine, David. "The European Marriage Pattern." Cengage, https://www.encyclopedia.com/international/encyclopedias-almanacs-transcripts-and-maps/european-marriage-pattern.

Levy, M. J. (1991). The Rights of the Individual in Habsburg Civil Law: Joseph II and the Illegitimate. Man and Nature / L'homme et la nature, 10, 105–112. https://doi.org/10.7202/1012627ar

Magocsi, Paul R. 2018. *The People from Nowhere: An Illustrated History of Carpatho-Rusyns*. New York: Carpatho-Rusyn Research Center.

Magocsi, Paul R. 2015. *With Their Backs to the Mountains: A History of the Carpatho-Rusyns*. Budapest-New York: Central European University Press.

Maksimovich, Walter , and Ivan Krasowskii . "A Dictionary of Lemko Surnames." L.V. Productions Limited, March 27, 2020. https://www.lemko.org/genealogy/krasowskii/.

Nowak, Maciej, Viktoriya Pantyley, Małgorzata Blaszke, Liudmila Fakeyeva, Roman Lozynskyy, and Alexandru-Ionut Petrisor. 2023.

"Spatial Planning at the National Level: Comparison of Legal and Strategic Instruments in a Case Study of Belarus, Ukraine, and Poland" *Land* 12, no. 7: 1364. https://doi.org/10.3390/land120713641

Our Ukrainian Cousins: A Historical Carpatho-Rusyn Perspective by Ron Matviyak. YouTube CGSI. Video, https://www.youtube.com/watch?v=GYhruM_lzG8.

Wikipedia. 2017. "Polish Names." Wikimedia Foundation. Last modified: November 28, 2017. https://en.wikipedia.org/wiki/Polish_name.

Popiel, Jan. "History of Dobra Szlachecka." The Dobra Szlachecka Society. The Dobra Szlachecka Society, Accessed May 25, 2023. https://www.dobra.org/history/history.html.

Interview with Thomas Prymak, Historian, Writer, and Scholar." SoundCloud. February 11, 2020. Video: https://soundcloud.com/krynytsya/thomasprymak.

Wikipedia. 2024. "Red Ruthenia." Wikimedia Foundation. Last modified: May 7, 2024. https://en.wikipedia.org/wiki/Red_Ruthenia

Wikipedia. 2024. "Ros River." Wikimedia Foundation. Last modified: March 28, 2024. https://en.wikipedia.org/wiki/Ros_(river).

Wikipedia. 2024. "Ruthenians." Wikimedia Foundation. Last modified October 24, 2024. https://en.wikipedia.org/wiki/Ruthenians.

Roser, Max. "Mortality in the Past: Every Second Child Died." Https://Ourworldindata.Org/Child-mortality-in-the-past. April 11, 2023.

Wikipedia. 2024. "Rus People." Wikimedia Foundation. Last modified: June 11, 2024. https://en.wikipedia.org/wiki/Rus%27_people.

Wikipedia. 2024. "Ruthenians." Wikimedia Foundation. Last modified October 24, 2024. https://en.wikipedia.org/wiki/Ruthenians.

Slomka, Jan. 2019. *Memoirs of a Peasant*. 3rd ed. Chicago, IL: Polish Genealogical Society of America.

"Soroka Name Meaning & Soroka Family History." Ancestry. May 9, 2020. Soroka Name Meaning & Soroka Family History at Ancestry.com®.

"Soroka last name popularity, history, and meaning." *NameCensus.com. Accessed on December 9, 2024. http://namecensus.com/last-names/soroka-surname-popularity/*

"Soroka Name Meaning & Soroka Family History." The Free Dictionary. The Free Dictionary, https://encyclopedia2.thefreedictionary.com/Soroka.

Stankiewicz, Janusz , and Magdalena Znamirowska. "How Surnames Came Into Being in Poland." November 28, 2017. Polishorigins.com/blog/how-surnames-came-into-being-in-Poland/.

Wikipedia. 2024. "Subdivisions of the Kingdom of Galicia and Lodomeria." Wikimedia Foundation. Last modified October 16, 2024.

Wikipedia. 2024. "The Polish-Lithuanian Commonwealth, 1466–1667; Https://Commons.Wikimedia.Org/." Wikimedia Foundation. Last modified: July 14, 2024. https://commons.wikimedia.org/.

"The Polish and Lithuanian Nobility." Nobility Titles. December 13, 2017. https://nobilitytitles.net/polish-and-lithuanian-nobility/.

"The Rus of Kyiv and the Varangians." Sons of Norway, March 18, 2013. https://sonsofvikings.com/blogs/history/vikings-in-russia-the-rus-of-kiev-and-the-varangians.

"The Splendor and Misery of the Last Tsarinas." YouTube. Video, https://www.bing.com/videos/riverview/relatedvideo?q=The+spendour+a nd+misery+of+the+last+tsarinas&mid=F8074C69AC59E7CA9D09F807 4C69AC59E7CA9D09&FORM=VIRE.

Wikipedia 2024. "Viking Age." Wikimedia Foundation. Last modified: June 24, 2024. https://en.wikipedia.org/wiki/Viking_Age.
Worsley, Lucy. 2013. *If Walls Could Talk: An Intimate History of the Home*. New York: Bloomsbury, USA

Wikipedia. 2024. "Ukrainian Nobility of Galicia." Wikimedia Foundation. Last modified: April 8, 2024.https://en.wikipedia.org/wiki/Ukrainian_nobility_of_Galicia#:~:text =According%20to%20one%20estimate%2C%20by,of%20the%20ethnic %20Ukrainian%20population.

Editorial Commentary. "Who Are the Rus?" Veritas Journal. March 7, 2022. https://veritasjournal.org/2022/03/07/who-are-the-rus/.

Wu, Tara. "Sweeping DNA Survey Highlights Vikings' Surprising Genetic Diversity." Smithsonian Magazine. Smithsonian, September 18, 2020. Sweeping DNA Survey Highlights Vikings' Surprising Genetic Diversity.

York, Hej. "Crow (and Raven): Wild Unknown Animal Spirit Deck." Unlocking Words. February 13, 2017. https://unlockingwords.wordpress.com/2017/02/13/crow-and-raven-wild-unknown-animal-spirit-deck/

Chapter 2
The History of Galicia

He could not dream of improving his fate but only of ending his suffering. Donna Gawell

In 1918, the Habsburg Empire collapsed, ending nearly seven centuries of rule and crushing any hope for Rusyn independence.. After generations of strategic marital alliances, conquest, and disfiguring inbreeding, the Austrian Empire drew its last breath as the emperor sailed into exile and his vast, authoritarian realm was carved into thirteen, ethnically defined nation-states. Between 1919 and 1921, a post-war conflict split the Lemko-Rusyn population between Polish and Soviet borders. The resulting treaty ignored the rights, status, and very existence of the Rusyn people, leaving them vulnerable to the policies of their newly established governments.

The outcome partly resulted from the Rusyn people's inability to agree on a unified course of action. The Lemko Rusyn Republic of Western Galicia sought unification with Russia or an independent Czech state. In contrast, the self-proclaimed Komańcza, or Eastern Lemko Republic, sought to align with an independent Ukraine. The Polish government suppressed the latter during a subsequent conflict with pro-Ukrainian forces (1918-1919), imprisoning its leaders and transforming its inhabitants into minions of the Second Polish Republic. Pro-Ukrainian political sentiments set the Sorokas apart from Russian allies in Western Galicia but also led to their eventual resettlement in Soviet Ukraine. These short-lived Republics help explain the Rusyn people's fractured identity.

Despite the Polish government's assurances to safeguard Rusyn cultural traditions, language, and religious practices, access to economic, educational, and religious opportunities overwhelmingly favored ethnic Poles. The Soviets made no pretense of respecting Rusyn traditions and instead demanded strict loyalty to a unified Russian Orthodox identity and allegiance to the communist state.

The Sorokas' political aspirations may have been more than a simple reflection of their nationalist ambitions, however. Rusyns often quip that they are from "nowhere" because their homelands have always been dominated by others. This, along with cultural, religious, historical, and geographic similarities, explains why some people assert that Rusyns and Ukrainians are part of the same ethnic family. Some argue that Ukrainians are Rusyns, while others claim Rusyns are Ukrainians. The debate remains highly contentious to the present day. Rusyns were only recently recognized as a distinct ethnic group in some Central and Eastern European countries; Russia and Ukraine continue to argue that Rusyns are Ukrainians. This left me to conclude that if we are not blood relatives, then we were once united in spirit.

What is more certain is that my grandparents came to the United States seeking a better life. However, even this timeworn phrase requires further examination. Better than what? With my forebears lying deep beneath the sod, only history could provide the answer.

Over the centuries, my ancestors endured constant oppression and generations of suffering. Despite being considered inferior to everyone other than Jews, their governments viewed them as a societal threat and implemented policies to prevent them from ever being regarded as equals. Discriminatory measures were especially harsh on those who refused to assimilate into Polish culture by learning the "state" language or attending the Roman Catholic Church. Unstable borders and military conscription tore families apart, while the ongoing presence of military forces introduced repeated cycles of famine, disease, and destruction. Immigration must have surely been seen as a welcome alternative. Leaving was easier than dismantling the societal institutions that had maintained the status quo for hundreds of years. Little did they know that the destruction of these institutions would lead to even greater suffering in the mid-twentieth century.

To understand the Rusyn people and the lives of my ancestors, it is essential to consider the historical context of their lives. As such, this chapter will concentrate on the history of Galicia.

My Grandparents' Galicia

Galicia's geopolitical history began as a principality of Kievan Rus. In 1245, it became an independent Kingdom of Galicia-Volhynia. About a century later, it was conquered by Polish forces and renamed Red Ruthenia. In 1559, it was incorporated into the Polish-Lithuanian Commonwealth. In the late 18th century, it was annexed by the Austrian Empire and renamed the Kingdom of Galicia and Lodomeria—a romantic name for a place that was anything but. In 1867, it became a province of the Austro-Hungarian Empire. In 1918, two-thirds of the region was returned to Poland, and during World War II, it became part of the Nazi Reichstag Galitzine (1941-1944). After World War II, Poland lost its eastern borderlands to the Soviets but gained former German territories in the west. And this summary overlooks the near-

The Political Instability of Galicia

1199–1245: Principality of Galicia-Volhynia
1245–1349: Kingdom of Galicia-Volhynia
1349–1569: Kingdom of Poland
1569–1772: Polish-Lithuanian Commonwealth
1772–1918: Kingdom of Galicia and Lodomeria
1918–1939: Republic of Poland
1939–1941: Soviet Occupation (eastern half)
1941–1944: Nazi German Occupation
1945–1991: Ukrainian Soviet Socialist Republic and
Polish People's Republic
1991– Independent Ukraine and Poland (Third Polish
Republic from 1989

Illustration 2.00
Source: Forgotten Galicia, bit.ly/3V7RC4R)

constant turmoil caused by failed invasions, the brutality of eastern nomadic tribes, and the effects of internal political conflicts. The region's turbulent history stems from its proximity to critical mountain passes that link Eastern and Western Europe, and its role as a buffer zone between rival empires.

Illustration 2.01: Territorial changes of Poland immediately after World War II - Wikipedia (43)

Paul Magocsi described Galicia as a *borderland of borders*. Given its strategic importance, one might have expected Galicia to thrive. And for a time, it did. However, with so many factions vying for control, Galicia, as my grandparents knew it, was backward and poor. Polish inhabitants called the region the *Land of the Naked and Hungry* (44). Peasants comprised 90% of the population. Galicia was home to two major communities—Kraków in the west and L'viv in the east, each serving as its capital at different times. Most residents of the rural landscape

(43) Wikipedia. 2025. "Territorial Changes of Poland Immediately after World War II." Wikimedia Foundation. Last modified January 9, 2025.

(44) Wikipedia. 2024. "Poverty in Austrian Galicia." Wikimedia Foundation. Last modified: June 15, 2024.
https://en.wikipedia.org/wiki/Poverty_in_Austrian_Galicia.

engaged in small-scale agriculture. According to JP Himka, in the late nineteenth century, Galicia accounted for 10% of the Austrian Empire's land and 15% of its population, or nearly 6 million residents. Approximately 40% of the population was Polish, 40% Ruthenian, and 10% Jewish, with the remainder being primarily German.

Illustration 2.02: Mid-19th-century map of Galicia. My grandparents were southeast of Krakow. (45)

While impoverished city dwellers died in crowded, disease-ridden slums, rural inhabitants routinely succumbed to starvation. Those in rural locations lived in small, bug-infested, thatched-roof cottages, which they shared with their livestock at seasonal times of the year. By 1880, rural Galicia had the highest population density in Europe. Peasant farms provided only a modest existence, but there were few alternatives. Ethnic Poles dominated civil service positions, thereby controlling the lives of the poor, disenfranchised Rusyn inhabitants. According to author Marty Rady, Vienna denied resident permits to Rusyns and Jews, resulting in about two-thirds of the city's population residing there

(45) Wikipedia. 2024. "The Germans from Galicia." Wikimedia Foundation. Last modified: June 15, 2024.

illegally, without access to welfare, decent housing, or the political influence to improve their situation. Thus, generations of peasants remained where they were—they had nowhere else to go.

Bread was critically important for survival. Even today, it plays a vital role in Rusyn holidays and family events (such as weddings and funerals) because it is considered a blessing from God. In Galicia, families were so impoverished that they sometimes mixed flour with ash or ground acorns to make it stretch. Potatoes were regarded as the region's second bread.

In a biography about Rusyn jazz pianist Bill Evans, his mother, Mary Soroka (who may be a possible relative), described Galicia at the end of the 19th century.

> *They lived in horrible conditions in turf huts with earthen floors. Only the parents had beds. They had an oven for cooking, but no chimney for the smoke to get out. In winter, the children slept on top of the stove to stay warm. They were dirt poor. And they lived in an area where the boundary lines kept changing with every conflict. One time, it was Russia; another time, it was Hungary; and then it would be Germany. These people did not know to whom they belonged. They were Russians living in Austro-Hungary, being ruled by Poles.* (46)

Beds were considered a luxury in most parts of Europe until the late 16th century. It was common for both lower- and upper-class individuals to share the same sleeping quarters, although wealthy individuals got to decide who slept next to them at night. Safety was prioritized over privacy, and medieval peasants had many

---

(46) Pettinger, Peter. 2002. *How My Heart Sings*. New Haven, Connecticut: Yale University Press.

fears and suspicions keeping them up at night. In Galicia, however, these conditions persisted well into the 20th century — the region's historical underdevelopment of Galicia cast a long shadow, and even today, it is marked by underemployment and limited infrastructure.

Disease and malnutrition were commonplace. Chronic undernourishment led to low productivity and high susceptibility to diseases like cholera and typhus. Vaccines were largely unavailable. Doctors, often lacking formal medical training, were either inaccessible, prohibitively expensive, or regarded as quacks. One source noted that a single doctor might be responsible for the health and welfare of an entire district. As a result, home remedies and a hefty dose of superstition were used to treat most medical issues. Rusyns who survived childhood developed robust constitutions. Those with serious health problems didn't survive. Women returned to work shortly after giving birth. The absence of daycare led to the deaths of unsupervised children from injuries sustained in the home. As a result, the local community encouraged children to start working at the age of six, tending flocks, caring for their siblings, or working as servants in neighboring homes and villages. (47) Children also helped with domestic chores such as tending animals, gathering firewood, or assisting with planting and harvesting crops.

Even as Galicia's political borders shifted, its property and resources remained in the hands of the landowning aristocracy. Before the establishment of the Kingdom of Poland, nobles (known as szlachta) convinced themselves they were descendants of the ancient Sarmatians — an elite

---

(47) Slomka, Jan. 2019. *Memoirs of a Peasant*. 3rd ed. Chicago, IL: Polish Genealogical Society of America. Pages 153-155.

society that historically dominated the Slavs. (48) Despite being Slavic themselves, this worldview encouraged them to behave as if only their interests mattered. Church leaders, known as *black priests* (i.e., priests who were aligned with the political system), like other members of the aristocracy, religiously upheld the rigid social order as being ordained by God. Rusyns, viewed as inferior, were considered incapable of governing themselves. Because Roman Catholicism was considered the one true faith, the government actively discriminated against Orthodox Christians, making it nearly impossible for non-Roman Catholics to aspire to a life outside the peasantry. (49) Non-Roman Catholics were regarded with suspicion. Peasants were forbidden from testifying against nobles in court. (50) The justice system allowed Rusyn peasants to be governed by those who acted with impunity. If aristocrats committed injustices against their tenants or serfs, the guilty party(s) might be sentenced to house arrest or receive penance from a local priest.

A Land and People Divided.

Galicia was named after the medieval city of Halych, which served as its center for many years. Galicia is the Latin translation of Halych, meaning "salt," a resource that has been mined in the region for centuries. Salt was crucial for tanning leather, preserving food; it was one of the few resources people couldn't produce themselves. Salt was so

---

(48) Wikipedia. 2024. "Szlachta." Wikimedia Foundation. Last modified: June 15, 2024. https://en.wikipedia.org/wiki/Szlachta.

(49) Brian Lenius interview

(50) Magocsi, Paul R. 2015. *With Their Backs to the Mountains: A History of the Carpatho-Rusyns*. Budapest-New York: Central European University Press. Page 66.

valuable that it acted as a form of currency. During wartime, salt was as important as gunpowder.

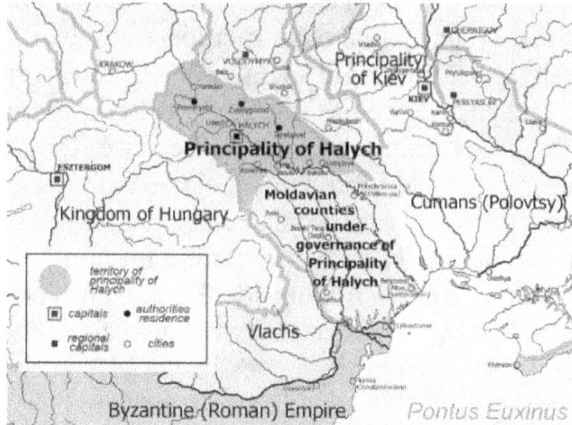

Illustration 2.03: Halych.
https://commons.wikimedia.org/wiki/File:Halych_Principal ity.jpg by Roman Frankiv

Russia, Lithuania, Poland, Austria, the Ottoman Empire, and Hungary coveted Galicia's fertile farmland, timber, white gold (salt), hardy peasants, and commercial trade routes connecting Kyiv to Constantinople—or, in other words, the Baltic to the Black Sea. For over 1,000 years, Constantinople, the world's most prosperous city, served as the hub of global trade and commerce. Situated along the Silk Road and a source of luxury goods, its fortified defenses, aqueducts, and cisterns rendered the city nearly invulnerable to attacks—until a Hungarian artilleryman joined with the Ottomans and using *basilica cannons* fired 1,200-pound projectiles capable of breaching its formidable stone walls.

Despite its vigorous trade network, the region, which became known as the Rus, proved challenging to govern. As a result, at some point in the ninth century, Rus communities invited, elected, or succumbed to Rurik (51), a Varangian (Viking) prince, to lead their struggling confederation. Rurik's descendants pursued aggressive expansionist policies, but his great-grandson, Vladimir, chose to unify the Rus through a shared religion. Vladimir reportedly considered various forms of religion, including Islam (rejected because it forbade alcohol consumption and favored circumcision), Judaism (rejected because the Jews had lost Jerusalem and presumably favor from their God), Byzantine Orthodoxy, and Roman Catholicism. Vladimir was supposedly most impressed with the aesthetics of the Orthodox Church. (52) While this fanciful tale may be true, the decision likely stemmed from more practical considerations; specifically, Vladimir's political and economic alliance with the Byzantine Empire. His fifth wife, Anna, the sister of the Byzantine Emperor, made Vladimir's conversion to Orthodoxy a condition of their marriage. His grandmother, canonized as St. Olga, is a revered saint in the Orthodox Church for her role in promoting Eastern Christianity. (53) Regardless of his motivation, Vladimir's edict divided Eastern and Western Europe until Peter the

---

(51) The first Russian Tsar, Ivan the Terrible, descended from Rurik.

(52) Wikipedia. 2024. "Vladimir the Great." Wikimedia Foundation. Last modified: June 24, 2024.
https://en.wikipedia.org/wiki/Vladimir_the_Great.

(53) St. Olga, also known as Olga of Kiev, was the grandmother of Vladimir the Great. She served as the regent of Kievan Rus' for her son Svyatoslav I and played a significant role in the early Christianization of the region. Her grandson, Vladimir the Great, later became the Grand Prince of Kiev and is known for officially converting Kievan Rus' to Christianity in 988.

Great attempted to modernize Russia with Western ideals. Since Vladimir imposed the Orthodox faith on his people from the top, pagan traditions and beliefs gradually evolved into expressions of Christian faith.

Galicia was a prosperous principality of Kievan Rus for about two centuries. At its peak, the Rus governed a territory stretching from the Baltic to the Black Sea, a span of 1,500 miles, making it the largest kingdom in medieval Europe. However, even a shared religion failed to establish lasting peace. *Partible inheritance laws*, which allocated property among surviving heirs, slowly fractured the Rus into competing principalities, each seeking to expand its influence. Additionally, the *rota system*, which transferred the throne from brother to brother rather than from father to son, led to acts of fratricide to secure succession rights. By the late 11th century, the Rus had fragmented into competing regional powers, each with its own leader and system of governance. As the Crusades diverted trade from Constantinople, the resulting economic decline of the Rus left it vulnerable to Mongol invasion. The Mongols, through raids and conquest, transformed much of the old Rus into vassals of the *Golden Horde*. Galicia-Volhynia, however, preserved its independence by not opposing Mongol rule and paying an annual tribute. Galician peasants were free to pursue seasonal economic opportunities to supplement their income, and some peasants even managed to acquire land.

Illustration 2.04: The Rus. (54)

Galicia then fell under Polish rule and remained in its control for the next 400 years. After Polish conquest, economic reliance on grain increased landowners' demands for free labor. Peasants were compelled to produce grain for Europe's growing urban centers. At the same time that

---

serfdom expanded in Eastern Europe, Western Europe industrialized and exploited the labor and resources of distant colonies. Waldemar Kugligowski's article on the history of Polish serfdom explains:

> In the early 16th century, Poland emerged as the most significant European exporter of cereal grains. The primary recipient of these grains was the Netherlands, and the revenue generated from this trade allowed the Polish nobility to accumulate wealth, as they had previously faced limited opportunities to engage in international markets. Thus, access to a vast and highly receptive market provided an impetus for increased production. To achieve this, large-scale farms were established, initially near major cities or along the banks of the Vistula River and its tributaries, which facilitated the transportation of grain. The expansion of export opportunities relied on increasing export acreages, developing extensive farms, and enlarging serfdom. This process solidified the system of serfdom on large farms, which became the economic foundation of the Commonwealth and endured for nearly three centuries. (55)

Galicia was also enmeshed in the religious power struggle sweeping across Europe. As Rome watched anxiously, Protestantism successfully challenged the church's authority, and the Islamic Ottoman Empire expanded its reach into Eastern Europe. The pope sought to expand his influence by dividing Orthodox Christians in Poland and

---

(55) Kuligowski, Waldemar . "A History of Polish Serfdom." Eurozine. February 13, 2018. https://www.eurozine.com/a-history-of-polish-serfdom/.

Russia. Rusyns were eager to improve their economic prospects and elevate their clergy to the status of Roman Catholic priests. (56) These efforts culminated in *the Union of Brest* in 1596, when Orthodox communities broke from their Eastern brethren and aligned with the Roman Catholic Church. Initially called the Uniate Church, it would later be known as the Greek Catholic Church, and later still, the Byzantine Catholic Church. Most Orthodox clergy quickly shifted their loyalties. According to Paul Magocsi:

> *Over time, the Greek Catholic priest evolved into a sort of village landlord, compelling his parishioners to contribute through agricultural labor and physical work. Consequently, the Greek Catholic priesthood emerged as the wealthiest class within Rusyn society. Joining this class was the only way for the son of a peasant serf to elevate his status lot.* (57)

Congregations quickly followed suit because the pope permitted them to practice their Eastern liturgical traditions. Priests could marry and have families (58), celebrate the liturgy in Slavonic, and follow the Julian Calendar. However, the government actively discouraged any remaining loyalty to the Orthodox faith. After the Union of Brest, Orthodox lands and properties were confiscated.

---

(56) Duly, William. *The Rusins of Minnesota*. Minnesota Rusin Association, 1993.

(57) Magocsi, Paul R. 1983. *The Rusyn-Ukrainians of Czechoslovakia*. W. Braumüller. Page 17.

(58) Orthodox priests and deacons can be married, but they must do so before being ordained. Once ordained, they are not permitted to marry. If a married priest's wife passes away, he is expected to remain celibate. However, bishops are traditionally chosen from among the monastic clergy, meaning they are usually celibate; though in early Christian history, concubinage or quasi-wives were tolerated.

Many Orthodox believers either worshiped in secret or fled to Russia to escape persecution. Orthodox priests who refused to join the Uniate Church lost their clerical status and were reduced to serfs. (59) Most Rusyns remained Greek Catholic until the 20th century, when some decided to return to the Orthodox faith.

With shifting borders, "nationality" was a meaningless concept. Family members could wake up and find themselves living on opposite sides of the border. After the Partitions of Poland (covered in a later section), passports became necessary to attend schools and visit nearby villages, disrupting the crucial relationships needed for survival. (60) Their region was known as the Red Rus by the Russians, Russian Poland by the Slavs, Little Poland by the Poles, Carpatho-Russia by the Americans, and Ruthenia by the Germans. My grandparents' ethnicity was reflected in official government documents in so many ways that I wondered if they knew themselves--until I discovered that Rusyn was not offered as a choice.

The Polish Manor Economy and Serfdom's Expansion

Galicia's social and economic structures remained essentially unchanged for generations, resulting in widespread poverty throughout the region. But what caused these systems to become so deeply ingrained in their way of life? Again, history provides the answer.

The fall of the Roman Empire threw Western Europe into turmoil. Viking, Mongol, and Tartar invasions, as well as barbarian attacks and rampant lawlessness, were the

---

(59) Beskid, Anthony. 2024. *The Origin of the Lems, Slavs of the Danubian Provenance.* London: Forgotten Books.

(60) Slomka. *Memoirs of a Peasant.* Page 219.

norm. The Roman Legions, which had long maintained order and secured international trade, vanished, as did the standard, minted currency that supported commercial exchange. Lacking engineers and an imperial army to build and maintain roads, bridges, and aqueducts, the Empire's infrastructure deteriorated. The technological knowledge required for such advancements was also lost. (61) The starving and fearful masses fled to the countryside, where independent barter economies emerged around large agricultural estates (manors) that were closely aligned with the Church.

In exchange for supplying food and protection, the proprietors of these estates became lords and masters over the nonlandowning peasants. They also owned or controlled all commercial activities relating to their enterprises. These informal understandings became generationally binding after the peasants were made into serfs. Landowner interests controlled the local economy because no larger institutions were keeping them in check; therefore, abuse and exploitation were common. Serfs served at the discretion of their masters, whose decisions could be arbitrary and unpredictable. Victims had to establish wrongdoing, but even then, it was often the same lord or steward who decided their fate. (62) While this system provided peasants with some predictability and security, it came at the cost of their freedom and human rights.

---

(61) The art of concrete was lost after 400 AD and not rediscovered until 1756 by British Engineer John Smeaton.

(62) Glinski, Mikolaj. "Slavery or Serfdom: Or Was Poland a Colonial Empire?" Culture. PL. October 8, 2015.
https://culture.pl/en/article/slavery-vs-serfdom-or-was-poland-a-colonial-empire.

With no uniform system of rule, Poland evolved into a pseudo-feudalistic governance structure. Three social classes were recognized: those who fought (nobles and knights, or szlachta), those who prayed (the clergy), and those who worked (peasants).

Illustration 2.05: Manor house in Lopuszna, Poland. Image from: widok-ogolny-przed-dworem.jpg (550×309) (tripadvisor.com)

The nobles pledged their fealty to serve the most powerful lord, the king, in exchange for land, while the peasants pledged their loyalty to the nobles. However, unlike other European states, Poland did not grant royal titles; in theory, all nobles were equal to the king. Some individuals, however, held more political influence than others. Although not officially titled, *magnates* were the wealthiest and most powerful political elites, building fortified strongholds and funding private armies to maintain their way of life. Magnates were sometimes referred to as "little kings" due to their significant power and influence.

In addition to maintaining the kingdom's defenses, the noble szlachta participated in civic governance by overseeing tax collections and appointing local officials. (63) Jewish lessees managed local business activities, such as taverns, mills, and inns, and acted as intermediaries between the szlachta and the peasants. One commentator observed that *"Serfdom created two near-nations—nobles and peasants—and between them a Jewish wall."* (64) Even long after serfdom had ended, there was little interaction between the landowner and the rural population—their lives resembled planets on paths that would never meet. (65)

Thus, the entire social and economic system was founded on a one-sided governance structure that was impervious to change. Opposition to the established social order was futile; therefore, a peasant's only options were to revolt, resist (pretend to be ignorant and perform substandard work), or flee. As a former serf explained:

> *No worse punishment could be found for men and women than serfdom. People were treated worse than cattle are today. They were beaten both at work and at home for the merest trifle. What I have heard from them could not be written down. It is unbelievable how men could thus torture their fellows! Every farmer had to do his dues at the manor house first, whether with his team or on foot. He could only work on his land, sowing and reaping at night. No excuse*

---

(63) Wikipedia. 2023. "Nobility Rights in Poland." Wikimedia Foundation. Last modified: April 8, 2023. https://en.wikipedia.org/wiki/Nobility_privileges_in_Poland.

(64) Wańkowicz, M. *Through Four Climates 1912–1972*, Warsaw 1972, p. 544.

(65) Gawell, Donna. 2024. *Our Galician Ancestors: The History and Culture of the People from Poland and Ukraine from the Middle Ages to WWI*. Independently Published. Page 209.

as to pressing needs at home was of any use. The overseer would come at once if one did not appear as ordered. If he found the wife busy cooking, he would throw a pail of water on the fire—or, in winter, would carry off the windows or doors. If that did not work, the overseer would eject the farmer from the home and homestead. Someone else would be put in his place. Nor was there any appeal anywhere since the lord of the manor owned everything. He was both land and water, even the wind, since only he could build a windmill to grind corn. Only when all his compulsory dues were done could the peasant sing the old song. I am not afraid that the landlord will molest me. (66)

Serfdom condemned individuals to a life of poverty and destroyed any hope of generational improvement. The ruling trifecta—Lord, State, and Church—claimed nearly all of a peasant's yearly income through tithes, taxes, and fees, and enforced a lifetime of servitude.

The lives of those benefitting from serfdom, however, reached a level of opulence almost unimaginable today. For example, Count Alfred Potocki, who owned Lancut Castle in southeastern Poland during the 19th and 20th centuries, was known for his lavish lifestyle. Potocki's horse stables were among the finest in Europe, featuring tiled floors, mahogany furnishings, and chandeliers. The property remained in the Potocki family until 1944.

---

(66) Slomka. *Memoirs of a Peasant*. Page 22

Illustration 2.06: Łańcut Castle (Wikipedia)

Illustration 2.07: Stanisław Antoni Szczuka, portrayed in a typical Sarmatian style; Source: Wikimedia/Wilanów Palace Museum. The wealthiest magnates wore crimson and scarlet clothing, earning them the nickname "the ***Crimson Ones***." (67)

During the 15th and 16th centuries, the szlachta strengthened its influence, transforming the absolute monarchy into a decentralized republic of nobles. In 1496,

(67) Wikipedia. 2024. "Stanisław Antoni Szczuka." Wikimedia Foundation. Last modified: August 27, 2024. https://en.wikipedia.org/wiki/Stanis%C5%82aw_Antoni_Szczuka.

the szlachta enacted the *Statutes of Piotrkow*, which legally transformed peasants into serfs—legislation partly driven by the labor shortages caused by the Black Death. Despite legal constraints, serfs were sold, gifted, or traded (with their offspring) to other nobles and estates, just like slaves.

Noble status was made a hereditary right. Non-noble property owners had to sell their estates to recognized members of the szlachta, seek ennoblement (which was rarely granted), or forfeit their ownership rights. (68) The magnates prohibited Jews from owning land and mandated that nobles hold leadership positions within the church. The szlachta-controlled parliament banned the king from enacting any law without its full consent. (69) Noble-led rebellions were considered legal if the king threatened any of their extensive privileges.

The Sejm also decreed that any noble engaged in trade or commerce would forfeit their privileged status. The Sejm elected foreign elites to serve as their king, partly because successive hereditary rulers failed to produce male heirs, but also to gain the upper hand. They made it increasingly difficult for the king to ennoble peasants, because such recognition required the consent of the Sejm.

With no system of checks and balances, the szlachta were free to negotiate secret alliances with foreign powers, inviting outside aggression to enrich themselves at the state's expense. Some allied with Russia, while others aligned with France, Austria, Hungary, or Prussia. By exercising their

---

(68) Wikipedia. 2024. "Magnates of Poland and Lithuania." Wikimedia Foundation. Last modified: March 6, 2024. https://en.wikipedia.org/wiki/Magnates_of_Poland_and_Lithuania.

(69) The Sejm was the Polish parliament, comprised entirely of szlachta.

golden freedoms (70), they could defeat any proposed legislation with one vote, known as the *liberum veto*, (71), which in turn allowed neighboring empires to dominate the Polish government through the payment of a single bribe.. The szlachta refused to levy taxes to support a centralized army because they feared it would undermine their power. Authors like James Michener observed that this "curious system" made Poland a continual target of foreign intervention. (72)

    Ironically, Poland was considered one of the most democratic kingdoms in Europe, with ten to twelve percent of its population participating in its governance. In contrast, only two to three percent of the population in England and France were part of the ruling class. (73) The sheer size and diversity of the szlachta, the liberum veto, an elected king, and the absence of an imperial army explain why Poland ceased to exist for 123 years. (between 1795 and 1918). Poland was "*too democratic for its own good.*" (74) The kingdom's central and strategic location, geography, and dysfunctional governance system made it an easy target for political opportunists.

---

(70) This system ensured that all nobles, regardless of rank or wealth, had equal legal status and significant political influence

(71) This rule allowed any member of the Sejm (the Commonwealth's parliament) to unilaterally block legislation. It was intended to protect the individual freedoms of the szlachta, but it ultimately led to legislative paralysis.

(72) Michener, James A. *Poland: A Novel*. Dial Press Trade Paperback, 2015. Page 23.

(73) Michener. *Poland*. Page 26

(74) Liulevicius, Vejas G., director. *A History of Eastern Europe*. The Great Courses, 2015.

In the 17th century, the magnates sought to raise taxes and expand serfdom. However, the general isolation of Rusyn villages, the presence of armed mountaineers, and the threat of Tartar invasion hindered their efforts. As a result, Rusyns became the freest yet poorest people in Central Europe.

The Commonwealth's economy declined in the 17th century due to the unfettered influence of the landowning aristocracy. Aristocrats prioritized their own wealth and power over the economic well-being of the Commonwealth, resulting in inefficient land use, decreased agricultural productivity, and inadequate investment in other economic sectors. The growing influence of the Sejm caused royal towns, like my grandfather's, to be among the first to suffer, as the parliament favored communities owned by its members over those benefiting the king. The rising power of neighboring states—specifically, Russia, Prussia, and Austria—ultimately led to the complete disintegration of the Commonwealth during the three *Partitions of Poland* between 1772 and 1795. The foreign powers that cannibalized the region said they were reclaiming what was rightfully theirs. Thus, geography would drive the quality of life of the Rusyn people for the next 123 years.

Life in the Austrian Empire

With the Partitions of Poland, most—but not all—of Galicia came under Russian control; however, my grandparents' villages became part of the Austrian Empire. Russia was less welcoming to its new inhabitants than the Austrians, referring to them as *"Little Russians."* The Tsar believed that his new subjects would assimilate into Greater Russian culture and ensured this inevitability by suppressing their language and culture and closing the Uniate Church. He viewed a separate Rusyn identity as a threat to imperial unity and Russia's expansionist foreign policy.

Austria, on the other hand, recognized its new inhabitants as a distinct ethnic minority, primarily to constrain the political influence of the Poles. (75) As the self-proclaimed successors of the Roman Empire, the Habsburgs allowed their newly acquired territories to keep traditional governance practices in exchange for their loyalty. This

---

The **Partitions of Poland** were a series of three divisions of the Polish-Lithuanian Commonwealth that occurred in the late 18th century, resulting in the elimination of Poland as an independent state for 123 years. Here's a brief overview.

• **First Partition (1772):** Initiated by Russia, Prussia, and Austria, this partition resulted in Poland losing approximately 30% of its territory and half of its population. The three powers defended their actions by claiming they were restoring order in Poland, which was viewed as weak and chaotic.

• **Second Partition (1793):** After internal reforms in Poland, including the adoption of the Constitution of May 3, 1791, Russia and Prussia intervened again. This partition further reduced Poland's territory, leaving it one-third of its original size.

• **Third Partition (1795):** After the failed Kościuszko Uprising, Russia, Prussia, and Austria decided to dissolve what remained of Poland. This final partition effectively removed Poland from the European map until it regained independence in 1918.

---

(75) Zalewski. *Galician Trails.* Page 12.

These partitions had a significant impact on Polish national identity and the growth of resistance movements until the re-establishment of the Second Polish Republic.

Source: Wikipedia. 2024. "Partitions of Poland." Wikimedia Foundation. Last modified June 6, 2024. https://simple.wikipedia.org/wiki/Partitions_of_Poland.

Image from: The partition of Poland – Poles – Te Ara Encyclopedia of New Zealand

Illustration 2.08: Partitions of Poland

changed when Maria Theresa and her son, Emperor Joseph II, implemented a series of administrative, military, economic, educational, financial, and legal reforms to modernize and strengthen the Habsburg Empire. Maria Theresa was deeply anti-Protestant and anti-Jewish—but she introduced reforms that were pragmatic and aimed at strengthening the state.. She established compulsory education to raise literacy to the fourth-grade level. She provided seminary training for Rusyn clergy. And she

---

Serfdom was a labor system in which peasants, known as serfs, were bound to the land owned by a lord. While serfs were not slaves, they were not truly free either; they were tied to the land and could not leave without the lord's permission. Key aspects of serfdom include:

1. **Labor Obligations:** Serfs worked on the lord's land several days a week. This labor was known as corvée. The corvée could include various tasks such as plowing, harvesting, and maintaining the lord's estate.

2. **Auxiliary Days**: In addition to the regular corvée, serfs were often required to perform extra labor on auxiliary days. These additional workdays were mandated by the lord, typically during peak agricultural seasons or for special projects. Landlords exploited this privilege to such an extent that it frequently applied to most weeks of the year.

3. **Personal Duties**: Serfs were also obligated to provide personal services to the lord, such as domestic work or skilled labor, based on their abilities.

---

4. **Personal Duties**: Serfs were also obligated to provide personal services to the lord, such as domestic work or skilled labor, based on their abilities.

5. **Fees and Taxes**: Serfs were required to pay various fees and taxes to the lord, including rent for the land they farmed, a share of their produce, and special levies for events such as marriages or inheritances.

6. **Restrictions**: Serfs had limited rights and freedoms. They needed the lord's permission to marry, move, or change jobs. Their children were born into serfdom as well.

Despite these obligations, serfs enjoyed certain protections. Lords were expected to provide justice and support their serfs during times of famine. Serfs retained the right to cultivate their own plots of land for the sustenance of their families.

Source: Wikipedia. 2025. "Serfdom." Wikimedia Foundation. Last modified April 19, 2025. Image from: widok-ogolny-przed-dworem.jpg (550×309) (tripadvisor.com).

Illustration 2.09: Serfdom

renamed the Uniate Church the Greek Catholic Church to ensure equal rights for followers of both Eastern and Western Catholic faiths--a calculated move to weaken Polish influence in Galicia and reinforce imperial unity. According to the Ancestry website, Maria Theresa also permitted peasants to seek justice through royal officials instead of their landlords' courts. In 1772, she capped the amount of unpaid labor landlords could demand of their serfs.

> *Landlords were forbidden from requiring more than one or two days of labor per week. Serfs received legal guarantees regarding plot and garden size, hunting rights, and free time. Industrious peasants could monetize their free time by selling handicrafts or services and fulfilling their landlords' obligations with money instead of labor. Religious tolerance and an emphasis on education led to a flowering of literature and culture.* (76)

Despite these efforts, Austrian tariffs and fees on grain markets and transportation channels suppressed the Galician economy. Overland travel through the mountainous terrain demanded considerable time and effort, leading to a preference for alternative transportation methods. Progress was slow, fodder was expensive, thieves posed a constant threat, and transportation animals were prone to injury and death. (77) All these factors contributed to Galicia's widespread economic impoverishment.

The Move to Multicultural Secularism

Her son, Emperor Joseph II, was arguably the most radical Enlightened Absolutist of his age. In 1781, he enacted the *Edict of Toleration*, which granted religious

---

(76) Empress Maria Theresa (1740 to 1780), a devout Roman Catholic, believed that religious unity was essential for a peaceful society. As a result, she did not advocate for religious toleration. Her successor, Joseph II, had more enlightened views.

(77) Armstrong, Dorsey, director. *The Black Death: New Lessons from Recent Research.* The Great Courses, 2022.

freedom to Protestants, Orthodox Christians, and Jews, thereby transforming the once-homogeneous population into a multicultural state. He closed monasteries to fund public education and social welfare benefits, to promote widespread prosperity and reduce the influence of the Roman Catholic Church. (78) Joseph created cadastral (land ownership) maps to collect taxes for the government and expand the imperial army. As Paul Magocsi explained:

> *The military played a significant role in the lives of citizens in the Empire. Before 1802, military service was for life, but not all those years were spent in active service. Those exempt from military service included the clergy, the nobility, the eldest son, certain government officials, and mining and iron production workers. After 1802, military service was reduced to 10 years. In 1868, universal military conscription was implemented. Every male citizen was required to serve a minimum of three years of active service. In 1912, this requirement was reduced to two years, plus ten years in the reserves.* (79)

According to the Family Search website, one benefit of military service, which was quite unusual at the time, was the absence of segregation and discrimination against nonconformist religious groups. Protestant, Orthodox, and Jewish people served alongside the Catholic majority. Soldiers from each group enjoyed all the rights of military membership, and many held high-ranking positions in the Austrian military.

---

(78) Davies, Norman. 2012. *Vanished Kingdoms: The Rise and Fall of States and Nations.* Penguin Books. Page 451.

(79) Magocsi, Paul R. "Austria Military Records." FamilySearch.com. https://www.Family Search.org/en/wiki/Austria_Military_Records.

Joseph aimed to create a unitary state with a uniform legal and administrative system, reducing the autonomy of Hungary, Bohemia, and other crown lands. In 1784, he made German the language of administration and education, sparking backlash in multilingual regions. Joseph issued over 6,000 edicts and 11,000 laws, aiming to standardize legal systems across his empire

Emperor Joseph's reforms created a seismic shift in the power dynamics of his empire. He abolished the nobles' golden freedoms, tax-exempt status, and judicial control. Non-citizen serfs were granted protection under a standard legal code. Tenant farming replaced serfdom, enabling peasants to remit monetary rents instead of relentless, unremunerated labor. After Emperor Joseph died in 1790, many of his reforms perished with him. The nobility despised Joseph and his far-reaching reforms. The immediate turnaround following his death demonstrates the transient nature of authoritarian rule and why peasants could never fully trust their government. (80) The only reforms that survived were in the religious realm, so the daily lives of peasants remained fundamentally unchanged. However, his actions would later spark successive rebellions calling for autonomy and human rights.

During the nineteenth century, the Russian, Polish, Prussian, and Hungarian governments secretly fueled ethnic tensions and social unrest within the Habsburg Empire. These actions ultimately led to the creation of the dual monarchy in 1867. In Galicia, anti-Austrian feelings were rare. Officially, anyone could request a meeting with the Emperor, so most peasants thought he was on their side. Anti-Polish feelings, however, were widespread. In 1846, the Polish nobility tried to form an alliance with their peasants in

---

(80) "The Habsburg Cadastral Survey and Map Initiative." Gesher Galicia, https://maps.geshergalicia.org/ref/habmap/.

a rebellion against the Austrian government. Recognizing their exclusion from the current political system, leaders of the Polish nationalist movement promised peasants a key role in their new republic, one free from serfdom. Fueled by recent memories of past injustices, the peasants turned on their masters instead. The timing of the nobles' uprising couldn't have been worse. A cholera epidemic, crop failures, and floods left peasants desperate and starving. According to Larry Wolff:

> To maintain order in the province, the Habsburgs offered the Polish elites significant autonomy in governing Galicia. This autonomy turned out to be a disaster, as the Poles put in charge turned out to be "particularly barbarous in their conduct toward the serfs." The ethnic, linguistic, religious, and social divides between the diverse groups intensified, culminating in a massacre of Polish landlords by their laborers in 1846. (81)

Nearly 2,000 members of the Polish nobility were killed, and 500 manor homes were destroyed. (82)

Post-insurrection

Shortly after the failed rebellion, the Austrians forcibly returned the peasants to their estates. However, as the Poles and Austrians competed for peasant loyalty, labor obligations (*corvée*) were abolished, and peasants had the right to own land. Wealthy peasants were even given the

---

(81) Wolff, Larry. 2012. *The Idea of Galicia: History and Fantasy in Habsburg Political Culture*. Stanford Press.

(82) Wikipedia. 2024. "Galicia Peasant Rising of 1846." Wikimedia Foundation. Last modified: March 10, 2024. https://en.wikipedia.org/wiki/Galician_Peasant_Uprising_of_1846.

right to vote. (83) Reforms aimed at curbing nationalist fervor included the right to elect local representatives and receive an education in one's mother tongue. To penalize the nobles for instigating the insurrection, serfs were released under relatively favorable terms. However, these reforms had a negligible effect on the daily lives of the peasants and, in some ways, made things worse.

For a century after the abolition of serfdom, the fundamental aspects of Galician villages—including landownership, the economic status of their residents, and the nature and extent of their interactions—remained the same as in previous centuries of serfdom. Reforms aimed at unifying the Empire fostered each region's political capacity to govern itself. Emancipation led to generational and gender-based tensions regarding dowries, inheritance, and family authority. Further, as author Stella Hryniuk observed:

> *Before the abolition of serfdom, Galician agricultural lands were divided into two legal categories— dominical land (land managed by the manor) and rustica land, which, although in law was the property of the estate, was deemed to belong to the peasants who farmed the land. Rustica land could only belong to the peasant class—those who were exclusively involved in agriculture. It could not be sold by the manor house separately from the estate. Property always passed to the eldest son. When serfdom was abolished in 1848, all rustica land was given to the peasants. The landowners were indemnified by a **special tax** levied on all taxpayers. The right to use shared meadows, pastures, and woodlands was left*

(83) Struve, Kai. "Citizenship and National Identity: The Peasants of Galicia during the 19th Century." Academia. www.academia.edu/1439246/Citizenship_and_National_Identity_the_Pe asants_of_Galicia_during_the_19th_Century. Pages 76-77.

unsettled. The two decades following emancipation from serfdom in 1848 were dominated by a struggle between landlords and peasants over the question of "servitudes," i.e., rights to forests and pastures. (84)

The special tax functioned like a 30- to 40-year mortgage, turning former serfs into heavily indebted tenants. While wealthy landowners kept the most fertile land for themselves (or sold it to influential outsiders), special tax receipts were allocated to the nobility as compensation for the relatively poor land they had given their tenants. This, along with environmental factors, led to ongoing indebtedness that turned the newly freed peasants into "economic serfs."

The ban on dividing inherited land was lifted in 1868, allowing property to be divided among surviving family members rather than passing to the eldest son. By the late 1800s, many peasant holdings had decreased to less than 1 hectare, far below the minimum of 2 to 5 hectares required. As a result, within a very short time, the peasants no longer had enough land to support their families—land had been subdivided *below the survival point.* (85) Beginning in 1868, villagers were banned from accessing open pastures and collecting firewood from the forests controlled by the manor. When the peasants complained, the Austrian courts sided with the Polish landowners. Peasant landholdings were also divided into non-contiguous strips, ensuring that no family received all the best land and allowing irrigation to be equitably shared. (86) Strip fields served as a form of crop

---

(84) Hryniuk, Stella. 1991. *Peasants With Promise: Ukrainians in Southeastern Galicia, 1880-1900*. Indiana University Press.

(85) Nugent, Walter. 1995. *Crossings: The Great Transatlantic Migrations, 1870-1914*. Indiana University Press. Page 84.

(86) Hryniuk. *Peasants with Promise*. Page 8.

insurance, but they also made farming more labor-intensive and time-consuming. Around the same time, factory-manufactured goods began to supplant cottage industries that produced textiles, needlework, and wood products. At one time, cottage industries provided a consistent and reliable source of income. (87)

By 1900, a small group of families controlled half of the region's arable farmland and forests. By the turn of the twentieth century, peasant landholdings had dwindled to an average of about five acres spread across twenty separate plots. (88) My maternal grandfather's family fell so deeply into debt that they lost the family farm. The effects of the land reforms quickly became evident. In 1892, an eyewitness described peasant laborers on three different noble estates:

> *His head covering is a mangy fur hood, often of squirrel skin. A sort of great robe hangs loosely below his knees, which is made of the skin of some animal, with fur or hair next to the body. The reverse side is covered with ancient layers of grease for protection against the snow and rain. He wears stockings of the coarsest material and high-legged, pointy shoes of monumental proportions, stuffed with hay, and wrapped with ropes of straw from above the knee to the ankle. These peasant animals are attached to every estate from a dozen to a score. They are disheveled, like hogs from the great house*

---

(87) Nugent. *Crossings*. Page 84.

(88) "An Austro-Hungarian Tragedy – The Kingdom of Galicia & Lodomeria (Part Two)." Europe Between East And West. https://europebetweeneastandwest.wordpress.com/2015/06/19/an-austro-hungarian-tragedy-the-kingdom-of-galicia-lodomeria-part-two/.

kitchen, in the corners of the stables, and lie among the other animals at night. (89)

As institutions came increasingly under the control of Polish nobles, Galicia received little oversight from Vienna's central government. The Austrian government's hands-off approach to Galicia led some historians to call the region an internal colony of the Austrian Empire. Galicia was expected to supply food, men, and horses for its imperial army (90) and to serve as a market for the Empire's industrialized west. Its terrain also served as a buffer zone between the Russian and Ottoman Empires. But investment in Galicia's industrial sector was nearly nonexistent. Aside from promoting cottage industries, the Austrians did little to encourage Galician enterprise. The only regional industrialization involved the production of alcohol. (91)

Wealthy landowners feared that industrialization would upend the social order and lead to demands for human rights. Social elites were upset that the wealth and influence of prosperous businessmen were surpassing their own. These concerns were particularly pronounced in the Hungarian province, where landowners prioritized agriculture over industrialization. Landowners saw little reason to educate the

---

(89) Gawell, Donna. "The Real World of Our Polish Ancestors in Serfdom: Clothing." February 8, 2022. https://donnagawell.com/2022/02/08/the-real-world-of-our-polish-ancestors-in-serfdom-clothing/.

(90) Wikipedia. 2024. "Kingdom of Galicia and Lodomeria." Wikimedia Foundation. Last modified: June 23, 2024. https://en.wikipedia.org/wiki/Kingdom_of_Galicia_and_Lodomeria.

(91) "An Austro-Hungarian Tragedy – The Kingdom of Galicia & Lodomeria (Part Two)." Europe Between East And West. https://europebetweeneastandwest.wordpress.com/2015/06/19/an-austro-hungarian-tragedy-the-kingdom-of-galicia-lodomeria-part-two/.

peasantry beyond what was necessary for survival, as they were more concerned with maintaining an excess supply of unskilled labor.

Before 1881, railways were privately owned and received little public assistance, further isolating Galician communities. The Emperor feared that railroads would bring an influx of radical thinkers and ignite a revolution. (92) Doing nothing was an inexpensive way to guarantee stability. The roads were so poor that traveling just a few miles took several days. Additionally, the Empire employed forced labor to maintain roads and assigned the cost of making improvements to local governments. Vienna viewed Galicia as a corrupt province with a multicultural population that was both dirty and strange. This perception was seemingly confirmed during Franz Joseph's 60th-anniversary celebration when a journalist covering the event reported:

> *Some spectators reported being shocked by the uncouth representatives of the poorer parts of the empire, who frightened children with their weather-beaten and haggard faces. The architect Adolf Loos felt he was witnessing barbarian tribes from the Middle Ages.* (93)

According to author Marty Radyn, Galicians were viewed as inferior because of their presumed Asian or Jewish (non-European) ancestry. Austrian officials characterized Galicia as "a barbaric place" and did not acknowledge it as part of their Empire. (94) Galician Jews were regarded with shame because of their extreme poverty and lack of education.

---

(92) Wikipedia. 2024. "Poverty in Galicia." Wikimedia Foundation. Last modified: June 23, 2024.
https://en.wikipedia.org/wiki/Poverty_in_Austrian_Galicia.

(93) Rady. The Habsburgs. Page 287

Most Galicians continued to engage in subsistence agriculture because they lacked the necessary skills, resources, and education to pursue alternative livelihoods. During a severe famine, just three years after my grandfather was born, the church declared it a sin for peasants to eat their horses. (95) The Catholic Church regarded horse consumption as a pagan custom, prompting Christian leaders to oppose it. Furthermore, horses were essential for transportation, farming, and labor, which made them far more valuable alive than as a source of food.

Despite the daunting challenges, Galician peasants showed remarkable resilience and an unparalleled capacity for suffering. An estimated 50,000 people died from starvation each year. (96) The average life expectancy was 27 years, compared to a decade or more in other parts of Europe. Between 1847 and 1889, a famine occurred roughly every six years. (97) The severity of the widespread starvation was comparable to that of British Ireland.

The region's impoverishment was described in disparaging terms, such as "Galician misery" (*nedza galicyjska*) and "Galician poverty" (*bieda galicyjska*). Meanwhile, the wealthy landowners remained seemingly content with the status quo, choosing to blame their

(94) Genealogica Polonica, Soroka Genealogist Report

(95) Wikipedia. 2024. "Famines in Austrian Galicia." Wikimedia Foundation. Last modified: February 27, 2024.

(96) Wikipedia. 2024. "Famines in Austrian Galicia." Wikimedia Foundation. Last modified: February 27, 2024.

(97) "An Austro-Hungarian Tragedy – The Kingdom of Galicia & Lodomeria (Part Two)." Europe Between East And West. June 15, 2015. An Austro-Hungarian Tragedy – The Kingdom of Galicia & Lodomeria (Part Two).

circumstances on sloth or alcoholism. To maintain an uneasy peace, the Austrians set the three main ethnic groups—the Poles, Ruthenians, and Jews—against each other, thereby *navigating a swirl of balanced discontent.* (98) In 1873, unwilling to grant the Poles the same autonomy as the Hungarians, the Austrians gave them Galicia instead. (99) However, this self-governing authority stifled meaningful change. As each ethnic group blamed the other, the realities of the situation required that Vienna uphold the interests of its most important political force—the landowning Poles. As Polish domination intensified, the peasant population became increasingly angry and dissatisfied.

Despite significant turmoil, affluent families dominated the political landscape even after the Empire's demise, until the communists abolished their privileges following World War II. Starvation and social unrest drove many peasants out of the country. An estimated 750,000 people crossed the Atlantic between 1880 and 1914. Paradoxically, Galicia experienced a 45% increase in population between 1869 and 1910; (100) growing even when Galicia could no longer feed itself.

Galicia remained part of the Austro-Hungarian Empire until 1918. The Great War accelerated its downfall, causing severe economic problems, crop failures, and widespread starvation.. Nevertheless, Franz Joseph's reign, which ended with his death in 1916, lasted 68 years, making

---

(98) "Galicia, Historic Region, Poland and Ukraine." The Columbia Electronic Encyclopedia. Infoplease.

(99) Magocsi. *Galicia: A Historical Survey and Bibliographic Guide.* Page 117.

(100) Wikipedia. 2024. "Kingdom of Galicia and Lodomeria." Wikimedia Foundation. Last modified: June 23, 2024. https://en.wikipedia.org/wiki/Kingdom_of_Galicia_and_Lodomeria.

him one of the longest-reigning monarchs in European history. Despite his lengthy rule, Franz Joseph was unable to address the rising demands for autonomy and independence from the various ethnic constituencies within his empire. (101) It's only fitting that his reputed last words were, *Does it have to be now?* (102)

After World War I, Russians, Poles, and Germans attempted to reassert their control over Rusyn lands. In March 1921, the Treaty of Riga annexed Eastern Galicia to Poland, effectively ending Rusyn aspirations for an independent state. (103)

Were Conditions Really That Bad in Galicia?

There are two distinct ways of remembering Galicia. One portrays it as an idyllic, innocent, and multicultural land, while the other depicts it as a landlocked, stagnant backwater from which many sought to escape. Those in the idyllic camp argue that the severity of conditions has been exaggerated, asserting that its people were not as hungry, poor, sick, or uneducated as countless historians have long claimed. They prefer to remember Galicia as a community that exemplified how multiculturalism and peaceful coexistence are compatible societal goals.

---

(101) A constitutional monarchy is a form of government where a constitution limits a monarch's power. The monarch shares power with the government, which is made up of elected officials and branches like the legislature and judiciary

(102) Rady. *The Habsburgs*. Page 289

(103) "World War One in Galicia: Katherine's Story." Rooted in Eastern Europe. August 4, 2014. https://eeroots.blogspot.com/2014/08/world-war-one-in-galicia-katherines.html.

The optimists assert that peasants feigned illiteracy to frustrate governmental authorities. According to U.S. census data, my grandparents, born in 1886 and 1891, completed the eighth grade. My grandmother's older brother, Steve (born in 1883), completed the third grade. Schools that opened between 1880 and 1890 reportedly had this effect. They also question the measure itself—peasants were literate in Rusyn or Ukrainian but illiterate in the state language.

They suggest that tax records are poor measures of wealth because they exclude leased or inherited properties. Historian Stella Hryniuk claimed that peasant farmers began diversifying their crops and using advanced farming techniques long before the wealthy estates. A family could therefore sustain itself with just two hectares of land thanks to improved production and increased livestock holdings, which she said fueled Galicia's population growth. (104)

In 1892, a newspaper report in The Pittsburgh Dispatch confirmed the dire condition of Galicia during my grandparents' childhood. An eyewitness observed:

> *Serfdom is not supposed to exist, but I have a well-founded suspicion that something very much like it is in vogue. The wages of such laborers are, at most, an average of twelve cents per day, although they are glad enough to get this. The estate laborer is in lifelong debt and is subject to prison and the lash if he attempts to escape his enslaver and his obligation. Wherever my host and I moved about these estates, these white enslaved people first bent and kissed the*

---

(104) Hryniuk, Stella. "Peasant Agriculture in East Galicia in the Late Nineteenth Century." *The Slavonic and East European Review*, (1985).

hems of our great coats and then stood silently with bare heads until we passed. (105)

The journalist went on to say that wages in the Galician oil industry were somewhat higher—36 cents a day—but considerably lower than those offered in the United States. So, which version of history should we believe?

I can only draw on my grandparents' experiences to answer that question. The Soroka and Syvak families were both poor, but the Sorokas, as landowners, were much better off than the Syvaks, who, as servants and tenant farmers, were slowly starving to death. There was a reason Galician peasants had the lowest military service rate: young men were often deemed unfit for duty. The surprising population growth may have resulted from factors yet to be considered. For example, Great Britain's industrialization lowered the average marriage age by nearly four years, from 27 to 23, during a woman's peak fertility. (106) Changes in inheritance laws might have led to earlier marriages and larger families. Cast-iron pots, a technological marvel of the nineteenth century, may have improved maternal and infant health by leaching iron into food. Migration from other parts of the Empire and improvements in agricultural practices, such as raising dairy cows to fertilize the fields, might also have contributed to the unexpected population growth.

The Sorokas lived and worked as a multigenerational team—a complex living arrangement driven by economic necessity rather than choice. Overcrowding undoubtedly influenced my grandfather's decision to leave the country. The Soroka family did everything possible to build a better life: delaying marriage, serving in the military, avoiding

---

(105) The Real World of Our Polish Ancestors in Serfdom: Donna Gawell

(106) Lucy Worsley.

alcohol, and even learning to speak German, Polish, and English. According to expert Paul Magocsi, wealth in Lemko villages was a function of an individual's hunger. Wealthy people were seldom hungry, while the poor were always on the brink of starvation.

Galicia was a land of diversity and contrast, where suffering varied only by degree. Ultimately, my grandparents' decision to leave for a better life may have meant having any life at all.

Chapter 2 References

Albert, Michael, Hyman Berman, C.W. Chrislock, and four others. 1981. *They Chose Minnesota: A Survey of the State's Ethnic Groups*. Minnesota Historical Society.

An Austro-Hungarian Tragedy – The Kingdom of Galicia and Lodomeria (Part Two). Europe Between East And West. https://europebetweeneastandwest.wordpress.com/2015/06/19/an-austro-hungarian-tragedy-the-kingdom-of-galicia-lodomeria-part-two/.

Armstrong, Dorsey, director. *The Black Death: New Lessons from Recent Research*. The Great Courses, 2022.

Beskid, Anthony. 2024. *The Origin of the Lems, Slavs of the Danubian Provenance*. London: Forgotten Books.

Davies, Norman. 2012. *Vanished Kingdoms: The Rise and Fall of States and Nations*. Penguin Books

Duly, William. The Rusins of Minnesota. United States: Rusin Association, 1993.

Wikipedia. 2024. "Famines in Austrian Galicia." Wikimedia Foundation. Last modified: February 27, 2024. https://en.wikipedia.org/wiki/Famines_in_Austrian_Galicia#:~:text=19th %20century%20saw%20the%20first,for%20years%2C%20up%20to%20 1848.

"Galicia, Historic Region, Poland, and Ukraine." The Columbia Electronic Encyclopedia. Infoplease, https://www.infoplease.com/encyclopedia/places/north-europe/poland/galicia-historic-region-poland-and-ukraine.

Wikipedia. 2024. "Galicia Peasant Rising of 1846." Wikimedia Foundation. Last modified: March 10, 2024. https://en.wikipedia.org/wiki/Galician_Peasant_Uprising_of_1846.

Gawell, Donna. 2024. *Our Galician Ancestors: The History and Culture of the People from Poland and Ukraine from the Middle Ages to WWI.* Independently Published.

Gawell, Donna. "The Real World of Our Polish Ancestors in Serfdom: Clothing." February 8, 2022. https://donnagawell.com/2022/02/08/the-real-world-of-our-polish-ancestors-in-serfdom-clothing/.

Genealogica Polonica, Soroka Genealogist Report

Glinski, Mikolaj. "Slavery or Serfdom: Or Was Poland a Colonial Empire?" Culture. PL. October 8, 2015. https://culture.pl/en/article/slavery-vs-serfdom-or-was-poland-a-colonial-empire.

Wikipedia. 2024. "Halych." Wikimedia Foundation. Last modified: June 6, 2024. https://en.wikipedia.org/wiki/Halych.

Hryniuk, Stella. 1991. *Peasants With Promise: Ukrainians in Southeastern Galicia, 1880-1900.* Indiana University Press.

Hryniuk, Stella. "Peasant Agriculture in East Galicia in the Late Nineteenth Century." *The Slavonic and East European Review*, (1985).

Wikipedia. 2024. "Kievan Rus." Wikimedia Foundation. Last modified:
June 15, 2024. https://en.wikipedia.org/wiki/Kievan_Rus%27.

Wikipedia. 2024. "Kingdom of Galicia and Lodomeria." Wikimedia
Foundation. Last modified: June 23, 2024.
https://en.wikipedia.org/wiki/Kingdom_of_Galicia_and_Lodomeria.

Kozłowski, M., & Himka, J. P. (1990). "Galicia Villagers and the
Ukrainian National Movement in the Nineteenth Century," John-Paul
Himka, London 1988 : [recenzja] / Maciej Kozłowski. *Studia
Historyczne, 33*(2).

Kuligowski, Waldemar . "A History of Polish Serfdom." Eurozine.
February 13, 2018. https://www.eurozine.com/a-history-of-polish-
serfdom/.

Liulevicius, Vejas G., director. *A History of Eastern Europe*. The Great
Courses, 2015.

Wikipedia. 2024. "Magnates of Poland and Lithuania." Wikimedia
Foundation. Last modified: March 6, 2024.
https://en.wikipedia.org/wiki/Magnates_of_Poland_and_Lithuania.

Magocsi, Paul R. "Austria Military Records." FamilySearch.Com.
https://www.familysearch.org/en/wiki/Austria_Military_Records.

Magocsi, Paul R. 1985. *Galicia: A Historical Survey and Bibliographic
Guide*. University of Toronto Press.

Magocsi, Paul R., 1983. *The Rusyn-Ukrainians of Czechoslovakia.* W.
Braumüller.

Magocsi, Paul R. 2015. *With Their Backs to the Mountains: A History of
the Carpatho-Rus and Carpatho-Rusyns*. Budapest-New York: Central
European University Press.

Michener, James A. *Poland: A Novel*. Dial Press Trade Paperback, 2015.

Wikipedia. 2023. "Nobility Rights in Poland." Wikimedia Foundation. Last modified: April 8, 2023. https://en.wikipedia.org/wiki/Nobility_privileges_in_Poland.

Nugent, Walter. 1995. *Crossings: The Great Transatlantic Migrations, 1870-1914*. Indiana University Press.

Pettinger, Peter. 2002. *How My Heart Sings*. New Haven, Connecticut: Yale University Press.

"Poland Social Life and Customs." Family Search. Accessed August 1, 2024.https://www.familysearch.org/en/wiki/Poland_Social_Life_and_Customs.

Pollack, Martin. "The Myth of Galicia." YouTube. Video, https://www.youtube.com/watch?v=_yxHexRa4tQ.

Wikipedia. 2024. "Partitions of Poland." Wikimedia Foundation. Last modified June 6, 2024. https://simple.wikipedia.org/wiki/Partitions_of_Poland.

Wikipedia. 2024. "Poverty in Austrian Galicia." Wikimedia Foundation. Last modified: June 15, 2024. https://en.wikipedia.org/wiki/Poverty_in_Austrian_Galicia.

Rady, Marty. 2020. *The Habsburg: To Rule the World*. Basic Books.

Wikipedia. 2025. "Serfdom." Wikimedia Foundation. Last modified April 19, 2025. Image from: widok-ogolny-przed-dworem.jpg (550×309) (tripadvisor.com).

Wikipedia. 2024. "Serfdom in Poland." Wikimedia Foundation. Last modified: June 9, 2024. https://en.wikipedia.org/wiki/Serfdom_in_Poland#:~:text=Serfdom%20in%20Poland%20became%20the,back%20to%20the%2012th%20century

Slomka, Jan. 2019. *Memoirs of a Peasant*. 3rd ed. Chicago, IL: Polish Genealogical Society of America.

Wikipedia. 2024. "StanisłAw Antoni Szczuka." Wikimedia Foundation. Last modified: August 27, 2024. https://en.wikipedia.org/wiki/Stanis%C5%82aw_Antoni_Szczuka.

Struve, Kai. "Citizenship and National Identity: The Peasants of Galicia during the 19th Century." Academia. www.academia.edu/1439246/Citizenship_and_National_Identity_the_Peasants_of_Galicia_during_the_19th_Century

Wikipedia. 2024. "Szlachta." Wikimedia Foundation. Last modified: June 15, 2024. https://en.wikipedia.org/wiki/Szlachta.

"The Habsburg Cadastral Survey and Map Initiative." Gesher Galicia, https://maps.geshergalicia.org/ref/habmap/.

Wikipedia. 2025. Territorial Changes of Poland Following World War II. Wikimedia Foundation. Last modified January 9, 2025. https://en.wikipedia.org/wiki/Territorial_changes_of_Poland_immediately_after_World_War_II.

Wańkowicz, M. *Through Four Climates 1912–1972*, Warsaw 1972.

Wikipedia. 2024. "Serfdom in Poland." Wikimedia Foundation. Last modified: June 9, 2024. https://en.wikipedia.org/wiki/Serfdom_in_Poland#:~:text=Serfdom%20in%20Poland%20became%20the,back%20to%20the%2012th%20century.

Wikipedia. 2024. "StanisłAw Antoni Szczuka." Wikimedia Foundation. Last modified: August 27, 2024. https://en.wikipedia.org/wiki/Stanis%C5%82aw_Antoni_Szczuka.

Wikipedia. 2024. "Szlachta." Wikimedia Foundation. Last modified: June 15, 2024. https://en.wikipedia.org/wiki/Szlachta.

Wikipedia. 2024. "The Germans from Galicia." Wikimedia Foundation. Last modified: June 15, 2024. https://sites.ualberta.ca/~german/AlbertaHistory/Galicians.htm.

Wikipedia. 2024. "Vladimir the Great." Wikimedia Foundation. Last modified: June 24, 2024.
https://en.wikipedia.org/wiki/Vladimir_the_Great

Wolff, Larry. 2012. *The Idea of Galicia: History and Fantasy in Habsburg Political Culture*. Stanford Press.

"World War One in Galicia: Katherine's Story." Rooted in Eastern Europe. August 4, 2014. https://eeroots.blogspot.com/2014/08/world-war-one-in-galicia-katherines.html.

Zalewski, Andrew (2012). Galician Trails: A Forgotten Story of One Family. Jenkintown, PA: Thelzo Press.

Chapter 3
The Lemko Way of Life

My ancestors were among several Slavic clans that settled in the Carpathian Mountains. In the early twentieth century, they were called Lemkos due to a shared language affectation, specifically their frequent use of the word "lem" (meaning "like") in daily conversation. Those living near Rusyn villages recognized them as a distinct ethnic community, while those with political agendas typically labeled them as Russians, Poles, Hungarians, or Ukrainians. In her book on 1930s Hungary, American author Eleanor Perenyi described Rusyns saying:

> *It was said that the Ruthenians were Ukrainian. This was hardly true. The language was different, and they had never belonged with the Russians or the Polish Ukrainians.* (107)

In some cases, it was the Rusyns themselves who embraced a new identity. As explained by author Starik Pollack:

> *Due to the policies of many churches and organizations, often supported by foreign interests, many descendants of Rusyns, including my family,*

---

(107) Perenyi, Eleanor. 1946. *More Was Lost.* New York Review Books, page 159. In 1843, the term Ruthenian became the official name for the Rusyns and Ukrainians in the Austrian Empire. However, the use of the term declined among Ukrainians in the mid-19th century and eventually fell out of use in Eastern and Central Ukraine. Today, Ruthenian only describes Rusyns.

*were pressured to adopt different identities. This
forced change in identity was evident in the adoption
of a Russian identity with the Orthodox Church, a
Ukrainian identity with the Greek-Catholic Church,
and a Polish identity with the Roman Catholic
Church. These external influences and the resulting
identity shifts have contributed to the complexity and
often contentious nature of Rusyn cultural identity.
(108)*

My understanding of my grandparents' Rusyn heritage was
limited to the inscription on our church's footstone. In 1947,
the church sponsored Ukrainian refugees (DPs) to increase
the size of its struggling congregation, supporting Pollack's
assertion that external circumstances confused American-
born descendants' understanding of their Rusyn heritage.

Rusyn Ancestry

Rusyns descended from nomadic Vlach tribes and
White Croats. Those who settled in higher elevations, called
Boykos and *Hutsuls*, typically lived in *zadruga* communes
governed by a family elder or patriarch. Zadruga communes
held property, herds, and money in common, with the eldest
member making decisions for the entire family. Lemkos
settled in the foothills and river valleys. The Boyko, Hutsul,
and Lemko communities engaged in seasonal trade and
participated in religious festivals, but were otherwise
distinguished by their geography, language, and culture.
While the Hutsuls and Boykos relied on animal husbandry
for sustenance, historical records suggest they traveled west
to sell cattle, pigs, lambs, and horses for profit.

---

(108) Pollock, Starik. "The Rusyns – the Forgotten Minority of Ukraine."
New Eastern Europe. October 8, 2020. Rusyns - the forgotten minority of
Ukraine - New Eastern Europe

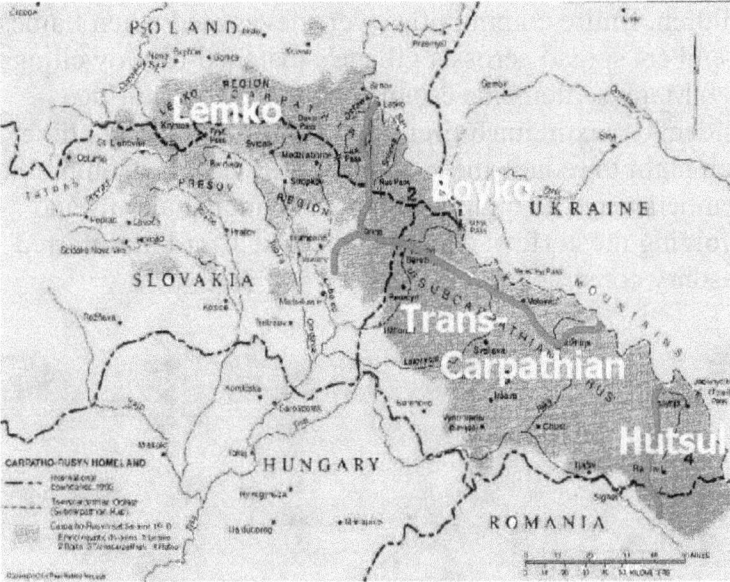

*Illustration 3.00: Geographic Homelands of Subgroups
(Source: https://www.pinterest.com/lbowka/lemko-Rusyn-heritage/*

Lemkos lived in multi-purpose cottages, with their living quarters and stables in separate sections of the same building. The family living quarters (*chyža*), an entry passage (*sini*), and a storehouse or pantry (*komora*) were thus separate from the threshing barn and grain storage area (*pelevnia*), a machinery and wagon barn (*sopa*), and stables (*staynia*). Typically, one side featured an exterior wall that supported a second outer wall (*zahaty*), which served as a windbreak and a storage area. Doors were low and narrow. To discourage rot, the exteriors and ceilings were coated with a thick mixture of brick dust and either crude or linseed oil. A cottage's structural lifespan averaged just ten years because of fires resulting from lightning strikes or domestic activities like drying hemp, baking bread, smoking tobacco, or the negligence of unsupervised children. Entire communities were devastated when flames or embers spread across a village's thatched-roof dwellings. (109) Many settlements established curfews requiring residents to extinguish fires and candles by a certain time each night to reduce the risk of accidental fires. Community members acted as night watchmen, sounding alarms and enforcing the curfew. Those who could afford it preferred masonry construction.

Illustration 3.01: Lemko Dwelling Interior (110)

(109) Slomka, Jan. 2019. *Memoirs of a Peasant*. 3rd ed. Chicago, IL: Polish Genealogical Society of America. Page 62.

(110) Danyliujk, Archyp. "Ethnography: The Lemko People." Pysanky.Info. https://www.pysanky.info/Lemko/Ethnography.html.

A Lemko Dwelling (111)

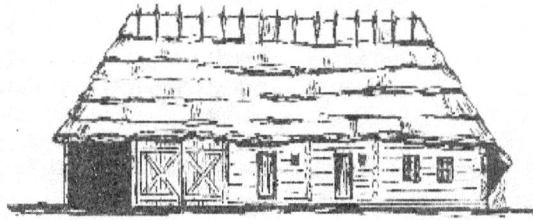

Long house. South façade

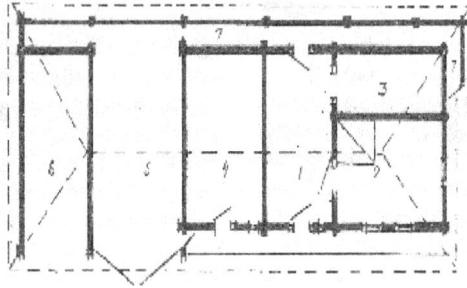

Long house ground plan. 1. Entry vestibule; 2. living space; 3. pantry; 4. stable; 5. threshing floor; 6. shed; 7. hay and grain storage.

Illustration 3.02: Lemko Dwelling. Drawing from the
Encyclopedia of Rusyn History and Culture by
Magocsi and Pop. The top depicts a basic tripartite
structure, and the bottom depicts an extended version.

    Most Rusyns were subsistence and livestock farmers, meaning they consumed what they produced. Only those with large landholdings grew cash crops or raised livestock to sell at market. According to Archyp Danyliujk:

---

(111) Caudill, Corrina. "Anatomy of a Lemko Longhouse." The Lemko Project. October 5, 2012. http://lemkoproject.blogspot.com/2012/10/the-anatomy-of-lemko-longhouse.html.

The most common Lemko occupations were farming and animal husbandry. Young animals were purchased in the Boyko or Hutsul region during the spring and sold in neighboring towns in the fall. After serfdom was abolished and grazing rights became more limited, dairy farming and grain agriculture gradually replaced animal husbandry. (112)

With mediocre soil and limited sunshine, the Lemkos planted only the hardiest of grains like rye, barley, oats, and buckwheat, along with potatoes, cabbage, and beans. Potatoes were particularly important because they could be grown in almost any soil, required minimal acreage, and fulfilled several nutritional needs. Potatoes and cabbage were staples of the Lemko diet. Potato skins provided a crucial source of protein, and cabbage was an essential source of vitamin C. Since white flour was prohibitively expensive, peasants made bread from coarser grains. They consumed pork, beef or mutton only on special occasions because cattle, chickens and sheep were vital for producing milk, eggs and wool for sale at markets and fairs. Pasta was another dietary staple. Coffee was brewed from burned crusts and milled wheat. According to Jan Slomka:

> *On every farm, they usually made barrels of cabbage into sauerkraut. In winter, we ate all of this and seasoned the fodder for the cows with the juice so they would not get fluke disease (which would reduce milk production and fertility).* (113)

---

(112) Oleksiak, Wojciech . "The Lost Homeland & Lasting Identity of the Lemko People." Culture.Pl, February 25, 2021. https://culture.pl/en/article/the-lost-homeland-and-lasting-identity-of-the-lemko-people.

(113) Slomka. *Memoirs of a Peasant.* Page 46.

Between November and February, villagers engaged in cottage industries to supplement their income. Women wove and embroidered fabrics, while the men transformed wood and metal into furniture, cooking utensils, and other household items. (114) According to historian Ted Nugent, nearly thirty years after the abolition of serfdom, ninety percent of Rusyn adults owned land (115) but typically had fewer than five acres. Lemko villages were situated in mountain valleys above the floodplain. Farmland was divided into strips along rivers and streams, creating a communal irrigation system that enabled efficient water distribution. (See Illustration 3.03).

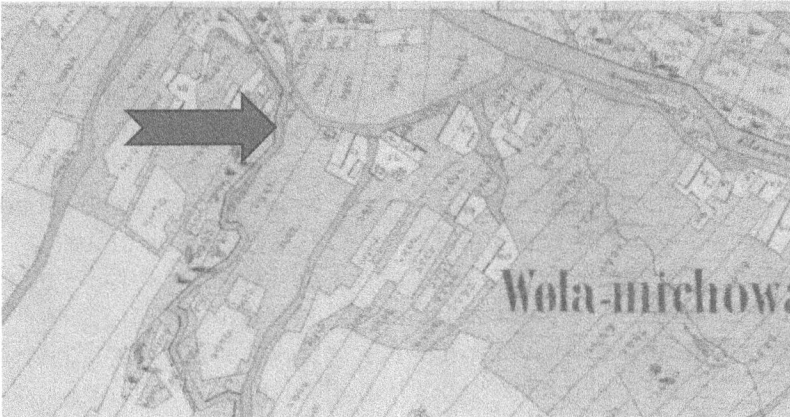

Illustration 3.03: Wola Michowa Cadastral Map. A blue arrow points to the Soroka homestead. In some areas, like the Hutsul regions, homes were built in a grazhda style, characterized by an enclosed courtyard.

---

(114) Magocsi, Paul R. 2015. *With Their Backs to the Mountains: A History of the Carpatho-Rusyns*. Budapest-New York: Central European University Press. Page 13.

(115) Nugent, Walter. 1995. *Crossings: The Great Transatlantic Migrations, 1870-1914*. Indiana University Press. Page 92.

A hereditary appointee, known as a *starosta* (mayor) or *kniaz* (prince), governed Rusyn communities in coordination with a village assembly or *viche*, a governance system that originated in Kievan Rus. The viche functioned as a deliberative body where citizens gathered to discuss community issues, including poverty, housing, crime, and education. The appointee received one-third of community-generated tax revenue, typically in labor, cheese, wool, and livestock, while the remainder was allocated to the magnate or king. Village priests kept census records to discourage consanguineous marriages. Their isolated rural communities sometimes led to higher rates of endogamy (marriage within the same group), but Rusyns didn't suffer from significant problems from inbreeding.

Villagers also gathered mushrooms, honey, beeswax, berries, and herbs to trade with Jewish merchants, who in turn sold them at local fairs or in village markets. Job opportunities outside of agriculture were limited; some found seasonal work as forest and quarry workers, while others secured positions in Galicia's oil fields (which had wells in the Lemko region) and in factories in Kraków. (116) After serfdom was abolished in 1848, Lemkos routinely crossed the Dukla Pass to harvest grain on the Hungarian plains.

---

(116) Magocsi. *With Their Backs to the Mountains: A History of the Carpatho-Rusyns*. Page 147.

Illustration 3.04: Galicia Oil Field, 1881. (117) Oil fields were found in the Lemko region.

Replicas of peasant dwellings offer insights into the daily lives of their inhabitants (see Illustrations 3.05). One example is a clay-plastered structure that was whitewashed annually (usually around Easter) with *vapno*, a mixture of calcium hydroxide (lime) and chalk, which brightened the interiors, acted as a disinfectant, and hardened clay floors. (118). A second example of a Lemko residence was built with split, half-round fir logs (with the rounded side facing out and the flat side facing in) and featured whitewashed mortar, clay, or moss filling the gaps between the logs. The

(117) Wikipedia. 2024. "The Petroleum Trail." Wikimedia Foundation. Last modified: April 25, 2024. https://en.wikipedia.org/wiki/Petroleum_Trail.

(118) "Life in the Galician Village of Bila: Sickness and Injury." Forgotten Galicia. Culture.Pl, November 12, 2018. https://forgottengalicia.com/life-in-the-galician-village-of-bila-sickness-injury/. Hardwood floors were impractical in peasant households since livestock was kept indoors during the spring birthing season. Only manor homes had hardwood floors.

logs were intentionally extended beyond the corners to serve as emergency fuel. (119) In both examples, spiders were welcome intruders because they killed other insects and protected residents from evil spirits.

An enclosed vegetable garden and drying field were nearby. They used willows to construct fences and baskets because they grew quickly and could bend and twist without breaking. Buckwheat, introduced from Asia, provided food for the family and nectar for the honeybees they housed in log apiaries. Honey farmers shared their bounty with family and friends but sold the valuable beeswax to the church and to noble families. (120) Beeswax candles produced less smoke and more illumination, but were too costly for daily use. They were favored for religious purposes because their clear, bright light symbolized the divine light of God. Tallow candles, the preferred choice of the peasantry, were inexpensive but emitted a foul odor and provided only modest illumination. Villagers gathered plums, pears, and apples from wild orchards or from trees they planted near their homes—fruits that could be dried for holidays and other special occasions. Most families grew hemp, a versatile and abundant plant that yielded fiber, seeds, and oil. Hemp was vital for making fabric and rope. Like most essentials, Rusyns made their fabric and clothing at home.

---

(119) Jan Slomka, *From Serfdom to Self-Government: Memoirs of a Polish Village Mayor*, 1842-1927, trans. William John Rose, (London: Minerva Publishing Co., 1941[Copyright expired]), page. 24.

(120) Slomka. *Memoirs of a Peasant.* Chapter 3.

Illustration 3.05: Lemko Residences (Naturalhomes.org/Lemko). Photo by Pawel Rzeznik.

Illustration 3.05: Lemko Residences (Naturalhomes.org/Lemko). Photo by Pawel Rzeznik.

Fabric-making began in October after the hemp had been allowed to decompose in a pond for several weeks. The fibers were then gathered and woven into cloth. (121) The resulting fabric (burlap) was used to for storage sacks and work clothes. However, because burlap offered little protection from the cold, peasants stuffed their clothing with hay. (122) Burlap was durable and resistant to mold and mildew, but was scratchy and uncomfortable. Only a Rusyn's finest clothing was made of linen flax. Laundry was a difficult, weekly chore. Clothes were soaked in tubs, rinsed in a pond, and then layered in a trough known as a *tryfus*. Fine hardwood ash was sprinkled between the layers and then covered with boiling lye. This process was repeated several times until the clothing was clean. (123)

Traditional clothing remained unchanged until after World War II. In addition to homespun cloth (in white and deep brown), garments were also made from sheepskin (for jackets, coats, jerkins, or vests, and caps) and cowhide or pigskin (for shoes and belts). (124) Garments were both practical and an important part of a Lemko's cultural identity.

---

(121) Forgotten Galicia: Life in the Village of Bila.

(122) Gawell, Donna. "The Real World of Our Polish Ancestors in Serfdom: Clothing." Https://Donnagawell.Com/Category/History-of-poland/Serfdom/. February 8, 2022.
https://donnagawell.com/category/history-of-poland/serfdom/.

(123) Slomka. *Memoirs of a Peasant*. Page 29.

(124) Brylak-Załuska, Maria . "The Festive and Everyday Attire of the Lemkos (Western Subregion)." SOKOL.
https://www.etnozagroda.pl/en_en/lemkos/the-festive-and-everyday-attire-of-the-lemkos-western-subregion.

Men wore a white linen shirt, linen or wool pants, a white or light blue vest, and a short jacket made of homespun wool. Of particular importance was the cloak (chicha) draped over the shoulders, worn by the gazda (peasant landowner) as a distinguishing badge from other villagers. All men wore a black hat (kalam) with a short brim.

Women's clothing included an undershirt (oplicha) and a blouse (koshelia), both of which were decorated with beads. Over this, women wore a corset-like vest made of black velvet or linen, adorned with silver-threaded embroidery patterns resembling plants. This was paired with a pleated skirt featuring a decorative base and an apron with decorative strips sewn onto it. In winter, women donned a coarse woolen vest or a heavy white sheepskin coat. Married women covered their heads with a small, close-fitting cap (chepets) worn over a shawl (khustka) or kerchief. Unmarried girls wore a necklace of tiny beads. Footwear for all genders consisted of leather moccasins and tall boots in winter. It was also common for peasants to go barefoot. (125)

(125) "The Lemkos – A People on the Edge." Postmark Ukraine. March 17, 2021. https://www.postmarkukraine.com/post/the-lemkos-a-people-on-the-edge.

Illustration 3.06: Traditional Rusyn Dress (126)

Because early homes traditionally lacked chimneys, doors were opened on cooking days to release the smoke. (127) Inhabitants crouched near the floor to avoid choking on the fumes. According to Jan Slomka, it wasn't until the 1870s that homes began to have proper chimneys. (128) Families used dried cow manure as fuel when it may have been more prudent to use it to fertilize their fields. Initially, clocks were considered unnecessary curiosities. Peasants worked from dawn until dusk, so knowing the exact time of day was of little importance. Every home had a rooster--that mostly got it right. Some families purchased clocks to prevent their stewards from taking advantage of them. (129)

---

(126) Kozak, Roman. "Folk Costume & Embroidery." https://folkcostume.blogspot.com/2018/10/overview-of-costumes-of-lemkos-Rusyns_31.html.

(128) According to internet sources, an estimated 80 to 90% of the heat generated by a fire is lost through a chimney, so having no chimney conserved fuel.

(128) Slomka, *Memoirs of a Peasant*. Page 24.

(129) Slomka, *Memoirs of a Peasant.* Page 25.

The living quarters were in the center of the home, featuring a large kitchen and an adjacent living room. The kitchen stove (*kuknya*), a square block of clay, served as the residence's only heating source; the loft provided warm sleeping quarters for children during the frigid winter months.

Illustration 3.07: Traditional Clay Oven. Image from:
https://www.booking.com/hotel/ua/pans-ka-
pich.html?activeTab=photosGallery

Furnishings might include a handcrafted wooden table, benches, and a few beds. Those who couldn't afford a place of their own rented a corner in a relative's cottage. Peasants generally slept on the floor. Blankets were considered a luxury, so they generally slept in their clothes. Only wealthier peasants could afford pillows and quilts. (130) Most Lemkos wore wool vests for warmth, which became so infested with fleas and lice by the end of winter that they were sold to Jews, who carefully cleaned them before

---

(130) Slomka. *Memoirs of a Peasant*. Page 27.

reselling them to the Rusyns the following season. Families positioned their beds against the walls and hung their clothes from hooks. They also stored their garments and personal treasures in artistically adorned chests (see Illustration 3.08).

Illustration 3.08: Malapolska Painted Trunk. Dowry Chest. Image from: https://Muzea.Malopolska.Pl/En/Objects-list/238

Icons were hung on the east wall or arranged in a shrine near the entrance. A beeswax candle was placed on a nearby windowsill with a blessed pussy willow to invoke God's protection. Young girls and elderly women were responsible for decorating outdoor surfaces to bring cheer to their otherwise drab surroundings. In some regions, it was traditional to paint exterior walls light blue.

Illustration 3.09: Lemko home in Smolnik ©Kasia Skóra & ©Robert Jurczyk. Notice the light blue exterior.

A Tree of Life typically adorned the entry door (see Illustration 3.10). Each stem represented a different family member. When a child was born, another branch was added. Painted birds on the gated doorways symbolized family love.

Illustration 3.10: Lemko Exterior Door with Tree of Life. Image from TRADITIONAL LEMKO DOMESTIC ARCHITECTURE (Carpatho-Rusyn.org) Volume 10 #2, 1987copyright © 1987 Archyp Danyljuk

Rusyns carved rosettes and religious symbols into the crossbeams of their homes for protection and good fortune. These carvings often included the cottage's construction date, the name of the family or carpenter, and other essential family details. An example of a Lemko crossbeam is shown in Illustration 3.11. (131)

Illustration 3.11: A rosette on a crossbeam found in a Lemko cottage (Rural Architecture Museum of Sanok, Poland)

Peasants owned little beyond the essentials of life. Among their treasured possessions was earthenware, a valuable luxury item they purchased from a local artisan. According to John Righetti, Rusyns adorned their pottery with folk art. The most common social outlet was visiting with neighbors at home or a local tavern. While the women sewed, villagers gossiped—so everyone knew each other's business.

---

(131) "A Protection Symbol for the Home: The Six-Petal Rosette on the Crossbeams of Galicia." Forgotten Galicia. October 22, 2022. https://forgottengalicia.com/a-protection-symbol-for-the-home-the-six-petal-rosette-on-the-crossbeams-of-galicia/.

Peasant Classes

A hierarchy of peasants characterized Austrian and Polish society. (132) In the early 20th century, especially after Poland gained its independence, the formal classification of peasants as a distinct social class began to fade. During the interwar period, land reforms and modernization efforts further diminished the importance of such classifications. However, because landholdings remained in the same families, these distinctions would not be entirely eliminated in rural areas until after World War II. Land was seldom bought or sold; instead, it was acquired through marriage, inheritance, or land grants for military service.

A person's social position was not solely determined by their income or accumulated wealth. Rusyn peasants, however, were deeply embedded in a system of mutual obligation and enforced labor, both to their landlords and to their village, at least until 1848, after which it was no longer forced but remained a part of village life. As a result, peasants were responsible for performing community service duties such as clearing forests, building churches, and maintaining roads and bridges. Rusyn villages retained traditional structures of mutual aid and shared responsibility, especially in mountainous areas where infrastructure and survival depended on cooperation. Wealthier peasants were typically expected to do more because they had the means to hire outside help. But then again, those without livestock faced twice the labor expectations of those who did. Even after serfdom was abolished, labor obligations persisted in some regions. This generally happened through informal

---

(132) Slomka. *Memoirs of a Peasant.* Page 21.

agreements or economic pressures, where peasants might work on estates in exchange for lower rents or other benefits.

Peasants were also required to pay taxes on surplus agricultural production, on the purchase of goods and services, and for being recognized as members of a community (i.e., poll taxes). The historic privileges of the nobility empowered them to negotiate with government authorities for lower tax burdens.

At the top of the peasant social hierarchy were *kmieci*, or independent farmers, who owned and leased large plots of land. They raised livestock and cash crops. If they were proficient in the state language, they also were granted the right to vote. The second tier, *zagrodnicy*, rented small parcels of land and cottages and worked as laborers on the larger estates. The lives of zagrodnicy, or tenants, most resembled those of serfs. *Chalupnicy*, or cottagers, were landless peasants who engaged in small-scale crafts, such as basket making, weaving, spinning, candle making, and pottery. They owned or rented small homes and raised fruits and vegetables for personal consumption. Unlike the zagrodnicy, they had greater autonomy and were permitted to sell their wares in the community market. Those who worked in lesser trades, such as blacksmithing, coopering, baking, butchering, tailoring, and milling, were known as *burghers*. Burghers enjoyed more freedom than peasants because of the critical role they played in the local economy. *Komornicy* were bailiffs or stewards who enforced legal judgments, seized assets, and managed evictions. They were considered petty gentry. Jewish leaseholders, known as *arendarze*, leased the rights to operate businesses owned by the landowners, such as taverns, mills, or tolls, for which they paid a fixed fee to the estate. Nobles avoided serving as shopkeepers or artisans because, by law, they would forfeit their noble status.

According to these definitions, the Sorokas were kmieci. My great-grandfather may also have worked in local law enforcement, and gained petty noble status. In addition to the acreage they leased, the Sorokas owned forty-nine parcels of land, including fields, forests, and pastures. James Michener described peasants like the Sorokas as:

> *Clever farmers who managed to acquire small pieces of land through adroit behavior, courage in warfare, or service to a magnate or king eventually sequestered enough land to generate a profit, allowing them to acquire more land until they became self-sufficient with their farms, horses, and rudimentary machinery.* (133)

Regardless of income, most peasants had servants, especially if they didn't have children. There was always plenty of work to be done, and everyone had to pitch in so that family members had "clothes on their backs and food in their stomachs."(134)

Old Country Medicine

Until germ theory revolutionized societal understanding of infectious diseases in the late nineteenth century, medical remedies in Galicia and across Europe varied widely, ranging from herbal medicines to more controversial substances, such as opium, morphine, arsenic, turpentine, and mercury.

In Lemkovyna, local homeopaths generally prescribed herbal remedies. Doctors were a last resort; even when available, most families could not afford outside medical assistance. When something was terribly wrong, they summoned a priest. Due to the rough terrain and

---

(133) Michener, James. 1984. *Poland: A Novel.* Fawcett. Page 26.

(134) Slomka. *Memoirs of a Peasant.* Page 162.

distance from medical facilities, Rusyns learned to be self-reliant, relying on fresh herbs they blessed at the church in early spring. Horse water, a poor iron supplement made by soaking rusty nails in a bucket of water, was believed to reduce fevers. Wounds were treated with spider webs. When seriously ill, they believed that their tangled hair would absorb the pain and support their recovery. (My mother wouldn't let us wash our hair when we were sick.) After six months, they removed the tangled mass and buried it in a private place. They also believed that disease spread by disguising itself as a child, an animal, a bird, or an old woman. When someone died, Lemkos covered their mirrors (like their Jewish neighbors) to prevent the deceased from haunting surviving family members. They would also tap the coffin against the outside door frame of the person's home to ensure their spirit would never return. Like other Eastern Europeans, they believed in the "evil eye." Interestingly, they didn't see any contradiction between their religious beliefs and magical convictions. Magic was the science of their age. Despite tensions between their superstitions and official church doctrine, Rusyn culture harmonized their Christian faith with their magical beliefs.

To relieve arthritis, my grandfather rubbed turpentine into his joints and basked in the sun. He ingested turpentine to fight infections and took a daily shot of rum to support his health. He seemed to enjoy giving a tablespoon of rum to family members, regardless of age. I remember gagging on it as a child! Medicine had to taste terrible to prove it worked. Spring water was believed to have magical healing powers. Poor sanitation and agricultural runoff contaminated the water supply, making spring water a healthier alternative.

Rusyns brewed a variety of teas from plants and herbs to treat specific ailments. According to our church's cookbook, they used dill to calm nerves, parsley for gallstones, sorrel for headaches, dandelion for anemia, elder for kidney and liver disease, rock rose for cancer, and sage for stomach troubles. Honey was believed to have mystical healing powers, and St. John's Wort was regarded as a cure-all. Wild mushrooms, rich in vitamin D and other essential minerals, were a dietary staple. Every summer, villagers would make raspberry syrup to treat fevers and flu, and they would use the flowers of the wild lilac shrub, known as habza, to remedy coughs and rheumatism. Tobacco was used to ease toothaches. My grandmother prepared a poultice of mustard seed and flour to draw out pus and toxins. They periodically washed their hair and bodies in lye to rid themselves of body lice.

My grandfather gathered herbs and tended sheep in the pastures near his home. During the winter, the family kept their flocks in nearby farm fields to clear weeds and drop manure; in the summer, they herded their flocks into mountain pastures, because higher-quality forage produced higher-quality wool.

Illustration 3.12: Heading to Pasture, Carpathian Mountains. Image from <u>Yurko Dyachyshyn / Юрко Дячишин - Carpathian shepherds</u>.

Shepherds built huts (see Illustration 3.13) to shield their livestock from harsh weather. They were also responsible for milking sheep (for cheese) and safeguarding their flocks from predators.

Illustration 3.13: Shepherd Hut (Pinterest)

My grandfather relished his time in the mountains. Michal, his parents, and his brothers Jan, Piotr, and Timothy, along with their wives and children, lived in the same home. Michal had two daughters and three sons. After his brother Maks died from sunstroke, his wife, Dominya, and their three children moved in with Michal's family. Jan later married Dominya, and together they had two boys. Piotr also had two sons. At various times, as many as twenty people occupied the same living quarters. When asked about the challenges of this living arrangement, my grandfather said, *"We had no choice."* The Sorokas collectively owned fields, forests, and pastures—some with access to the tributaries of the Oslawa River. (See Appendix F for land records and maps.) However, the ongoing hardships of living and working together provided my grandfather with yet another reason to immigrate to the United States.

Illustration 3.14: Rusyn peasants at home in the 1930s. (135)

Lemko Culture

With so much of their lives influenced by outside forces, Rusyns employed a variety of talismans to ward off bad luck and evil spirits. Over time, pagan-inspired folk customs and superstitions were reinterpreted as expressions of their Christian faith. For instance, ringing bells three times to ward off evil spirits was reinterpreted to symbolize the Holy Trinity. Coral bead necklaces represented martyrdom, sacrifice, and the blood of Christ. A woman's head covering demonstrated her submission to God.

(135) *Transcarpathia in the Photographs of the Magazine "LIFE" in 1938-1939 (Photo).* Photograph. *Uzhgorod.Net.Ua*)

Illustration: 3.15 Coral Beads (Pinterest)

Pysanky, or elaborately decorated eggs, are talismans that originated in pre-Christian times and represented renewal, rebirth, and the coming of spring. The simplest pysanky were made by adhering vegetation and flowers to an egg and dyeing them in water boiled with onion skins.

Illustration 3.16: Simple Pysanky (Pinterest)

Those with fine motor skills used melted beeswax to create designs before dipping them in progressively darker dyes, resulting in a complex variety of symbolic images. Natural materials were gathered throughout the year to manufacture the necessary dyes. Tree bark made brown, tea shades of green, dried blackberries a yellow-orange hue, and hollyhocks a shade of blue. Dyes were often mixed with vinegar to intensify their colors.

Wax application techniques varied by region. Lemkos used a drop-pull method with a horseshoe nail to symbolize Mary's tears. The Hutsuls employed a metal tool known as a *kistka* to create line-pysanky rich in Christian symbolism. The Boykos crafted intricate patterns by attaching colorful glass beads. After the church blessing, pysankas were given to friends and family throughout the year. Young girls presented their finest pysanky to boys as a token of their affection.

Embroidery

Women also embroidered symbolic motifs on clothing and household linens to bring good fortune. (136) By embroidering during the less stressful times of the year, they believed they channeled positive energy into their work. (137)

---

(136) Sibirtseva, Maria . "The Meaning Behind Traditional Patterns in Ukrainian Embroidery." Culture Trip. December 28, 2017. https://theculturetrip.com/europe/ukraine/articles/the-meaning-behind-traditional-patterns-in-ukrainian-embroidery.

(137) Slomka. *Memoirs of a Peasant.* Page 31.

Illustration 3.17: Hutsul, Lemko, and Boyko pysanky. (Pinterest)

Illustration 3.18: Traditional Embroidery. Designs varied by region and village. (Pinterest)

Roosters and birds symbolized the beginnings of a new family. Geometric shapes represented the divine. Flowers, branches, and leaves reflected a family's purity and hopes for future prosperity.

Illustration 3.19: The Ruthenian peasant, pictured at Ellis Island, is notable for her head covering, coral beads, and embroidered shirt. (138)

---

(138) Image from:
https://www.ggarchives.com/Immigration/EllisIsland/1907-05-ALookAtSomeOfOurImmigrants.html

During the first quarter of the harvest, Lemko's shaped pirohy, a traditional Rusyn dumpling and talisman, into a crescent to emulate the new moon. Pirohy were believed to give reapers "moon energy."

Folk music from pagan times was also reworked to bear Christian meaning. Folk songs, as oral traditions, were well known to Rusyns of all ages. Their songs reflected local history and influenced community ideals. They also served as an emotional release, helping them to cope with difficult circumstances. Their musical instruments included the sopilka (reed pipe), the trembita (long alpine horn), and the fifty-five-string bandura (see Illustration 3.20). (139)

Illustration 3:20: Bandura (Pinterest)

Religion

In 863, the Byzantine Emperor dispatched missionaries Cyril and Methodius to convert the pagan Slavic tribes to Christianity. Cyril invented a modified Greek alphabet that bears his name (i.e., the Cyrillic alphabet) to translate sacred texts into Slavic-sounding words. Despite their impact on the Christian landscape of Eastern Europe,

(139) "Ukrainian Musical Instruments." Green Tour. https://greentourua.com/ukrainian-musical-instruments/.

their efforts caused schisms between the Catholic and Orthodox Churches. The Western church relied on the Latin text. The rift became official after the Patriarch of Constantinople and the Pope of Rome excommunicated each other in 1054. (140) As a result, two distinct forms of Christianity emerged, each with their own mode of spiritual expression. Eastern Christianity invites direct and experiential knowledge of God through the use of iconography, chanting, and incense. In contrast, Western Christianity emphasizes intellectual rigor and structured theology, positioning its spiritual leaders as intermediaries and interpreters of God's word. Attending a Greek Catholic Church service offers an ethereal experience, while the rituals of the Roman Catholic Mass reinforce the church's strongly hierarchical character.

     My grandparents' social and spiritual lives were centered around the church, such that my father often complained they didn't spend enough time at home. Nevertheless, their faith provided them with a sense of community, a personal identity, and a way of communicating with God. (141) The church required an astonishing 18 weeks of fasting; however, compliance, at least in Europe, was nearly universal. Holy days gave the faithful a day off from

---

(140)"East-West Schism Christianity." Britannica. May 13, 2024. https://www.britannica.com/event/East-West-Schism-1054. The Great Schism of 1054, which separated the Eastern and Western Christians, was due to a combination of theological, political, and cultural factors, especially the supreme authority of the pope.

(141) Wikipedia. 2024. " Russian Icons." Wikimedia Foundation. Last modified: April 7, 2024. https://en.wikipedia.org/wiki/Russian_icons. Icons are all reproductions of prior work, with the artist serving only as a reproduction tool.

work. The origin of the word "holiday" is derived from "holy day."

Illustration 3.21: One of my grandfather's icons. (Personal Photo)

A Rusyn's life was based on a recurring cycle of religious feasts and fasting, which were crucial for salvation, spiritual growth, and fulfilling one's purpose in life. In my grandparents' world, religion was the lens through which everything was explained, from the mundane to the divine. Religious holidays marked the passage of time, and various saints were thought to protect believers from harm. In the old country, village (or white) priests taught the young to read and write, demonstrated modern farming methods, and advocated for social justice within their communities.

The church also had a significant impact on my family, though not in the ways you might expect. Practical considerations often overshadowed our religious devotion. My mother, sister, and I cleaned the sanctuary, while my father maintained the church, rectory, and grounds. The congregation sold pierogis and cabbage rolls on weekends, held seemingly endless rummage sales, and operated a concession at the St. Louis County Fair. My father gathered pussy willows for Easter, and we baked leavened bread for communion. My sister and I participated in a church-affiliated dance troupe. My mother sewed our costumes, and we occasionally performed in public.

Illustration 3.22: Ukrainian Dancers. From left to right: The author, Mary Kaye Leschak Kuzma, and my sister, Connie. (Personal Photo)

My sister and I were painfully aware of our inferior status in our predominantly Roman Catholic community. When our church closed in 1974, we had no choice but to attend the Roman Catholic Church, where it was clear (at least initially) that we were the wrong sort of Catholic. According to John Goman, the Rusyns who settled in Minneapolis and Northern Minnesota came from several villages in Poland's Sanok and Lesko administrative districts. Along with my grandfather, the Leschaks, Kotiks, Kers, and Franchaks all originated from Wola Michowa; the Dundas and Ivancas hailed from Smolnik (which they spelled Smilnik); and the Fesniks, my great-grandmother's family, were from nearby Maniow. Consequently, many of the churches and community founders were friends or relatives who arrived in Chisholm with my grandparents sometime between 1910 and 1913.

Rusyns were the first immigrants to arrive in the United States without their clergy because they planned to return to Europe. When circumstances became untenable due to global wars, immigration restrictions, and the spread of communism, they established parishes in the United States with whatever personal resources they could provide. Some mortgaged their homes and sold their personal belongings to raise the necessary capital. Our church was just a few blocks from the Russian Orthodox Church. Given the economic constraints on immigrant families and the similarities in liturgical practices of the two religious institutions, why didn't all Rusyns attend the same church?

A Second Religious Fissure

Between 1890 and 1929, the Pope in Rome began backpedaling on a longstanding agreement that permitted Greek Catholic communities to own church property and preserve their Eastern liturgical practices, including married priests. As a result, in 1891, Archbishop John Ireland of St. Paul, Minnesota refused to acknowledge Greek-Catholic widowed priest Alexis Toth's credentials, citing the American Catholic Church's prohibition on married priests in the United States. As a result, Ireland is sometimes jokingly referred to as "*The Father of the Orthodox Church in America.*" Thousands of Greek Catholics returned to the Russian Orthodox Church

According to John Goman, Chisholm's Galician-Rusyn community officially split in 1914 when their fraternal association adopted a strong pro-Russian (Orthodox) philosophy. (142) Greek Catholics were expelled

---

(142) Sadly, these animosities persist to the present day, particularly in Europe.

in the process. (143) As a result, two parishes were formed, effectively undermining the viability of both. Between 1915 and 1990, St. Nicholas Russian Orthodox Church employed 31 different clergy, plus a multitude of itinerant priests when the salaried position was vacant.(144) The Greek Catholic Church fared slightly better because one of its mid-century priests was particularly good at raising outside funds

Rusyns in other Minnesota communities experienced similar conflicts and built churches of the Orthodox and Greek Catholic faiths in the same or nearby neighborhoods. In some communities, the religious divide was so contentious that police officers were invited to attend weekly services to curb potential violence. In Chisholm, the Orthodox and Byzantine churches were constructed for roughly the same amount of money in roughly the same year (1916-17). (145) However, while Orthodox congregations generally received in-kind support (146) from the Russian Tsar, Chisholm's did not receive any promised support because their churches were constructed during the Russian Revolution. The Tsar's generosity was rooted in the hope that when Rusyns returned from America, they would spread the Orthodox faith in their homelands. The actual number of converts gained with this policy is unknown.

Byzantine Catholic Churches, with members from both Galicia and Subcarpathia, with "mixed congregations" were permitted to join either the Rusyn or Ukrainian districts

---

(143) The Vatican lifted its ban on married priests for Eastern Catholic Churches on November 17, 2014.

(144) Goman. *Galicians on the Iron Range*. Page 82.

(145) Duly. *The Rusins of Minnesota*. Page 64.

(146) Known as *rolling rubles*, gifts from the Tsar typically included bells and chandeliers, which were believed to consecrate the church

of the church. Our congregation chose the Ukrainian jurisdiction because of its strong Ukrainophile leanings. (147)

Illustration 3.23: St. Peter and Paul's Byzantine Catholic Church (148)

The Oliver Mining Company supported all of the religious institutions attended by its employees. However, even with outside support, our church did not pay off its mortgage until 1942. Our church's footstone was inscribed with the following information in both Rusyn and English.

---

(147) According to the pastor of the Byzantine Church in Minneapolis, in the 1980s, the congregation was Rusin, but since only Ukrainian priests could be found to serve there, it came to be regarded as a Ukrainian Church.

(148) Image from the public domain:
https://commons.wikimedia.org/w/index.php?curid=33108623

Osnovana	**Established**
28 Maja 1916 Roku	May 28, 1916
Ruska Parokhija	Rusyn Parish
Svjat. Petra I Paula	St. Peter-Paul
Greko-Kath. Cerkove	Greek Catholic Church
Chisholm, Minn.	Chisholm, Minn

*Illustration 3.24: A Greek Catholic iconostasis that visually teaches the
word of God instead of using text. Image
from:orthochristian.com/96581.html*

The religious schism also divided families. My
grandfather's cousin, Andrew Soroka, was a founding
member of the Orthodox Church in Bramble. He and his
wife are buried in the adjacent cemetery.

Because religious holidays hold great significance for
Rusyn families, I have shared my grandfather's memories of
his family's Christmas traditions in Appendix A and
included a summary of our Easter traditions and recipes in
Appendices B and D.

St. Peter and Paul Byzantine Church was added to the National Register of Historic Places in 1980 for its cultural significance on the Iron Range. The church closed after the bishop determined that it could no longer afford a full-time priest. The consecrated assets, including the crystal chandelier, pews, and iconostasis, were distributed to churches in North Dakota and Pennsylvania. However, the building itself still stands at 530 Central Avenue. The Russian Orthodox churches in Chisholm and Bramble are open to the public only during designated times of the year.

Chapter 3 References

A Protection Symbol for the Home: The Six-Petal Rosette on the Crossbeams of Galicia." Forgotten Galicia. October 22, 2022. https://forgottengalicia.com/a-protection-symbol-for-the-home-the-six-petal-rosette-on-the-crossbeams-of-galicia/.

Brylak-Załuska, Maria . "The Festive and Everyday Attire of the Lemkos (Western Subregion)." SOKOL. https://www.etnozagroda.pl/en_en/lemkos/the-festive-and-everyday-attire-of-the-lemkos-western-subregion.

Caudill, Claudia. "The Anatomy of a Lemko Longhouse." The Lemko Project. October 5, 2012. https://lemkoproject.blogspot.com/2012/10/the-anatomy-of-lemko-longhouse.html.

Danyliujk, Archyp. "Ethnography: The Lemko People." Pysanky.Info. https://www.pysanky.info/Lemko/Ethnography.html.

"East-West Schism Christianity." Britannica. May 13, 2024. https://www.britannica.com/event/East-West-Schism-1054.

Wikipedia. 2024. "Egg Decorating in Slavic Culture." Wikimedia Foundation. Last modified: April 27, 2024. https://en.wikipedia.org/wiki/Egg_decorating_in_Slavic_culture.

Gawell, Donna. "The Real World of Our Polish Ancestors in Serfdom: Clothing." Https://Donnagawell.Com/Category/History-of-Poland/Serfdom/. February 8, 2022.

Goman, John. 1990. *Galician-Rusins on the Iron Range*. Rohart Services Desktop Pub.

Kozak, Roman. "Folk Costume & Embroidery." https://folkcostume.blogspot.com/2018/10/overview-of-costumes-of-lemkos-rusyns_31.html.

Wikipedia. 2024. " Russian Icons." Wikimedia Foundation. Last modified: April 7, 2024. https://en.wikipedia.org/wiki/Russian_icons.

Life in the Galician Village of Bila: Sickness and Injury." Forgotten Galicia. Culture.Pl, November 12, 2018. https://forgottengalicia.com/life-in-the-galician-village-of-bila-sickness-injury/.

Magocsi, Paul R. 2015. *With Their Backs to the Mountains: A History of the Carpatho-Rus and Carpatho-Rusyns*. Budapest-New York: Central European University Press.

Michener, James A. *Poland: A Novel*. Dial Press Trade Paperback, 2015.

Miller, Yvette A. "Catherine the Great and the Jews: 5 Facts." Aish. https://aish.com/catherine-the-great-and-the-jews-5-facts/.

Nugent, Walter. 1995. *Crossings: The Great Transatlantic Migrations, 1870-1914*. Indiana University Press.

Old folk medicine in the Western Carpathians, https://www.magurskiewyprawy.pl/2021/10/dawne-lecznictwo-ludowe-w-karpatach.html

Oleksiak, Wojciech. "The Lost Homeland & Lasting Identity of the Lemko People." Culture.Pl, February 25, 2021. https://culture.pl/en/article/the-lost-homeland-and-lasting-identity-of-the-lemko-people.

Perenyi, Eleanor. 1946. *More Was Lost*. New York Review Books.

Wikipedia. 2024. "Russian Icons." Wikimedia Foundation. Last modified: April 7, 2024. https://en.wikipedia.org/wiki/Russian_icons.

Pollock, Starik. "Rusyns – the Forgotten Minority of Ukraine." New Eastern Europe, October 8, 2020. Rusyns – the forgotten minority of Ukraine.

Wikipedia. 2024. "Saints Peter and Paul Church (Chisholm, Minnesota)." Wikimedia Foundation. Last modified: June 8, 2024. https://en.wikipedia.org/wiki/Saints_Peter_and_Paul_Church_(Chisholm, _Minnesota).

Sibirtseva, Maria. "The Meaning Behind Traditional Patterns in Ukrainian Embroidery." Culture Trip, December 28, 2017. https://theculturetrip.com/europe/ukraine/articles/the-meaning-behind-traditional-patterns-in-ukrainian-embroidery.

Skóra, Kasia. "Ancient Folk Medicine in the Western Carpathians." Magura Expeditions: Travel, Mountains, and Photography, October 9, 2021.

Slomka, Jan. 2019. *Memoirs of a Peasant*. 3rd ed. Chicago, IL: Polish Genealogical Society of America.

"The Lemkos – A People on the Edge." Postmark Ukraine, March 17, 2021. https://www.postmarkukraine.com/post/the-lemkos-a-people-on-the-edge.

Wikipedia. 2024. "The Petroleum Trail." Wikimedia Foundation. Last modified: April 25, 2024. https://en.wikipedia.org/wiki/Petroleum_Trail.

"Ukrainian Musical Instruments." Green Tour. https://greentourua.com/ukrainian-musical-instruments/.

Wikipedia. 2023. "Zadruga." Wikimedia Foundation. Last modified: October 7, 2023. https://en.wikipedia.org/wiki/Zadruga.

Chapter 4
My Grandparents' Villages

In the early twentieth century, roughly one thousand communities dotted the Carpathian landscape, including around 300 villages in the Lemko region of southeastern Poland. Typical Rusyn communities had fewer than a thousand inhabitants. Most lived in medieval conditions on land controlled by local clergy or influential landowners.

Polish King *Sigismund the Old* established Wola Michowa in 1546. (149) During the post-Mongol reconstruction period, new and restored settlements in the Carpathian Mountains were established on land owned by the king, on *royal lands*, or on land owned by equally powerful nobles. (150) Wola Michowa was established along a lucrative trade route connecting Sanok to Slovakia. Its proximity to the Hungarian border and the village's commercial district made it critically important for military operations, trade, forestry, and agriculture. Neighboring mountain passes transformed the community into a regional administrative hub and a center for multicultural exchange. The Dukla Pass, 37 miles west of Wola Michowa, offers the lowest navigable route through the Carpathian Mountains.

---

(149) Wikipedia. 2023. "Wola Michowa." Wikimedia Foundation. Last modified: November 29, 2023. https://en.wikipedia.org/wiki/Wola_Michowa.

(150) Magocsi, Paul R. 2015. *With Their Backs to the Mountains: A History of the Carpatho-Rusyns*. Budapest-New York: Central European University Press. Page 59.

(151) The Lupkow Pass is just 8 miles distant. Both sites witnessed significant military conflict, most recently during the two World Wars. Commodities transported through the Dukla Pass included wine, beer, horses, dried fruit, cheese, iron, fabric, yarn, skins, herring, and honey. Before World War I, wagons served as the primary mode of transportation; people largely traveled on foot. The Dukla Pass remains an important trade route between Slovakia and Poland. The Lupkow Pass holds historical significance but is largely irrelevant in today's geopolitical landscape.

The village's social justice practices were based on a type of customary law known as *Wallachian law* (152), based on the customs and traditions of communities inhabited by Romanian shepherds and farmers. (153) A royal appointee (either a kniaz or prince, or a starost, i.e., constable, steward, or mayor) served as the village's highest-ranking government official, managing community affairs alongside an elected village assembly. The magnate or monarch hired agents to oversee their towns and estates. The lives of nobles and peasants seldom intersected, so manor homes were generally situated in more densely populated urban areas where social opportunities abound. A peasant's life afforded few opportunities for enjoyment; only the church provided respite from the daily grind. The starost served as the regional magistrate. Because land ownership spelled the difference between leading a free, independent life and that

---

(151) Wikipedia. 2024. "The Dukla Pass." Wikimedia Foundation. Last modified February 21, 2024. https://en.wikipedia.org/wiki/Dukla_Pass.

(152) Wallachian law was a medieval legal system in Eastern Europe. Its principles included the right to self-governance, collective use of forests and pastures, military service in exchange for self-governance, and local administration.

(153) Wikipedia. 2024. "Customary Law." Wikimedia Foundation. Last modified: March 2, 2024. https://en.wikipedia.org/wiki/Customary_law.

of being a tenant or serf, property rights were the focus of most legal disputes. Entire communities were punished for the criminal activities of their members, so guilty parties were quickly apprehended. According to one Rusyn immigrant, a vigilante court would try the offending party and impose corporal punishment. (154) Elected community leaders served as tax collectors and were personally responsible for any discrepancies in funds or payments in-kind.

The king appointed Kniaz Piotr Kmit (1477–1531) to oversee the region's colonization. As one of the wealthiest and most distinguished Polish nobles of his day, Kmit managed multiple estates and townships. (155) Mich Rusyn, the son of the kniaz from nearby Smolnik, was appointed as Kmit's local representative or *freeholder*, for which he received settlement privileges. (156) Freeholders were more deferential than higher-level aristocrats, and because they lived in the community, freeholders were more responsive to regional needs. As members of the petty gentry, they were often assigned military responsibilities. Their inflated sense of importance made them objects of ridicule, as their lives were fundamentally no different than those of other peasants. (157)

---

(154) "Life in the Galician Village of Bila: Sickness and Injury." Forgotten Galicia

(155) Wikipedia. 2022. "Piotr Kmita Sobieński." Wikimedia Foundation. Last modified: November 25, 2022. https://en.wikipedia.org/wiki/Piotr_Kmita_Sobie%C5%84ski.

(156) Settlement privileges might include exemption from taxation, military services, and/or the right to own serfs.

(157) Wikipedia. 2024. "Petty Nobility." Wikimedia Foundation. Last modified: June 8, 2024. https://en.wikipedia.org/wiki/Petty_nobility.

The village was divided into a commercial district, originally called Wola Novae, and a rural community named after its original freeholder, Mich. The market was established at the confluence of the Oslawa and Chliwne Rivers. The community received a town charter in 1731; however, it was revoked by the Austrian Empire in 1785, following the region's annexation in the Polish Partitions.

Illustration 4.00: Wola Michowa Marketplace. Image from Undiscovered Bieszcady.

A Town Charter

1. **Legal Recognition:** The charter formally recognized the settlement as a town, granting it a unique legal status.

2. **Self-Governance:** Towns with charters often had the right to self-governance, which included electing their political officials, such as mayors and councils, and establishing local laws and regulations.

3. **Economic Privileges:** Charters often granted towns the right to hold markets and fairs, which were crucial for trade and economic growth. This might also include exemptions from certain taxes or tolls.

4. **Judicial Rights:** Towns with charters could establish their own courts and judicial systems, allowing them to manage local disputes and legal matters independently.

5. **Military Obligations**: In some cases, towns were required to provide military support to their lord or monarch in exchange for their charter.

6. **Land Ownership**: Charters empowered towns to own and manage land, including the option to lease or sell property.

Traditionally, a charter granted a settlement and its inhabitants the right to certain privileges. Townspeople were burghers instead of serfs. Towns were "free" because the king or emperor protected them, and they were not part of a feudal fief.

Source: Wikipedia. 2024. "Municipal Charter. Wikipedia Foundation. Last modified: June 24, 2024. Wikipedia. https://en.wikipedia.org/wiki/Municipal_charter

Illustration: 4.01 Critical Aspects of a Town Charter

In Old Polish, *wola* means freedom. (158) Settlers were granted land free of feudal obligations for a period of 20 to 25 years, during which they could not be bound as serfs. (159) Feudal responsibilities were waived to promote settlement and reinforce the region's defenses. Even after the feudal waiver expired, wola communities rarely enforced feudal work expectations because residents simply refused to comply. Wola Michowa remained an agricultural community for more than three centuries. In the late 1800s, a narrow-gauge railway was constructed to transport lumber from the nearby Bieszczady Mountains. (160)

---

(158) Wikipedia. 2024. "Wola Settlement." Wikimedia Foundation. Last modified: May 24, 2024. https://en.wikipedia.org/wiki/Wola_(settlement).

The exact number of Wola communities remains undocumented, but several hundred were established to promote settlement and agricultural development.

(159) Wikipedia. 2024. "Villein." Wikimedia Foundation. Last modified: May 11, 2024. https://en.wikipedia.org/wiki/Villein.

(160) Madrecki, Barnaba. 2013. *Undiscovered Bieszczady Real Exist Travel Guide.*

Illustration 4.02: Narrow-gauge railroad in Cisna, Poland. Notice the small engine and absence of passenger cars. (161)

Kraków is barely 100 miles from my grandfather's village, yet it took 36 hours to reach by industrial train. While Rusyn isolation provided some benefits, it nearly doomed the war-torn region after World War I, when sickness and famine struck with a vengeance.

In 1914, Wola Michowa was a large, diverse community. The village belonged to the Roman Catholic diocese in Komańcza, but also had a sizable Greek Catholic population and two Jewish synagogues. One synagogue served Orthodox Jews (*Kahal*), while the other served *Hasidic* Jews. Each Jewish sect maintained its own temple because of variations in theological beliefs, liturgical practices, cultural traditions, and interpretations of Jewish law. Synagogues had to be within walking distance because any form of work, including exercise, was prohibited on the Sabbath. At the end of the 19th century, 240 of the 840

---

(161) *Green Narrow-gauge Railway, Steam Train in Cisna, Poland. Dreamstime.* https://www.dreamstime.com/royalty-free-stock-images-narrow-gauge-railway-steam-train-cisna-poland-green-image36410089 At the time, passenger trains traveled an average of twenty-five miles per hour.

inhabitants—nearly 30%—were of Jewish descent. (162) Poland's centuries-long tradition of religious tolerance and the Jews' pivotal role in commercial enterprise explain the region's substantial Jewish population. Wola Michowa hosted six annual fairs where wine and livestock, including horses, cattle, and pigs, were bought and sold. (163) The Dukla Pass offered the easiest and most direct way to import Hungarian wine, a commodity prized by the Polish gentry.

Illustration 4.03: Sausage market in a Rusyn community. Image from the Polish National Digital Archive. Institution | NAC

The village owned the marketplace. By the end of the 19th century, 120 homes surrounded a central market square. My grandfather's home was number 42, indicating they were among the earliest settlers.

---

(162) Undiscovered Bieszczady

(163) Soroka Genealogy Information provided by Genealogica Polonica

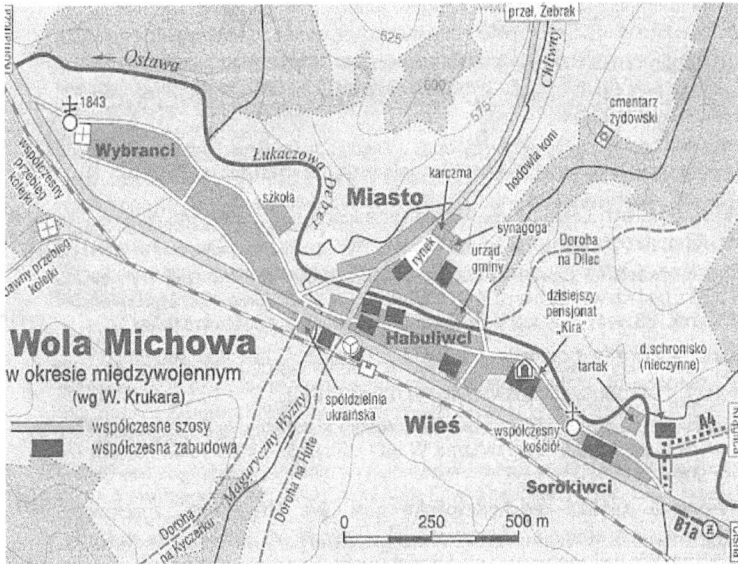

Illustration 4.04: The Town (miasto) of Wola Michowa. Note the two synagogues, a Greek Catholic Church, a Jewish cemetery (cmentarz), a sawmill (tartak), a rail station (kolejki), a market square (rynek), an inn (karczma), a government office (urzad gminy), a school (szkola), steel works (Doroha na Hute), a guest house (kira), a Ukrainian Cooperative (spoldzielnia ukrainska), and a horse breeding business (holowla koni) (164)

Jewish Importance

In the thirteenth century, Polish kings, eager to boost economic activity after years of military conflict, granted Jews exclusive rights to serve as the kingdom's moneylenders. In exchange for legal protections, Jewish bankers offered substantial loans to Polish kings on generous terms. Jews were also given exclusive control over the production and sale of alcohol, a major source of Poland's

---

(164) Undiscovered Bieszczady

tax revenue. Anyone found guilty of hurting a Jew incurred the same penalties as someone who harmed a noble. Additionally, Jews who converted to Catholicism were occasionally raised to noble status.

Jews also held a near monopoly on managing landed estates, mills, taverns, and inns. They served as tax collectors, livestock traders, and stewards—occupations that required literacy, math, and investment skills, which, according to Jay Orbik, were considered "*beneath the dignity of Christian gentlemen.*" The Catholic Church forbade charging interest on investments or loans because authorities believed it was sinful to profit on the mere passage of time. Prohibited from owning land, Jews were the only residents with cash assets; everyone else was property-poor. Christian peasants and aristocrats viewed commercial activity as immoral. As a result, they sold their production to Jews and then complained that Jews profited from their labor. (165) Nevertheless, the prevailing sentiment was that a noble was nothing without a Jew, and that every noble needed his "*Moshke,*" the Polish term for Moses. (166) Wola Michowa attracted Jewish refugees from the Russian Pale of Settlement, which at its peak represented 40% of the world's Jewish population. (167) The majority of those who settled in Wola Michowa were Hasidic Jews, a kind of Judaism that is

(165) Slomka, Jan. 2019. *Memoirs of a Peasant.* 3rd ed. Chicago, IL: Polish Genealogical Society of America. Page 104.

(166) "The Jews Come To Poland." JewishHistory.Org. https://www.jewishhistory.org/the-jews-come-to-poland/.

(167) Wikipedia. 2024. "Pale of Settlement." Wikimedia Foundation. Last modified: June 17, 2024. https://en.wikipedia.org/wiki/Pale_of_Settlement.

open to everyone, and not limited to the educated and well-read.

The Jewish Pale

The Polish Partitions created an unforeseen "Jewish problem" for the Russian government when former Commonwealth communities became part of its empire. Russian authorities were outraged when their newly settled Jewish residents refused to convert to Orthodox Christianity. They also condemned Jewish business practices for destroying Russian-owned enterprises. (168) The Russian Imperial family was particularly anti-Semitic, and Empress Elizabeth (1741–1762) sought to exile every Jew from her borders. Her successor, Catherine the Great, chose to forcibly relocate them to the westernmost perimeter of the Russian Empire, which she called the *Pale of Settlement.* Russian Jews were prohibited from living outside the Pale without a government exemption. Within the Pale, Jews were forbidden from traveling to cities like Kyiv without an imperial pass. (169) Russia prohibited Jews from owning land or working as teachers, lawyers, or civil servants, but these restrictions were not consistently enforced. Considered second-class citizens, crimes against Jews largely went unpunished.

The Pale became the epicenter of Russian pogroms. While the extent of the Russian government's involvement remains unclear, officials were slow to respond and, at times, joined the rioters themselves. According to Lisa Cooper,

---

(168) Manekin, Rachel. "Galicia." Https://Yivoencyclopedia.Org/Article.Aspx/Galicia.

(169) Miller, Yvette A. "Catherine the Great and the Jews: 5 Facts." Aish. 7https://aish.com/catherine-the-great-and-the-jews-5-facts/.

author of **A Forgotten Land**, preadolescent Jewish boys were forced into the Russian military, some as young as ten years old. (170) Given the 25-year service requirement, parents would do almost anything to keep their sons out of the military, where Jewish traditions would be forbidden, and they would never see their families again. Cossacks were routinely sent to the Pale to cause chaos, loot settlements, and kill residents. Cooper's great-great-grandfather survived one of these incidents when the leather belt a Cossack used to hang him from a kitchen beam snapped before he could suffocate.

Illustration 4.05: The Pale of Settlement. (Notice its proximity to Galicia.Image from: https://litwackfamily.com/the_pale.htm

Conditions in the Austrian-controlled sector were somewhat better. While the Austrian government did not initially uphold the Commonwealth's former civil liberties, it steadily expanded them. Jews were liberated and granted complete legal equality in 1867, which allowed them to live

---

(170) Cooper, Lisa. 2013. *A Forgotten Land: Growing Up in the Jewish Pale: Based on the Recollections of Pearl Unikow Cooper.* Jerusalem: Penina Press.

and worship anywhere they wished. As a result, many Jews illegally fled the Pale and moved to Galicia and other Austrian communities. By 1857, approximately 449,000 Jews resided in Galicia, accounting for 10% of its population.

Reasons for Business Disdain

In many traditional societies, peasants and nobles viewed business and commerce with suspicion. Profiting from what they did not produce was seen as immoral. Merchants were also viewed as not contributing to society by performing traditional roles.

1. **Social Hierarchy**: Traditional societies were often organized around rigid hierarchies, with nobles at the top and peasants at the bottom. Engaging in business was perceived as a threat to this social order, as it could accumulate wealth and power outside of the established system hierarchy.

2. **Moral and Religious Beliefs**: Many religious and moral teachings of the time emphasized humility, modesty, and the importance of maintaining one's social role. Given its focus on profit and competition, business was often regarded as contrary to these values.

3. **Economic Stability**: Peasants, primarily engaged in agriculture, depended on stable and predictable economic conditions for their survival. Business and trade could bring volatility and uncertainty, which were unfavorable.

4. **Control of Resources**: Nobles controlled land and resources, preferring to maintain this control rather than allowing others to gain wealth and influence through business. This control reinforced their power and status.
5. **Cultural Values**: In many cultures, the ideal life is one of simplicity and self-sufficiency. Engaging in business is often associated with greed and materialism, which are frowned upon.

Source: "Societal Structure and the New Urban Economy." Decameron Web. Brown University, February 25, 2010. https://www.brown.edu/Departments/Italian_Studies/d web/society/structure/merchant_cult.php.

Relationships with the Jews

Some historians describe the relationship between Jewish and Christian communities as neighborly, while others describe them as contentious. Jews and Rusyns mingled at local markets, sometimes intermarried, and as neighbors, developed shared cultural practices, vocabulary, recipes, and customs. My grandfather said that Jews and Christians in his community got along quite well because they were poor like everyone else.

Generally speaking, Jews were not among the wealthiest merchants; instead, they played secondary roles as traders, suppliers, and distributors, ranging from established shopkeepers to traveling street vendors. Jews also brokered small transactions between clients and merchants, often selling agricultural products. (171) Some Christians viewed them with suspicion and were quick to blame them for God's wrath. Because they did not assimilate into the local community, Jews were often seen as "guests" or outsiders, regardless of how long they had lived in their communities. Their style of dress also set them apart from their Christian neighbors. Religious leaders in both communities discouraged interaction because they worried their traditions might be forgotten or that their people might be tempted to convert. The Jewish community, with its different Sabbaths, holidays, and calendars, made it difficult for them to socialize or share meals with their Christian peers. Nevertheless, many families have stories about how they supported each other's religious traditions, and there is no evidence of pogroms occurring in Rusyn communities.

Because of Jewish widespread literacy, they could advocate for their interests, making them targets of community hostility. Literate Jews might be assigned light military duties (e.g., desk work) or serve in civic roles that exempted them from military service altogether. However, the most significant criticism of Polish Jews stemmed from their involvement in the *propinacja*, a monopolistic system that granted gentrified landowners' control over the production and sale of alcohol. Jews were seen as trustworthy partners because they abstained from hard spirits. Propinacja, abolished in 1910, required peasants to

(171) Teller, A. (2010, October 28). Trade. YIVO Encyclopedia of Jews in Eastern Europe. Retrieved June 12, 2024, from https://yivoencyclopedia.org/article.aspx/Tade.

buy a fixed quantity of alcohol from their landlords (*forced consumption*) and prohibited them from purchasing alcohol from competing estates. The alcohol requirement varied by region and by landowner policy.

Tokens redeemable for alcohol were issued as compensation, guaranteeing that a portion of the peasants' earnings were returned to their employer's estate. The most popular drink was ninety-proof alcohol, known as *nalevkas*, a fruit- or herb-infused vodka. (172) Vodka was especially prized because a bushel of potatoes could produce twelve liters of alcohol and was easy to distill. (173) According to Jay Orbik:

> *One of the unfortunate outcomes of the inns and alcohol production was rampant alcoholism among the peasants. This became a significant political, social, and religious issue. The Jews were accused of luring peasants to buy more drinks by offering them credit; of usury for charging exorbitant interest (as much as 50%); of foreclosing on the farms of the peasants when they defaulted; and of contributing to the moral and social decay of the peasantry.* (174)

In the early 19th century, journalist Edgar Wakeman said that the typical peasant drank roughly a gallon of alcohol a week. As cases of alcoholism and domestic violence increased, clergy urged their congregations to take sobriety oaths. Jews were accused of exploiting their

---

(172) Pollack, Martin. "The Myth of Galicia." YouTube. Video, https://www.youtube.com/watch?v=_yxHexRa4tQ.

(173) Orbik. Alcohol Production and Distribution. Page 10.

(174) Orbik. Alcohol Production and Distribution. Pages 10-11.

intoxicated community members through forged credit agreements and unfair business practices aimed at confiscating their property. (175) While Jan Slomka praised Jewish community members for their frugality, ambition, fiscal restraint, sobriety, and disciplined lifestyle, he also expressed dissatisfaction with Jewish business practices, describing them as crooked and unethical.

The golden age of Galician Jews ended with World War I. In 1921, approximately 93,000 Jews lived in the Carpathian-Rus, but many emigrated to the United States due to economic hardship and anti-Semitism, which became unbearable in the years after the war. (176)

Illustration 4.07: Jewish Shopkeeper. Image from:
http://uzhgorod.net.ua/news/70678

---

(175) Slomka. *Memoirs of a Peasant*. Page 112.

(176) Hykle, Douglas. "History of Tluste/Tovste from a Jewish Perspective." Tovoste. https://www.tovste.info/JewishHistory.php.

Noteworthy Historical Events

Wola Michowa is best known for three historical events. The first was its brief period of independence as part of the Eastern Lemko Republic (also known as the Komańcza Republic). (177) Between November 1918 and January 1919, thirty-three Lemko villages, including Wola Michowa and Smolnik, petitioned to join an independent Ukrainian state.

Wola Michowa is also remembered for the atrocities committed during World War II. On July 10, 1942, the Nazis burned the community to the ground, executed 75 Jews, and transported the rest to labor camps, where they would ultimately perish. (178) My grandfather's village was only 125 miles from the horrors of Belzec and Auschwitz. The Nazis desecrated the Jewish cemetery, repurposing headstones for roads and other building projects.

(177) Wikipedia. 2024. "Komańcza Republic." Wikimedia Foundation. Last modified: March 30, 2024. https://en.wikipedia.org/wiki/Koma%C5%84cza_Republic.

(178) "Jewish Communities Destroyed in the Holocaust: Poland." Jewish Virtual Library. https://www.jewishvirtuallibrary.org/jewish-communities-destroyed-in-the-holocaust-poland.

Illustration 4.08: Nazi extermination camps located in Poland. (179)

Finally, Wola Michowa is known for the involuntary resettlement (or ethnic cleansing) of its Rusyn population in 1947. (180) The objective of *Operation Vistula* was to weaken Rusyn support for Ukrainian insurgents by forcibly deporting non-ethnic Poles.

---

(179) Image from: https://en.wikipedia.org/wiki/File:WW2-Holocaust-Poland.PNG

(180) Wikipedia. 2024. "Operation Vistula." Wikimedia Foundation. Last modified: May 16, 2024.
https://en.wikipedia.org/wiki/Operation_Vistula.

Smolnik (Smilnik)

My grandmother was born in Smolnik, a village in the Oslawa River Valley, near my grandfather's farm. The village got its name from the region's pine tar, which was used to produce turpentine, methyl alcohol, and other derivatives. *Smol* is a Slavic term for "resin." (181)

Jacek Kulczycki was appointed the community's freeholder in 1531. When it was first established, Smolnik was heavily forested. Like Wola Michowa, settlers were granted land free of feudal obligations in exchange for clearing it for agriculture. Smolnik became the third royal village established in the Beskid Mountains and quickly became the largest community in the Sanok eldership. By 1876, approximately 1,000 people resided in 156 cottages. Smolnik's boundaries extended to the source of the Oslawa River, encompassing eight smaller communities. According to parish records, my grandmother, Marya Syvak, was born on April 3, 1891, making her the youngest of five children. However, some official documents stated that she was born in March 1890, so this required further investigation.

Several sources said that it was common for a peasant's reported age to be off by a few years in either direction. (182).Most Rusyns prioritized name days (*imieniny*), or the saint's day after whom they were named, over birthdays. Peasants who shared the same name day

---

(181) "The Bieszczady Gate - Smolnik And Oslawa." Magura Expeditions - Travel, Mountains, Photography. https://www.magurskiewyprawy.pl/2020/01/brama-bieszczadow-smolnik-nad-osawa.html.

(182) "Grandma Said She Was from Poznań": Decoding Stories About Ancestors from Poland." January 26, 2017. https://fromshepherdsandshoemakers.com/2017/01/.

celebrated it together as a village. Peasants were also known to lie about their age for practical reasons, such as avoiding military conscription, forced labor assignments, or to be permitted to work as adults.

Thus, my grandmother may have intentionally inflated her age for some work-related reason, or perhaps her actual birthday simply wasn't important to her. What is more certain is that my grandmother was the daughter of Max Syvak and Marianna Petruniak, both peasant farmers from Smolnik. They married in 1879 when Max was 26 and Marianna was 22. Their children — Joannes (born 1881), Stephanus (born 1883), Eudocia (born 1888), Anna (born 1889), and Marya — were all born in the same home. The couple lost two children: Joannes, who died in the year he was born, and Eudocia, who perished at age 12 in an epidemic. The cause of Eudocia's death was attributed to night air. According to medieval medical theory known as *miasma,* cholera and other diseases were believed to be caused by contaminated air. (183) The term malaria literally means bad air.

Max Siwak was born in Smolnik in 1853. His mother was a widow at the time of his birth, so he was recorded as illegitimate. His social status may have also stemmed from Tatianna and his presumed father's failure to marry in the church until after he was born. Tatianna was 41 years old at the time of his birth, so Max would be her only child. Max's last name would later be reflected as Syvak.

Mary Petruniak was born in Smolnik in 1857. She was an only child. Her parents were Jacobus Petruniak (1814) and Euphemia Jachwak (1831). They married in 1850 when Euphemia was 19 and Jacobus was 36. Therefore, my

(183) Wikipedia. 2024. "Miasma Theory." Wikimedia Foundation. Last modified: June 1, 2024. https://en.wikipedia.org/wiki/Miasma_theory.

grandmother's entire family consisted of peasant farmers from Smolnik.

Illustration 4.09: Smolnik Region Image from www.mapofpoland.pl.

The Surname

Syvak is an Eastern European and Jewish surname meaning "grey-haired man." In Slovenian, "Syvak" means to "cobble" or "sew." (184) According to Brian Pozun, the surname has Roma origins that can be traced to Northern India. The dark hair and eyes of the Roma people starkly contrasted with the typical Lemko's fair complexion, light hair, and blue eyes. (185) However, because Tatianna did not have children with her first husband, this is a moot point. Max's actual father's name was Stanko, which in Slavic means "fragrant." According to my aunt, the Syvaks were acquainted with the Soroka family because they traveled to Wola Michowa for milling and postal services. Family members also resided in Wola Michowa.

---

(184) "Sivak Family History." Ancestry.Com. https://www.ancestry.com/name-origin?surname=sivak.

(185) Pozun, Brian. "Our Rusyn Gypsies." Medium, April 8, 2020. https://medium.com/@bpozun/our- Rusyn-gypsies.

Max immigrated to the United States to work in the Minnesota iron mines shortly after Marya was born. He broke his back in a mining accident, returned to the old country, and spent his remaining years languishing in bed. He died in 1902 at the age of 49. The financial pressures of having a disabled father and a mother with a drinking problem forced the Syvak children to take jobs as servants and field hands from a very young age. Unsurprisingly, all of my grandmother's siblings immigrated to the United States within a decade of Max's death. The fate of my great-grandmother is unknown. Details regarding my grandmother's family are summarized in Appendix E.

The Impact of the World Wars

After World War I, residents of Wola Michowa and Smolnik became unwilling participants in a conflict involving Polish forces and the Ukrainian Nationalist Army. The Poles wanted to restore their former republic, while the Ukrainians wanted their own nation. The Rusyns were wary of each side because they had been accused of treason at the beginning of the war. Before World War I, the Poles promoted Ukrainian nationalism as a means of opposing Austrian control. After World War I, the Poles seized their property and religious institutions and closed their schools and seminaries. When the Germans invaded Poland in 1939, the Nazis restored the civil liberties of the Rusyn Ukrainians in hopes of gaining German allies.

During Operation Barbarossa in June 1941, Hermann Goering forced Rusyns, Poles, and other Slavs to work in Germany's war industries. Known as *ostarbeiters* (foreign slave workers), children as young as ten were forcibly abducted from their homes. (186) Ostarbeiters were abused

---

(186) Wikipedia. 2024. "Ostarbeiter." Wikimedia Foundation. Last modified: June 27, 2024.

and raped, leading to thousands of unwanted pregnancies. They were held in barracks and given meager rations. Anyone who attempted to flee was executed. Because Eastern Europeans were considered "subhuman," the Nazis also used them for "medical experiments." The exact number of ostarbeiters is uncertain, but it is estimated to be between 2 and 3 million people.

Following World War II, Polish hostility led to the forced relocation of Lemkos and Boykos to Soviet Ukraine and former German villages in northwest Poland (1944-1951). The purpose of *Operation Vistula* was to achieve majority support for the Second Polish Republic by ensuring that Rusyns made up no more than 10% of the population of any Polish settlement. Many Lemkos, including my grandfather's siblings, were deported to Ternopil in western Ukraine. Approximately 140,000 Rusyns were resettled. Rusyns who had been coerced into working as ostarbeiters were regarded as traitors in Soviet Ukraine.

In the early morning hours, Polish authorities rounded up deportees and loaded them onto cattle cars that took several months to reach their destinations. Those who resisted deportation were either sent to former concentration camps in Silesia or killed.

Illustration 4.10: Operation Vistula. File: Operation Wisła. 1947.jpg - Wikimedia Commons

According to one eyewitness account:

> *The boxcar had no windows, toilet facilities, or food or water (except what people brought). There was nowhere to sit or sleep except on the floor. It was sweltering hot—no breeze, fresh air, or relief from the heat in the evenings. There was no privacy to do the everyday things a body needs. And the people went days, sometimes weeks, or more without seeing daylight. Not long before, the enclosed air had become unbearably foul with the stench of farm animals, sweating people, and animal and human waste. Illness and disease soon became rampant. But there was no medicine. The attitude of those in charge was "if they die, they die,"—which many did.* (187)

Despite promises that individuals could bring up to two tons of personal belongings, they were only permitted to bring what they could manage themselves. The Polish

---

(187) "Operation Vistula 1947." Displaced Persons Camps. Michigan Family History Network, http://dpcamps.org/operationVistula.html.

Army destroyed or confiscated the property they left behind, which they had buried in the hope that they would be permitted to return home. Deportees were told they could choose their final destination, but others made those decisions for them. They were assured they would receive housing and tax exemptions. Instead, they were forced to live in makeshift dugouts or the corners of occupied homes and work on collective farms. Ultimately, none of the governments promises were fulfilled. The only Rusyns unaffected by the ethnic cleansing program were from the Prešov Region of Slovakia. A few displaced Rusyns returned home in the late 1950s. (188) The Polish government did not acknowledge any wrongdoing until the 1990s and only began to recognize Rusyns as a distinct ethnic minority in 2011.

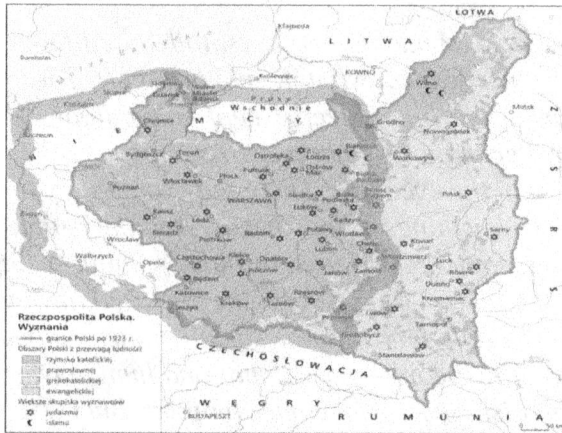

Illustration 4.11: Poland: 1923-1939 and post-1945 from the Facebook Galicia Family Group. Eastern Galicia ultimately fell under Soviet control following an agreement among Roosevelt, Churchill, and Stalin. Many Poles were resettled in the "regained territories" in southwestern Poland, after the German population had been expelled.

---

(188) Wikipedia. 2024. "Lemkos." Wikimedia Foundation. Last modified: June 28, 2024. https://en.wikipedia.org/wiki/Lemkos.

Many Rusyn settlements suffered considerable damage during each world war. After ethnic displacement, the new Polish residents struggled to cultivate the poor-quality soil. When they left, Rusyn communities suffered an almost total decline. Currently, Wola Michowa has 90 residents, while Smolnik has 182.

Tourism is helping to revitalize the Carpathian Mountains. The region's attractions include hiking, skiing, and seeing the beautiful wooden churches built by the area's early inhabitants. *Tserkvas* are recognized as UNESCO World Heritage sites and are celebrated for their medieval church-building traditions and ornate iconography. (189) They were built entirely of wood because, in 1681, the Habsburg Emperor decreed that only Roman Catholic churches could be constructed of stone. (190) St. Michael the Archangel Church in Smolnik was constructed in 1791, near an oak tree where it is said St. Michael appeared. (191) The Tserkva in Wola Michowa was destroyed by fire and replaced in 2011 with a simpler, modern structure.

(189) "Wooden Tserkvas of the Carpathian Region in Poland and Ukraine." UNESCO, June 21, 2013. https://whc.unesco.org/en/list/1424. Tserkvas were built using the horizontal log technique, developed during the Middle Ages, which features interlocking joints instead of nails, as nails were associated with the crucifixion of Jesus Christ.

(190) Mutschlechner, Martin . "Faith and Power – the Nobility and the Catholic Church." https://www.habsburger.net/en/chapter/faith-and-power-nobility-and-catholic-church.

(191) Warnke, Agnieszka . "Poland's Most Beautiful Wooden Prayer Houses." Culture.Pl's. February 2016.

Illustration 4.12: Lemko Greek Catholic Tserkva in Kwiatoń, (192)

Chapter 4 References

Wikipedia. 2024. "Bieszczady Mountains." Wikimedia Foundation. Last modified: March 20, 2024. https://en.wikipedia.org/wiki/Bieszczady_Mountains.

Cooper, Lisa. 2013. *A Forgotten Land: Growing Up in the Jewish Pale: Based on the Recollections of Pearl Unikow Cooper*. Jerusalem: Penina Press.

Nugent, Walter. 1995. *Crossings: The Great Transatlantic Migrations,* 1870-1914. Indiana University Press.

Wikipedia. 2024. "Customary Law." Wikimedia Foundation. Last modified: March 2, 2024. https://en.wikipedia.org/wiki/Customary_law.

Wikipedia. 2024. "Galician Jews." Wikimedia Foundation. Last modified November 8, 2024. https://en.wikipedia.org/wiki/Galician_Jews.

"Grandma Said She Was from Poznań": Decoding Stories About Ancestors from Poland." January 26, 2017. https://fromshepherdsandshoemakers.com/2017/01/.

---

(192) Image from:
https://en.wikipedia.org/wiki/Wooden_Tserkvas_of_the_Carpathian_Region_in_Poland_and_Ukraine

Goman, John. 1990. *Galician-Rusins on the Iron Range*. Rohart Services Desktop Pub.

Hykle, Douglas. "History of Tluste/Tovste from a Jewish Perspective." Tovoste. https://www.tovste.info/JewishHistory.php.

"Jewish Communities Destroyed in the Holocaust: Poland." Jewish Virtual Library. https://www.jewishvirtuallibrary.org/jewish-communities-destroyed-in-the-holocaust-poland.

Wikipedia. 2024. "Komańcza Republic." Wikimedia Foundation. Last modified: March 30, 2024. https://en.wikipedia.org/wiki/Koma%C5%84cza_Republic

Wikipedia. 2024. "Lemkos." Wikimedia Foundation. Last modified: June 28, 2024. https://en.wikipedia.org/wiki/Lemkos

Life in the Galician Village of Bila: Sickness and Injury." Forgotten Galicia. Culture.Pl, November 12, 2018. https://forgottengalicia.com/life-in-the-galician-village-of-bila-sickness-injury/.

Magocsi, Paul R. 2015. *With Their Backs to the Mountains: A History of the Carpatho-Rus and Carpatho-Rusyns*. Budapest-New York: Central European University Press.

Madrecki, Barnaba. 2013. *Undiscovered Bieszczady Real Exist Travel Guide*.

Manekin, Rachel. "Galicia." Https://Yivoencyclopedia.Org/Article.Aspx/Galicia.

Slomka, Jan. 2019. *Memoirs of a Peasant*. 3rd ed. Chicago, IL: Polish Genealogical Society of America.

Teller, A. (2010, October 28). Trade. YIVO Encyclopedia of Jews in Eastern Europe. Retrieved June 12, 2024, from https://yivoencyclopedia.org/article.aspx/Tade

Michener, James A. *Poland: A Novel*. Dial Press Trade Paperback, 2015.

Wikipedia. 2024. "Miasma Theory." Wikimedia Foundation. Last modified: June 1, 2024. https://en.wikipedia.org/wiki/Miasma_theory.

Miller, Yvette A. "Catherine the Great and the Jews: 5 Facts." Aish. https://aish.com/catherine-the-great-and-the-jews-5-facts/.

Wikipedia. 2024. "Municipal Charter. Wikipedia Foundation. Last modified: June 24, 2024. Wikipedia. https://en.wikipedia.org/wiki/Municipal_charter

Mutschlechner, Martin . "Faith and Power – the Nobility and the Catholic Church." https://www.habsburger.net/en/chapter/faith-and-power-nobility-and-catholic-church.

Nugent, Walter. 1995. *Crossings: The Great Transatlantic Migrations, 1870-1914*. Indiana University Press.

Orbik, Jay M. "Alcohol Production and Distribution in the Rural Augustow District in the 19th Century." *East European Genealogical Society Newsletter* (2020): 10-11.

"Operation Vistula 1947." Displaced Persons Camps. Michigan Family History Network, http://dpcamps.org/operationVistula.html.

Wikipedia. 2024. "Operation Vistula." Wikimedia Foundation. Last modified: May 16, 2024.https://en.wikipedia.org/wiki/Operation_Vistula.

Wikipedia. 2024. "Ostarbeiter." Wikimedia Foundation. Last modified: June 27, 2024. https://en.wikipedia.org/wiki/Ostarbi

Wikipedia. 2024. "Pale of Settlement." Wikimedia Foundation. Last modified: June 17, 2024. https://en.wikipedia.org/wiki/Pale_of_Settlement.

Wikipedia. 2024. "Petty Nobility." Wikimedia Foundation. Last modified: June 8, 2024. https://en.wikipedia.org/wiki/Petty_nobility.

Wikipedia. 2022. "Piotr Kmita Sobieński." Wikimedia Foundation. Last modified: November 25, 2022. https://en.wikipedia.org/wiki/Piotr_Kmita_Sobie%C5%84ski.

Polianski, Fr. Ioann (2012). Lemkovina: A History of the Lemko Region of the Carpathian Mountains in Central Europe. Translated by Paul Best, Michael Decerbo, and Walter Maksimovich. Higganum, Connecticut: Carpathian Institute and Lemko Association.

Pollack, Martin. "The Myth of Galicia." YouTube. Video, https://www.youtube.com/watch?v=_generally yxHexRa4tQ.

Pozun, B. "Our Rusyn Gypsies." Medium, April 8, 2020. https://medium.com/@bpozun/our-rusyn-gypsies.

Rusinko, E. (2024). *Andy Warhol's Mother: The Woman Behind the Artist* (1st ed.). University of Pittsburgh Press.

"Sivak Family History." Ancestry.Com. https://www.ancestry.com/name-origin?surname=sivak.

Wikipedia. 2024. "The Dukla Pass." Wikimedia Foundation. Last modified February 21, 2024. Dukla Pass - Wikipedia. https://en.wikipedia.org/wiki/Dukla_Pass.

"The Bieszczady Gate - Smolnik And Oslawa." Magura Expeditions - Travel, Mountains, Photography. https://www.magurskiewyprawy.pl/2020/01/brama-bieszczadow-smolnik-nad-osawa.html.

"The Jews Come To Poland." JewishHistory.Org. https://www.jewishhistory.org/the-jews-come-to-poland/

Wikipedia. 2024. "Ukrainian Collaboration with Nazi Germany." Wikimedia Foundation. Last modified: June 27, 2024. https://en.wikipedia.org/wiki/Ukrainian_collaboration_with_Nazi_Germany.

Wikipedia. 2024. "Villein." Wikimedia Foundation. Last modified: May 11, 2024. https://en.wikipedia.org/wiki/Villein.

Warnke, Agnieszka. "Poland's Most Beautiful Wooden Prayer Houses." Culture.Pl's. February 2016.

Wikipedia. 2023. "Wola Michowa." Wikimedia Foundation. Last modified: November 29, 2023. https://en.wikipedia.org/wiki/Wola_Michowa.

Wikipedia. 2024. "Wola Settlement." Wikimedia Foundation. Last modified May 24, 2024. https://en.wikipedia.org/wiki/Wola_(settlement).

"Wooden Tserkvas of the Carpathian Region in Poland and Ukraine." UNESCO, June 21, 2013. https://whc.unesco.org/en/list/1424.

Chapter 5
The Cossacks & Nationalist Movements

The small landowners and peasants either joined the Cossacks or looked to them for protection and leadership. With their rich cultural heritage, the Cossacks became a symbol of freedom and independence. Albert Seaton

My father and great-grandfather were named after the patron saint celebrated during the month of their birth. This tradition, popular among Orthodox Christians, both honors the saint and provides lasting spiritual protection to those who share their name. *Michaelmas* honors St. Michael, the warrior saint who protects God's people from physical and spiritual harm. Both men were appropriately named, as they served as family caretakers and in their country's armed forces.

My father was occasionally rebellious, but was mostly polite, gentle, and restrained. My great-grandfather was nicknamed a "*Cossack*," partly because he exhibited all the manly attributes associated with that descriptor: gruff, powerful, passionate, and known for his fierce temper, which his children and other family members learnt to respect. Michal reportedly said the Sorokas "*lived very well under the Tsar.*" He urged my grandfather to flee the growing social unrest in Europe before the First World War began, an inevitability that European rulers ignored until the moment of its declaration.

I always wondered what these comments meant. Did he call the Austrian Emperor a tsar? Was part of the Soroka family partitioned into the Russian Empire and enlisted as Cossacks? Was a Soroka involuntarily impressed into the

Russian military? Or was his remark influenced by the nineteenth-century belief that the Tsar would liberate the Rusyns from their Austrian and Polish oppressors? This hope was shared by many after the Austrian Emperor conceded Galicia to the landowning Poles and declared it a self-governing province of the Austrian Empire.

Tsarist policies were seen as more accommodating to Orthodox Christians than those of other European nations. The Russian Empire even recognized Cossacks as a distinct ethnic group. In contrast, Cossacks in the Polish-Lithuanian Commonwealth were relentlessly persecuted by the ruling class. According to Albert Seaton, the economic status of Russian Cossacks varied over time, but:

> *Although not wealthy in Tsarist Russia, Cossack communities were generally more prosperous than Russian peasants. They participated in various economic activities, including horse breeding, grain farming, and tobacco cultivation. In exchange for their military service, they received financial support and tax exemptions from the Tsar, along with access to shared communal land and rights to hunt and fish. Their economic independence was an essential aspect of their identity.* (193)

There is evidence of Cossack resettlement in Lemkovyna. Father Polianski observed:

---

(193) Seaton, Albert. 1972. *The Cossacks (Men-at-Arms)*. New York: Osprey Publishing. Pages 21-22. For a more detailed discussion of the Russian Cossacks, see Appendix C.

*The descendants of those old Lemkos have retained such a vital life force that they have assimilated many German, Wallachian, and **Cossack colonists** who found refuge in their mountains.* (194)

Plus, the Congress of Poland, a puppet state of the Russian Empire, was situated just 100 miles northeast of my grandfather's village. According to historical records, *Vasily Soroka* (195) was a leader in the Pugachev Rebellion that challenged the legitimacy of Catherine the Great. However, aside from my grandfather's observation that family members, including my grandmother, had "Cossack eyes," I wondered if there was any definitive proof of familial ties to Cossacks, Russian or otherwise.

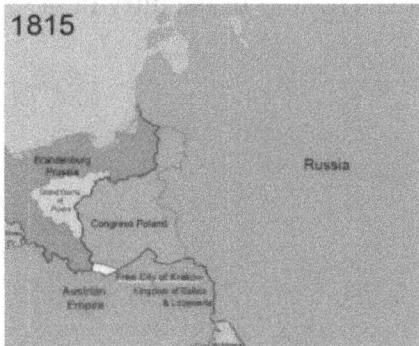

Illustration 5.00: Congress of Poland (196)

---

(194) Polianski, Fr. Ioann. 2012. *Lemkovina: A History of the Lemko Region of the Carpathian Mountains in Central Europe.*

(195) Soroka was known for his leadership and bravery, rallying Cossacks and peasants to join the cause against the oppressive regime. His actions during the rebellion made him a key figure in the fight for social and economic justice. He was captured and executed in 1775.

(196) "Grandma Said She Was from Poznan": Decoding Stories About Ancestors from Poland." From Shepherds and Shoemakers. January 27, 2017. https://fromshepherdsandshoemakers.com/2017/01/.

Cossacks in the Carpathians

While not necessarily Russian in origin, the Carpathian region had a long history of banditry and criminal gangs, which were often romanticized in peasant folklore. These brigands, sometimes referred to as rebels or freedom fighters, exploited the challenging terrain of the Carpathians, utilizing the region's natural defenses to their advantage. They rebelled against oppressive governments and often turned to banditry during times of economic hardship. Unlike organized Cossack military units, these brigands acted more like social bandits, embodying the struggles and resistance of the local people against economic and political pressures. With a surname that possibly means "prone to thievery," perhaps there was a history of banditry in the Soroka family.

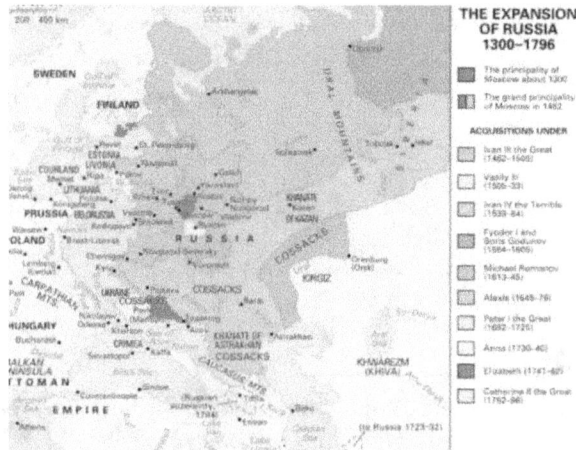

Illustration 5.01: Expansion of Russia (Britannica). Note the Cossack regions near the Carpathian Mountains. (197)

---

(197) Andreyev, Nikolay. "Ivan the Terrible." Brittanica. Accessed November 18, 2024. https://www.britannica.com/biography/Ivan-the-Terrible.

A second Minnesota Rusyn family, however, had a broader and less literal interpretation of the term:

> *Luka said he left the old country to avoid conscription into the Austrian army.* **They told him he was too short to be a Cossack and would have been assigned to clean the stables**. *This may have been an imaginative recollection, as they adopted the Russian identity alongside their fellow parishioners at St. Mary's, since it is unclear whether the Austrian army had Cossacks. Perhaps the original reference was to the Hussars and was adapted to fit the adopted Russian narrative. (Samanisky-Urista Family History)*

So perhaps Rusyns merely reappropriated the Russian term for those serving in the cavalry. But could there be anything more to it than this? What insights can be gained from the historical records?

Early History

The term "Cossacks" was first used to describe Tartar raiding parties who pillaged European settlements in the 11th and 12th centuries. The term is derived from the Turkic-Tatar word *kazak*, which means "free man" or "adventurer." Cossacks began as small, disorganized bands of opportunists that attacked larger settlements, kidnapping residents and holding them for ransom or selling them in Ottoman slave markets. They avoided the customary responsibilities that would subject them to political authority, such as landownership, and resided on the Eurasian steppe just outside the borders of autocratic empires. (198)

---

(198) O'Rourke. *The Cossacks*. Page 32.

The mostly featureless frontiers of the Russian and the Polish Empires made them especially vulnerable to Cossack invasions. The Eurasian steppes along what is now Russia's southern border served as an ancient highway for wandering hordes in search of economic booty (see Illustration 5.02). The absence of natural barriers, such as mountain ranges or large bodies of water, combined with its broad expanse, rendered the Russian border extremely difficult to defend. The Polish-Lithuanian Commonwealth was equally susceptible to invasion, repeatedly attacked by Tartars, Ottomans, and Mongols over several centuries. (199)

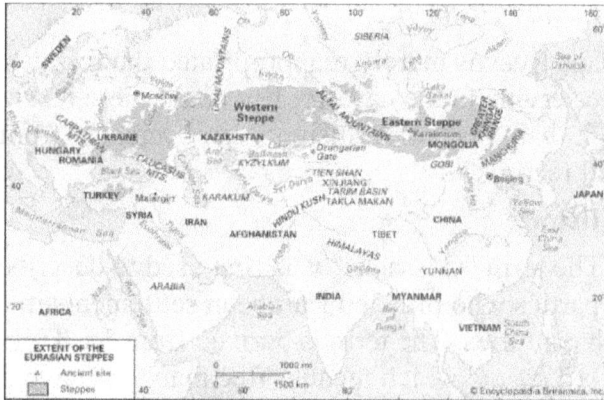

Illustration 5.02: Eurasian Steppes. (200) The steppes served as an ancient highway for wandering hordes on horseback.

---

(199) Wynar, Lubomyr. "Registered Cossacks." Encyclopedia of Ukraine. https://www.encyclopediaofukraine.com/display.asp?linkpath=pages%5CR%5CE%5CRegisteredCossacks.html

(200) "The Steppe." Britannica. https://www.britannica.com/place/the-Steppe.

Cossacks were renowned for their courage, resilience, exceptional riding skills, and willingness to make sacrifices for the greater good. In addition to their reputation as skilled horsemen, they were also proficient mariners. Their boats, *chaiki*, were small, shallow-draft ships, similar to Viking and other pirate vessels.

Illustration 5.03: Cossack Chaika (201)

As time progressed, Cossacks established self-governing communities, particularly in areas north of the Black Sea. Their distinct identity was characterized by a rich tapestry of music, poetry, and sporting traditions, reflecting their martial prowess and rugged lifestyle. Their squat-and-kick dance epitomized their vibrant culture. They were avid drinkers, convinced that alcohol could alleviate virtually every ailment. (202)

---

(201) Wikipedia. 2024. "Chaika." Wikimedia Foundation. Last modified: June 3, 2024. https://en.wikipedia.org/wiki/Chaika_(boat).

(202) Many of their customs were inherited from Mongolian warriors who lived in Genghis Khan's egalitarian society. He grew his clan by

Since we are talking about Cossacks, we will tell you what we know about how they act under certain circumstances. I saw Cossacks suffering from fever who used nothing but a half charge of gunpowder to recover; after diluting it in half with vodka, he stirred and drank well, then went to bed to wake completely healthy the following day. I had a driver who did it more than once and recovered thanks to these drugs, which neither doctors nor pharmacists were aware of. (203)

Although gunpowder and alcohol had more symbolic meaning than medicinal properties, both were important in Cossack society.

Women would eventually come to play vital roles in Cossack communities, managing agriculture and livestock, and safeguarding their homes when the men were out on campaign. Their autonomy and influence in Cossack society were notably distinct from the more limited roles of women in other parts of Europe. People of all ages and genders had parts to play on the perilous frontier. In his novel **The Cossacks**, Leo Tolstoy (204) praised Cossack women for their virtue, independence, and strength.

---

destroying the nobles of competing tribes and integrating the common people into his community. The Khan was also religiously tolerant.

(203) Essar, Dennis F., and Andrew B. Pernal. "The First Edition (1651) of Beauplan's Description D'Ukranie." *Harvard Ukrainian Studies 14*, no. 1/2 (1990): 84-96.

(204) Tolstoy, Leo. 1863. *The Cossacks*. First published in the magazine The Russian Messenger, but late in book form by multiple publishers. Tolstoy lived with the Cossacks from 1851 to 1855.

Slavic Cossacks

Slavic Cossacks originated from a diverse mix of individuals seeking refuge in Central and Eastern Europe's frontier regions.

Among the first to join Cossack communities were fugitives, deserters, and escaped criminals who fled to border regions to avoid punishment. As the szlachta expanded its pro-Catholic policies and introduced serfdom into what is now Western Ukraine, runaway serfs also joined Cossack communities. Additionally, seasonal migrants, traveling into the hazardous yet profitable borderlands to gather fish, honey, beaver pelts, salt, and caviar to sell in European markets, also settled in Cossack communities. The high costs of trading in government-regulated communities prompted many seasonal travelers to settle on the frontier year-round.

As their influence grew, neighboring empires began to regard them as a threat. As a result, the Polish and Russian Empires hired Cossack *mercenaries* to defend their borders. The Cossacks were a highly effective and inexpensive military force, but they proved difficult to manage. They fought for whichever side treated them best and even switched sides during battles to secure a victory. (205) Their primary source of income, however, came from raiding communities south of their homes.

Despite their growing reliance on Cossack military forces, government authorities generally regarded them as reckless brigands whose unruly behaviors caused

---

(205) Seaton. *The Cossacks.* Page 9.

unnecessary conflicts with the Ottoman Turks (206) leading at least one Polish statesman to observe:

> *One must treat this foolish rabble in three ways. For the officers, gifts. The conservative Cossacks and those who have homes favor. Remind them of the fatherland's integrity and the freedom they and their heirs will enjoy. As for the wild rebels, the have-nots who live only from booty—these must be curbed by annihilation and fear of the sword.* (207)

Evolution of Cossack Militias

Frustrated by their unruly behavior, the Polish and Muscovite governments began *registering* or enlisting Cossacks in their regular armed forces. By 1620, thousands of Cossacks had been organized into military colonies (208) along the Dnieper River and the southeastern borders. Each government allocated registered Cossacks free land, tax exemptions, and the privilege of self-governance. The registration system provided authorities with a way to harness the military prowess of the Cossacks while regulating their numbers, movements, and aggression. (209)

---

(206) Dawson, Andrew H., and Kazimierz M. Smogorzewski. "The Cossacks of Poland." Britannica. January 20, 2025. https://www.britannica.com/place/Poland/The-Cossacks.

(207) O'Rourke. *The Cossacks.* Page 71.

(208) Wikipedia. 2025. "Registered Cossacks." Wikimedia Foundation. Last modified January 11, 2025. https://en.wikipedia.org/wiki/Registered_Cossacks.

(209) "A Brief History of the Cossacks." Flames of War. January 11, 2022.https://www.flamesofwar.com/Default.aspx?tabid=112&art_id=696
.

Registered Cossacks were expected to swear fealty to the king and obey the orders of their military commanders, while unregistered Cossacks were relegated to serfdom. This subjugation caused significant unrest and several uprisings. Insurgencies were also caused by the government's failure or unwillingness to increase their numbers, compensate them for their services, fulfill their promises, or provide adequate land grants to compensate their families for their prolonged absences.

These arrangements continued until the mid-17th century, when the Cossacks defeated the Poles in the Cossack-Polish War (1648-1657). The Polish king was forced to recognize an autonomous Cossack Hetmanate in present-day Ukraine. Due to ongoing Polish oppression, the Hetmanate would later ally with Russia.

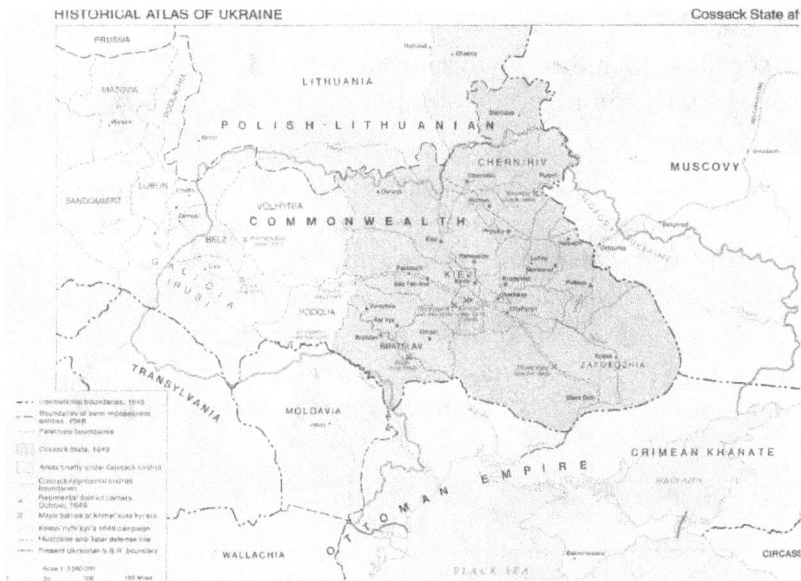

Illustration 5.04: Cossack Hetmanate inside the Polish Lithuanian Commonwealth. Image from Khmelno.jpg (1726×1210)

Types of Cossacks

By the early 1500s, two kinds of Cossacks had emerged: *Town Cossacks* and *Free Cossacks*. Town Cossacks (*gorodovye kazaki)* served as frontier police. In addition to their military duties, Town Cossacks patrolled border crossings to curtail smuggling and other illicit activities. Jan Slomka said that these patrols rarely shot anyone but frequently extorted bribes. Town Cossacks received government subsidies, including land, salaries, food, and military resources. Over time, their roles evolved into hereditary positions passed down from father to son. In frontier areas, some Town Cossacks were even elevated to petty gentry status. According to Albert Seaton:

> *The Poles also began to raise Town Cossacks in a very similar pattern to Muscovy's. Over time, these Town Cossacks would be found in all frontier areas, not only on the open southern flank.* (210)

According to author-historian Martyn Rady, the Austro-Hungarians continued this tradition after the Polish Partitions:

> *Staffed by farmers who held land in exchange for military service and other duties. The frontiersmen were a mix of migrants and refugees who had settled over centuries in a mosaic of different national groups. Their officers were predominantly German or, at the very least, Germanized Slavs. The main task of the frontier troops was to guard the border. (211)*

---

(210) Seaton. *The Cossacks*. Page 7.

(211) Rady, Marty. 2020. *The Habsburg: To Rule the World*. Basic Books. Page 304.

Free Cossacks remained adventurers and explorers who claimed new territories for their government and secured overland trade routes. The Russian Stroganov family (212) paid Free Cossacks to safeguard the white gold (salt) and soft gold (furs) trade and to claim Siberia for the Russian Empire. Free Cossacks continued to resist any commitment that might jeopardize their independent way of life.

Why Rusyns Aspired to be Cossacks

According to historian John Righetti, many Rusyn families claim to have Cossack ancestry, as it was once a source of tremendous pride. Cossacks had the same social autonomy as nobles, while peasants had no social status and few personal freedoms. The peasants regarded Cossacks as heroes and defenders of an independent way of life. During traditional peasant wedding ceremonies, groomsmen even carried a Cossack whip. (213)

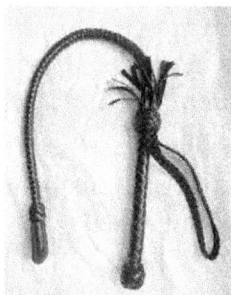

Illustration 5.05: A Cossack Whip (nagaika). Promotional photo.

---

(212) In the 16th century, the Stroganov family funded an expedition led by the Cossack leader Yermak Timofeevich to conquer the Siberian Khanate, marking the beginning of Russian incursions into Siberia.

(213) Slomka, Jan. 2019. *Memoirs of a Peasant*. 3rd ed. Chicago, IL: Polish Genealogical Society of America. Page 137.

While peasants averted their eyes in a noble's presence (to do otherwise was a punishable crime), Cossacks were bold and insolent—an attitude that social elites found especially hard to tolerate from former serfs. In addition to their brash and haughty mannerisms, the Cossacks posed a more substantial threat to the established social order. Cossack-led communities proved that peasants were capable of ruling themselves. Cossack agriculturists posed an economic threat to noble landowners. Cossack villages provided peasants with a way to escape serfdom. And the mere suggestion of a Cossack rebellion:

> ... was often enough for the enserfed masses to shake off their sullen obedience to a hated system, declare themselves Cossacks, and wreak bloody vengeance on their oppressors. The extreme violence of Cossack-inspired revolts and the immediate shedding of blood distinguished them from most other revolts in Europe at the time. The memory of the abrupt transition from glowering docility to mob fury terrorized the nobility. (214)

Cossacks defeated Turkish forces and even Napoleon himself, but why did governments believe they were worth the social turmoil they unleashed?

Initially, Cossack land grants were in unsettled frontiers that few willingly chose to inhabit. (215) Cossack households were responsible for supplying military equipment, including horses, uniforms, and other essentials.

---

(214) O'Rourke, Shaun. 2007. *The Cossacks*. Manchester University Press. Page 62.

(215) O'Rourke. *The Cossacks*. Page 71.

They also bore the economic loss when their men went out on campaign. Cossack commanders were required to deliver trained conscripts and military supplies to meet the needs of their government. As a result, Cossacks offered inexpensive yet reliable military support. This was especially important in the Commonwealth, where the szlachta-controlled parliament resisted tax increases for wars or other coordinated acts of aggression.

By the end of the 19th century, government intervention had diminished the dignity and unity of Cossack communities. (216) Their growing reliance on government subsidies made them complicit in the very systems they had historically condemned. When ordered to suppress peasant strikes and social unrest, their governments unleashed the Cossacks on those they considered their brothers. The once-proud warriors, who represented freedom and resistance, now enforced the very oppression they once aimed to destroy. The military hierarchy created unequal societal and economic roles in their formerly democratic society.

Later Developments

Throughout the 17th century, Poland and Austria reduced their reliance on Cossacks by training army regulars to replace them; however, Cossacks remained a significant military force within the Russian Empire.

After the Bolshevik Revolution in October 1917, Cossacks mobilized against Soviet forces during the Russian Civil War (1918-1920) to defend their traditional way of life. The Bolsheviks viewed the Cossacks as *bourgeois*, akin to the landed gentry, and regarded them as enemies of the state. In the early 1920s, Soviet authorities initiated a campaign to

---

(216) O'Rourke. *The Cossacks.* Pages 60-61.

eradicate the Cossacks, which included mass executions, deportations, and various forms of repression.

Cossacks by Another Name

The Polish Commonwealth established two cavalry divisions to replace Cossack mercenaries—*Hussars* and *Kozaks*. (217) Galicia was a principal source of cavalry recruits for several reasons. First, Galicians were skilled horsemen, so they were drafted to defend the *Military Frontier*. (218), a borderland region that the Habsburg monarchy established as a defense against the Ottoman Empire. This region (1553 to 1881) was primarily inhabited by soldiers and their families, who received land grants in exchange for their military service.

Galicians also excelled at breeding two distinct kinds of military horses. Because of its temperament, stamina, and versatility, the *Malapolska*, or the *Little Poland* horse, was ideal for cavalry units. The *Hucul* horse was admired for its ability to withstand harsh winters, steep terrain, and heavy loads. Peasants and highlanders, like the Lemkos, engaged in informal breeding to meet military demands. According to Stella Hryniuk, many Galicians received subsidies for breeding horses for the military. (219) One source said of the Malapolska horse:

---

(217) Following the partitions of Poland, the Austrian government also established several light cavalry divisions—Hussars and irregulars known as Ulans and Grenzers, the Austrian equivalent of Kozaks, who served as both light cavalry and infantry.

(218) Wikipedia. 2024. "Imperial and Royal Ulans." Wikimedia Foundation. Last modified October 28, 2024. https://en.wikipedia.org/wiki/Imperial_and_Royal_Uhlans

(219) Hryniuk, Stella. 1991. *Peasants With Promise: Ukrainians in Southeastern Galicia, 1880-1900*. Indiana University Press. Page 152.

For centuries, Polish armies needed these home-bred horses. While in times of peace, they were employed for general work, during wars, they were mainly deployed on the eastern borders. These horses were speedy fighters, unafraid of any terrain. (220)

Illustration 5.06: Malapolska Horse (221)

Wola Michowa was a regional commercial center where horses, cattle, and other livestock were bought and sold. If Soroka-owned pastures near the horse breeding operation serve as evidence of involvement, this may also explain part of our Cossack narrative.

Elite and Light Infantry

Hungarian cavalrymen were the first soldiers to be called ***Hussars***, a term based on a Serbian word meaning "brigand." The concept later spread to other European nations, including France, Russia, and Poland, which customized their hussar divisions to meet their specific

---

(220) "Malopolski Horse." http://www.malopolskihorse.com/history.html.

(221) Wikipedia. 2024. "Malopolski." Wikimedia Foundation. Last modified August 24, 2024. https://en.wikipedia.org/wiki/Malopolski.

military needs. Originally called "winged hussars" due to the raptor feathers they attached to their armor, the Polish Hussars were part of the notorious "heavy cavalry," whose primary objective was to shatter enemy lines with overwhelming force. Their wings served as both psychological warfare and repelled enemy lariats. An armored knight charging into battle on a noble steed was thought to intimidate and demoralize opponents, at least until gunpowder and artillery fire rendered armored knights obsolete.

Illustration 5.07: Polish Winged Hussar 1503-1702
Image from: https://en.wikipedia.org/wiki/Polish_hussars

Hussars were recruited from elite society due to their costly military accoutrements, which included purebred horses, armor, ornate uniforms, and weaponry, and their traditional role in public military displays.

Kozak light infantry specialized in irregular warfare and admitted soldiers from all social classes, as long as they could equip themselves with a horse, a pistol, a whip, a knife, and a spear. Kozak is the Polish equivalent of "Cossack." Polish Kozaks lived in what is now Belarus,

Latvia, Western Russia, Ukraine, Estonia, Northern Moldova, and Slovakia. Kozak battalions were agile military units that performed either on horseback or in loose formation infantry (skirmishers) until the army regulars arrived. Kozaks served ten to fourteen years in active duty and an additional twenty years in the reserves. Unlike Hussars, the military obligations of Kozaks prohibited them from marrying or leaving their village posts while on active duty—so they either married before their service began, or after their military service was complete.

Polish genealogist Wojciech Makowiecki found my second great-grandfather's military service record. Hryce Soroka served in the light infantry from 1830 to 1841 (excluding his time in the reserves). Light infantry soldiers, known as Ulans and Grenzers in the Austrian military, were smaller, more agile men, skilled in both sharpshooting and conducting battle on horseback. (222) Some became quite wealthy toward the end of the 19th century, due to subsidies from the Austrian government. (223) Hryce may have fought in the Italian Insurrection of 1831 and the Egyptian-Ottoman War from 1839 to 1841. Although both campaigns were Austrian victories, the number of casualties is unknown.

---

(222) Wikipedia. 2024. "Light Infantry." Wikimedia Foundation. Last modified: July 3, 2024. https://en.wikipedia.org/wiki/Light_infantry

(223) Schlesinger, Tessa. " Russia's Three-Century Relationship with Ukraine." Medium. May 12, 2023. https://medium.com/tessas-web-log/Russias-three-century-relationship-with-ukraine-19143aeb4021.

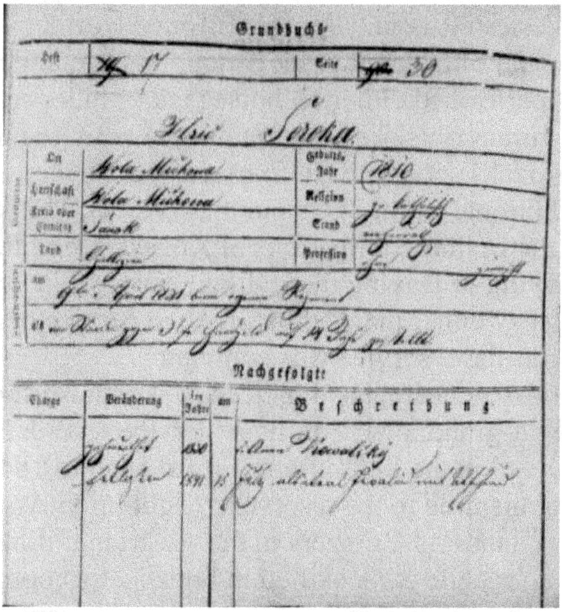
Grundbuchs-

Heft 17 | Seite 30

Soroka

Ort: Wola Michowa | Geburts-Jahr: 1810
Herrschaft: Wola Michowa | Religion
Kreis oder Comitat: Sanok | Stand
Land: Galizien | Profession

Nachgefolgt

Charge	Veränderung	im Jahre	am	Beschreibung

Illustration 5.08: Hryce Soroka's Grundbuchblätter (personnel sheets) for the Austrian army. At that time, cavalrymen served for 11 years, with four in active service and the remaining seven in the reserves.

The 40th Infantry Regiment in Galicia was part of the military forces of the Austrian Empire during the early 19th century. This regiment primarily recruited soldiers from various regions within Galicia, including Wola Michowa. The soldiers of the 40th Infantry Regiment were typically trained for traditional battlefield roles, such as forming battle lines, engaging in close combat, and executing coordinated maneuvers included:

1. **Infantrymen**: The main force was equipped with muskets and bayonets.

2. **Grenadiers**: Elite troops recognized for their strength and bravery, frequently leading assaults.

3. **Light Infantry**: Specializing in skirmishing and reconnaissance, operating in more adaptable formations.

These disciplined soldiers played crucial roles in the regiment's military campaigns throughout the 19th century.

Source: "An Overview of Galician Military Records between 1781-1865." April 7, 2022. https://galicia-gen.com/galician-military-records-between-1781-1865/.

Illustration 5.09: 40th Infantry Regiment.

My great-grandfather Michal's military records were unavailable, so I had to rely on oral history. Family members said that Michal served in Germany for many years. The Austrian Empire exerted considerable influence over several German states until the mid-nineteenth century, including

Bavaria, Württemberg, Baden, Saxony, Bohemia, and Moravia. These military forces fought alongside the Austrian army in the Austro-Prussian War (1866). However, Austria's influence over German principalities diminished after the Prussian victory and subsequent German unification.

To curb the expanding influence of the enlightened French, Germany, Russia, and Austria formed the *League of Three Emperors* in 1871. (224) The League was established to contain nationalist movements, particularly those of the Serbs and Poles, and to maintain a "balance of power" on the European continent. In 1879, Germany and the Austro-Hungarian Empire formed a *Dual Alliance*, pledging to defend one another if Russia attacked and to remain neutral if Russia did not intervene. This alliance would later expand to include Italy, and then be called the *Triple Alliance,* in 1882. (225) Thus, Germany continued to influence Austrian politics until 1918. Ironically, these alliances, meant to reduce military conflict, unwittingly propelled the continent into World War I.

---

(224) Wikipedia. 2024. "League of Three Emperors." Wikimedia Foundation. Last modified: June 20, 2024. https://en.wikipedia.org/wiki/League_of_the_Three_Emperors.

(225) This military alliance led to the Franco-Russian Alliance, which would later expand to include the United Kingdom. The **Triple Entente**, as it became known, aimed to counterbalance the threat posed by the Triple Alliance.

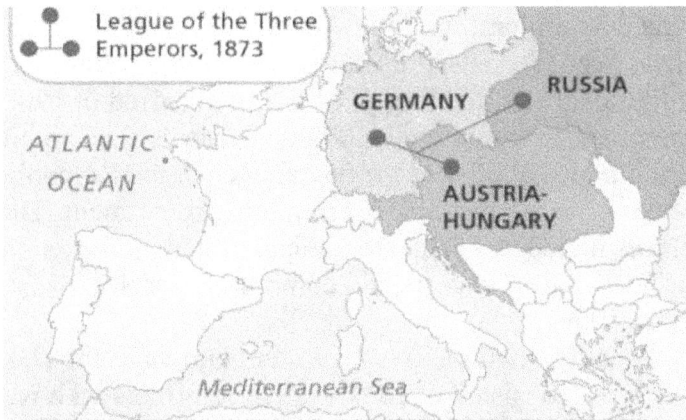

Illustration 5.10: League of Three Emperors. Image from: https://www.blinklearning.com/coursePlayer/clases2.php?idclase =451764686&idcurso=4518350

Thus, my great-grandfather (and his father) may have been called Cossacks because they served in a Cossack-style military unit, embodied Cossack traits (fierce, independent, Orthodox, defiant), or had ancestral ties to regions where Cossack and Lemko identities blurred, common in borderland settlements. The Carpathian Mountains served as a cultural boundary only in a limited sense. The historical influence of Cossack forces in border settlements, combined with pro-Ukrainian sentiments and societal respect for Cossacks, must have contributed to our family legend. Perhaps my great-grandfather also served as a police officer or "Town" Cossack after finishing his military service. Because it was a hereditary role, it may provide another reason my grandfather chose to leave the country.

Nationalism

Polish dominance, disputes over servitude, and calls for a second Polish Republic helped to fuel nationalist movements throughout Galicia. The vicious cycle of debt, land subdivision, and population growth, only partially alleviated by emigration to the United States, along with conflicts over forests and pastures, triggered a series of agricultural strikes, the largest of which occurred in 1902 and involved approximately 200,000 peasants. The abolition of serfdom also abolished the advantages of the Ruthenian elite, exacerbating the ranks of mounting resentment. These privileges included a separate judicial system and exemption from "humiliating" and unpaid community service responsibilities. (226)

The first nationalist movement, known as the ***Old Ruthenians***, consisted of conservative reformers who were loyal to the Greek Catholic Church and the Austrian Empire. They opposed Polish rule, demanded equal rights, and aimed to improve the education of the Rusyn people. Their clerical leaders focused on Rusyns residing inside Galician borders. (227) As dissatisfaction with the Old Ruthenians' inability to effect positive change intensified, however, nationalists shifted their loyalties to either the ***Russophile*** or the ***Ukrainophile*** movements.

Momentum for the Russophile movement accelerated after the Russian government suppressed the Polish Uprising of 1863. (228) Russophiles believed their best chance for independence was to unite with the only autonomous Slavic nation at that time. (229) The larger *Pan-Slavic* movement advocated for all Eastern Slavs to be part of the same Russian state, regardless of their geographical location,

---

(226) Slomka. *Memoirs of a Peasant*. Page 41.

(227) Hryniuk. *Peasants with Promise*. Page 89.

(228) Wikipedia. 2024. "Ukrainophilia." Wikimedia Foundation. Last modified: April 30, 2024. https://en.wikipedia.org/wiki/Ukrainophilia

(229) Russophiles were part of the Pan-Slavism movement, concerned with promoting integrity and unity for all Slavic people.

language, or political beliefs. The Tsar provided financial support for the Russophile movement to expand the Orthodox faith. Initially, the Austrian government backed the Russophile movement to counter Polish and Hungarian pro-Catholic influences. (230). Later, it endorsed the Ukrainophile movement as concerns intensified over Russia's growing political influence. (231)

The Ukrainophile movement sought to unify all Ruthenians (Ukrainians and Rusyns) through a shared language and Cossack traditions, while improving the lives of their people across Europe. The Poles supported the Ukrainophiles to create divisions within the Old Ruthenian and Russophile movements and to garner their support for a second Polish Republic.

The Russophile and Ukrainophile movements differed in both philosophy and method. The Ukrainians adopted a bottom-up strategy, while the Russophiles employed a top-down approach. The Russophiles believed that only the promise of Russian military and financial assistance would liberate them from their Polish, Hungarian, and Austrian overlords. In contrast, the Ukrainophiles believed the solution lay in empowering the lower social classes through education, credit unions, and fraternal insurance cooperatives. They encouraged collective action through a shared language and cultural identity. Thus, Ukrainophiles advocated for teaching the Ukrainian language in Rusyn schools. In fact, Wola Michowa had a Ukrainian cooperative.

---

(230) Wikipedia. 2024. "Galician Russophilia." Wikimedia Foundation. Last modified: April 20, 2024. https://en.wikipedia.org/wiki/Galician_Russophilia.

(231) Wikipedia. 2024. "Russophilia." Wikimedia Foundation. Last modified: May 26, 2024. https://en.wikipedia.org/wiki/Russophilia.

As Russian military forces advanced in Eastern Galicia from 1914 to 1915, the army launched a brutal campaign to Russify the local inhabitants, persecuting both Jews and Greek Catholics. The Russian Army deported thousands of Rusyn priests and intellectuals to Siberia. (232) Their ruthlessness alienated many Russophile supporters as the Tsar was no longer viewed as a Rusyn ally.

When Austria's military establishment failed to expel Russian troops from Galicia at the onset of World War I, Orthodox Lemkos were accused of treason. Austria's military incompetence was blamed on the Lemkos' supposed pro-Russian sympathies. Civil authorities considered the Cyrillic alphabet, religious icons, and even Russian-sounding names to be evidence of subversive intent. Polish authorities exploited Austrian fears to gain greater control over Galician communities. They offered financial rewards for neighbors to inform on each other. Some of the accused faced immediate execution. Thousands more perished from exposure, illness, and starvation in detention camps like Thalerhof and Terezin. According to one historical account:

> On the eve of World War I, the Austro-Hungarian government was suspicious of the Russian Empire. The Orthodox movement was gaining strength in Galicia, particularly in the Lemko Region, as some immigrants returned from the United States, where many had converted to the Orthodox Church. The Austrian government suspected these new Orthodox adherents to be Russian sympathizers. The Lemkos

(232) Wikipedia. 2023. "The Russian Occupation of Eastern Galicia," Wikimedia Foundation. Last modified: September 28, 2023. https://en.wikipedia.org/wiki/Russian_occupation_of_Eastern_Galicia.

> *comprised only 2% of the Galician population but*
> *made up 30% of the prisoners at Thalerhof.* (233)

Those who identified as Ukrainian were supposedly released, but Ukrainian nationalists were also imprisoned and murdered.

Roman Berezovskyj	Lev Kobylianskyj	Pantaleimon Zhabiak
, greek-cath. priest from Protesy, county Zhydachiv, b. 9/26/1874 in Vaniatiche, widower, father of three, no prior record.	clerk from Senechol, c. Dolynsk b. 1/27/1857 in Nadvorne gr-cath., single, no prior record	peasant, b. 1867 in Senechol' married, father of five, no prior record

Illustration 5.11. Thalerhof Intern Camp—Wikipedia

I found no evidence of treasonous charges being levied against the Soroka family. While there were undocumented deaths, I was unable to identify any Sorokas among the records of those who died in the camps. Church records also confirmed that my great-grandmother died in house number 42 in 1931. I could not locate the death record for my great-grandfather, but family members said he died in

(233) Wikipedia. 2024. "Thalerhof Internment Camp." Wikimedia Foundation. Last modified: June 12, 2024.
https://en.wikipedia.org/wiki/Thalerhof_internment_camp.

1911. My grandfather's siblings survived because church records indicate they all married after World War I.

Illustration 5.12: Maria Soroka and Wasyl Iwanysko, 1919 (Personal Photo)

My grandfather's sister, Sophia, and her husband, Steve Kerr, immigrated to Canada in 1936 and settled in Windsor, Ontario. She had three children. After her first husband died in 1959, she married Peter Suszyryba, a widowed Rusyn who had also immigrated from a nearby village. Maria's daughter, Ann, corresponded with my grandfather until his death in 1974; however, her address is no longer valid. Maria's family was deported during Operation Vistula because her address was in Soviet Ukraine.

Among my grandfather's papers was a photo of Ewa Soroka's funeral, who I believe was my grandfather's sister-in-law. The fate of the other Soroka family members or their descendants after World War II is unclear, but this photograph suggests that at least some had survived the war. By remaining in Poland, they avoided the horrors of the Great Famine, also known as the Holodomor (1932-33), a Stalin-orchestrated famine intended to crush Ukrainian resistance to collectivized agriculture. An estimated 17.5 million people died in the Holodomor. Survivors resorted to cannibalism.

Illustration 5.13: Ewa Soroka's funeral. The beautifully painted coffin and the brick structure in the background suggest that the family was doing well at the time the photo was taken. It's also noteworthy that Lemko tradition dictated her burial attire, which was an ethnic costume. Although the exact year this photo was taken is unknown, it is believed to be from the 1950s or 1960s. (Personal Photo)

Had Franz Ferdinand and his progressive views survived the assassination attempt in 1914, my family history and that of the European continent might have taken a different turn. Franz Ferdinand advocated for the creation of the *United States of Austria* to appease the empire's diverse population. After the Soviets withdrew from World War I, the Allies no longer considered Russia a threat, making the vast Austro-Hungarian Empire unnecessary for countering Russian dominance. As a result, the Allies divided the former empire into less powerful, autonomous nation-states. Ironically, these nations would later fall behind the Soviet-controlled Iron Curtain after World War II. The Soviets established communist governments and maintained strict control over the political, economic, and social life in these nations.

Illustration 5.14: Proposed United States of Greater Austria, a federalized Austro-Hungarian Empire, superimposed on the major ethnic groups of the empire. Image from United States of Greater Austria - Wikipedia

Chapter 5 References

"A Brief History of the Cossacks." Flames of War. January 11, 2022.https://www.flamesofwar.com/Default.aspx?tabid=112&art_id=696

Andreyev, Nikolay. "Ivan the Terrible." Brittanica. Accessed November 18, 2024. https://www.britannica.com/biography/Ivan-the-Terrible.

Wikipedia. 2024. "Chaika." Wikimedia Foundation. Last modified: June 3, 2024. https://en.wikipedia.org/wiki/Chaika_(boat).

Wikipedia. 2024. "Congress of Poland." Wikimedia Foundation. Last modified: June 30, 2024. https://en.wikipedia.org/wiki/Congress_Poland.

"Cossack Family Values." Nicholas Kotar. February 11, 2016. https://nicholaskotar.com/2016/02/11/cossack-family-values/.

Dawson, Andrew H., and Kazimierz M. Smogorzewski. "The Cossacks of Poland." Britannica. January 20, 2025. https://www.britannica.com/place/Poland/The-Cossacks.

Edwards, Mike. "Cossacks Facts and Details." https://factsanddetails.com/russia/Minorities/sub9_3c/entry-5101.html.

Essar, Dennis F., and Andrew B. Pernal. "The First Edition (1651) of Beauplan's Description D'Ukranie." *Harvard Ukrainian Studies 14*, no. 1/2 (1990).

Wikipedia. 2024. "Galician Russophilia." Wikimedia Foundation. Last modified: April 20, 2024. https://en.wikipedia.org/wiki/Galician_Russophilia.

"Grandma Said She Was from Poznan": Decoding Stories About Ancestors from Poland." From Shepherds and Shoemakers. January 27, 2017. https://fromshepherdsandshoemakers.com/2017/01/.

Wikipedia. 2024. "Imperial and Royal Ulans." Wikimedia Foundation. Last modified October 28, 2024. https://en.wikipedia.org/wiki/Imperial_and_Royal_Uhlans.

Wikipedia. 2023. "The Russian Occupation of Eastern Galicia," Wikimedia Foundation. Last modified: September 28, 2023. https://en.wikipedia.org/wiki/Russian_occupation_of_Eastern_GaliciaJue v.

Hopler, Whitney. "Meet Archangel Michael, Leader of All Angels." Learn Religions, March 29, 2017. https://www.learnreligions.com/meet-archangel-michael-leader-of-angels-124715.

Hryniuk, Stella. 1991. *Peasants With Promise: Ukrainians in Southeastern Galicia, 1880-1900*. Indiana University Press

Wikipedia. 2024. "League of Three Emperors." Wikimedia Foundation. Last modified: June 20, 2024. https://en.wikipedia.org/wiki/League_of_the_Three_Emperors.

Wikipedia. 2024. "Light Infantry." Wikimedia Foundation. Last modified: July 3, 2024. https://en.wikipedia.org/wiki/Light_infantry.

Magocsi, Paul R. 1983. *Galicia: A Historical Survey and Bibliographic Guide*. Toronto: University of Toronto Press.

"Malopolski Horse." http://www.malopolskihorse.com/history.html.

Wikipedia. 2024. "Malopolski." Wikimedia Foundation. Last modified August 24, 2024. https://en.wikipedia.org/wiki/Malopolski.

Wikipedia. 2024. "Military Frontier." Wikimedia Foundation. Last modified September 17, 2024. https://en.wikipedia.org/wiki/Military_Frontier.

O'Rourke, Shaun. 2007. *The Cossacks*. Manchester University Press.

Wikipedia. 2024. "Polish Cavalry." Wikimedia Foundation. Last modified: June 1, 2024. https://en.wikipedia.org/wiki/Polish_cavalry.

Polianski, Fr. Ioann (2012). Lemkovina: A History of the Lemko Region of the Carpathian Mountains in Central Europe.

Rady, Marty. 2020. *The Habsburg: To Rule the World*. Basic Books.

Sang, Michael. "From Horseback to Tank Warfare." War Insights, March 25, 2024. https://warinsights.com/from-horseback-to-tank-warfare-the-evolution-of-cavalry-traditions-in-the-british-army/.

Slomka, Jan. 2019. *Memoirs of a Peasant*. 3rd ed. Chicago, IL: Polish Genealogical Society of America.

Seaton, Albert. 1972. *The Cossacks (Men-at-Arms)*. New York: Osprey Publishing.

Schlesinger, Tessa. "Russia's Three-Century Relationship with Ukraine." Medium: May 12, 2023. https://medium.com/tessas-web-log/russias-three-century-relationship-with-ukraine-19143aeb4021.

"The Steppe." Britannica. https://www.britannica.com/place/the-Steppe

Wikipedia. 2024. "Thalerhof Internment Camp." Wikimedia Foundation. Last modified: June 12, 2024. https://en.wikipedia.org/wiki/Thalerhof_internment_camp.

Wikipedia. 2023. "The Russian Occupation of Eastern Galicia." Wikimedia Foundation. Last modified: September 28, 2023. https://en.wikipedia.org/wiki/Russian_occupation_of_Eastern_Galicia_(1914%E2%80%931915).

Tolstoy, Leo. 1863. *The Cossacks*. The Russian Messenger and others.

Wynar, Lubomyr. "Registered Cossacks." Encyclopedia of Ukraine. https://www.encyclopediaofukraine.com/display.asp?linkpath=pages%5CR%5CE%5CRegisteredCossacks.html

Wikipedia. 2024. "Russophilia." Wikimedia Foundation. Last modified: May 26, 2024. https://en.wikipedia.org/wiki/Russophilia.

Wikipedia. 2024. "Ukrainophilia." Wikimedia Foundation. Last modified: April 30, 2024. https://en.wikipedia.org/wiki/Ukrainophilia.

Wikipedia. 2024. "United States of Austria." Wikimedia Foundation. Last modified: June 3, 2024. https://en.wikipedia.org/wiki/United_States_of_Greater_Austria.

Chapter 6

Immigrating to the United States

Because they never owned anything, they left the country.
They were pretty much like slaves. John Pachan (234)

Wage migration has been a pillar of the European economic system for centuries. However, as steam power and cheap iron and steel transformed agrarian economies into industrial powerhouses, safe and inexpensive transportation extended 19th-century migration pathways to the United States. (235)

Between 1850 and 1920, thirty million immigrants arrived on American shores. As Midwestern officials and railroad executives promoted free 160-acre homesteads, the initial wave came from Northern and Western Europe and settled in agricultural states like Texas, Minnesota, and Wisconsin. During the 1870s, a growing number of immigrants, particularly from Southern and Central Europe, settled on the Eastern Seaboard, working in the nation's expanding industrial sector. (236) Their earnings helped retire family debts and improved the immigrants' economic and marriage prospects. (237) Despite the challenges of tenement living and factory work, most immigrants believed

---

(234) Duly, William. *The Rusins of Minnesota*. Minnesota Rusin Association, 1993. Page 41.

(235) Nugent, Walter. 1995. *Crossings: The Great Transatlantic Migrations, 1870-1914*. Indiana University Press. Page 26.

(236) Nugent. *Crossings*. Page 92.

(237) Nugent. *Crossings*. Page 88.

that opportunities in the United States were superior to those in Europe. There was the possibility of dressing in upper-class clothing, a plentiful supply of food, and an increasing number of non-agricultural job prospects. (238) Even so, seventy-five percent of European immigrants didn't plan to become American citizens. Family loyalty was strong, and their newfound wealth had the potential to transform the lives of everyone they loved. Many sacrificed physical comforts to save as much as they could in the shortest time possible. They planned to stay for three to four years, just long enough to make the journey worthwhile. As cost and distance became less of a concern, migratory destinations began to include South America and Australia. The sheer number of people involved in these journeys does not diminish their extraordinary character. They came for their families' sake as much as for their own.

In 1906, the average male immigrant was twenty-three, while the average female immigrant was nineteen. My grandfather crossed the Atlantic just one month shy of his twentieth birthday. My grandmother waited until 1911, when her older brother had saved enough money to buy her a ticket, and she was old enough to travel alone (the minimum age was 16). If either grandparent had stayed in Europe, one or both would have probably died. Agricultural imports were negatively impacting local economies and threatening the established social order. Revolutionary fervor was sweeping through Russia and the Balkan Peninsula. Political tensions and ethnic conflicts were erupting across the Austro-Hungarian Empire. The Ottoman Empire was in a state of serious decline. While social unrest was nothing new, its scope and intensity began to have far-reaching effects. The United States feared that revolutionary sentiments would

(238) Rusinko, E. (2024). *Andy Warhol's Mother: The Woman Behind the Artist* (1st ed.). University of Pittsburgh Press.

reach its shores. Ellis Island opened in 1892 to control immigration. The Naturalization Act of 1906 raised and standardized the requirements for American citizenship. Immigration quotas were established to ensure that new arrivals were primarily from Northern and Western Europe. The ease of crossing the Atlantic Ocean was becoming increasingly uncertain.

Immigration was a family decision because of its cost and multi-generational impact. Entire villages saved money to send their loved ones to the United States to reduce poverty, unemployment, and overpopulation. It wasn't long before families and communities became heavily reliant on remittances from the United States. Most individuals saved four years for the journey, which included $30 for transportation and $25 for living expenses, or about $2,000 today. Even this modest sum made immigration unthinkable for those whose wages barely kept them from starving to death.

> *A muscular servant girl who would wash, scrub, attend to the garden and cattle, and help with the harvesting received about $10 a year, with a giant cake and possibly a pair of boots, no less huge, as a premium.* (239)

Landless laborers had little hope for improvement because the entire social and legal system was stacked against them. According to Fr. Polianski (240), the laws in

---

(239) Steiner, Edward A. 1923. *The Immigrant Tide: Its Ebb and Flow*. Republished by Ulan Press (August 31, 2012). Pages 21-22. Steiner went back and forth on steamships crossing the Atlantic, traveling on steerage as an ordinary passenger, avoiding the cabins and reenacting time and again the experience of immigration that he had gone through as a young man.

(240) Polianski, Fr. Ioann (2012). *Lemkovina: A History of the Lemko Region of the Carpathian Mountains in Central Europe*.

Rusyn villages stipulated that housemaids who refused job offers were to be expelled from the community. Servants and manual laborers were housed in communal dormitories or barns, where disease and malnutrition were common. Nobles coerced female servants into sexual liaisons to "strengthen peasant bloodlines," resulting in illegitimate children without the means of support. Landowners could withhold wages, abuse, injure, or exploit their servants without fear of repercussions. Rape was prosecuted only when the perpetrator was someone other than the victim's employer. Even then, the court awarded financial damages to the employer, rather than to the victim herself. A German businessman impregnated my maternal grandmother, but she left Europe after her illegitimate son died. She was fortunate that he bought her a ticket so she could leave the country.

The first to go were young men. Women soon followed as the number of available marriage prospects in their community dwindled. Most men left for economic reasons, while others left to avoid conscription. Although the military service requirements in the Austro-Hungarian Empire had been reduced to three years, universal conscription made service inevitable, and no one could predict when the laws might change. Abuse and disease-related deaths were common in the Austrian military. According to Fr. Polianski:

> *The military courts did not recognize any due process. Justice was administered without witnesses, a defense, or the defendant's presence. Ordinary soldiers were mercilessly beaten where they stood with whatever was available. Facial beatings were often so severe that eardrums and noses were crushed. It is not surprising that the peasants viewed military service as a form of penal servitude to be*

avoided at all costs, even at the risk of mutilation, imprisonment, or death. (241)

In **A Forgotten Land,** author Lisa Cooper said that Russian Jews amputated trigger fingers and toes and even had their teeth removed to avoid conscription. Her great-great-grandfather was among them. Her family also persuaded a Ukrainian family to adopt one of her uncles so that he might be awarded a military exemption as the family's eldest son. (242) Jewish adolescents were routinely abducted and placed in Christian homes to ensure their continued military eligibility. Galician authorities conducted unannounced visits to prevent men from fleeing military service.

> *The recruitment process was rigorous and involved local authorities. One of the most striking details of the process was the use of extreme measures to prevent evasion. On recruitment day, officials, accompanied by village leaders, went door to door before dawn, detaining those selected for service. To prevent escapes, recruits were sometimes bound with ropes or shackled.*
>
> *These harsh measures underscored the seriousness of meeting conscription quotas. (243)*

In addition to rampant and violent abuse, conscripted men also contracted pneumonia, tuberculosis, scarlet fever, dysentery, cholera, and typhus, which, if not fatal,

---

(241) Polianski. *Lemkovina: A History of the Lemko Region,* Pages 196-97.
(242) Cooper, Lisa. 2013. *A Forgotten Land: Growing Up in the Jewish Pale: Based on the Recollections of Pearl Unikow Cooper.* Jerusalem: Penina Press.
(243) "Military Recruitment in Galicia." Galicia Genealogy. https://www.galiciangenealogy.com/military-recruitment-in-galicia/.

significantly shortened their lives. Although the Austrian Empire avoided any prolonged external conflicts between 1866 and 1914, it experienced significant social unrest inside its borders. (244) Military expenditures consumed so much of the government's tax revenues that there were few resources for funding infrastructure improvements outside of Vienna. The ongoing conflict among the Poles, Ruthenians, and Jews ultimately convinced Austria to grant self-governance to Galicia in 1873. Influential Poles thereafter controlled the governance structure, causing widespread dissatisfaction.

Initially, the Habsburgs permitted residents to leave the country to alleviate famine, disease, and ethnic strife. However, as the number of departing males reached menacing proportions, the Austrian government began imposing travel restrictions. Steamship companies were banned from promoting immigration. Village priests railed against the immorality and dangers of the new world. Beginning in 1900, immigrants needed a government-issued passport. (245). In 1913, immigration for military-aged men was paused for one year. In response, young male immigrants adopted false identities, recycled family members' travel permits, and bribed government officials. They disguised themselves as itinerant peddlers or religious pilgrims and crossed poorly defended borders. Soon, the number of unlawful departures outnumbered those authorized to leave. (246) As a young Josephat Jobko explained:

---

(244) Kotlarchik, Carl. "A Guide for Locating Austro-Hungarian Military Records." https://ahmilitary.blogspot.com/2014/10/a-guide-for-locating-austro-hungarian.html.

(245) The U.S. government did not require passports until 1917.

(246) Magocsi, Paul R. 1984. *Our People: Carpatho-Rusyns and Their Descendants in North America*. Toronto: The Multicultural History

The Austrian government was against people moving to other countries, particularly young boys who should serve in the military. This is why our small group took off for America secretly and without passports. (247)

Josephat and his friends, who were then 14, pretended to be attending a religious event in Krakow but instead bribed Polish authorities to smuggle them into Germany. From Berlin, they traveled to Bremen and then to the United States. About 225,000 Rusyns immigrated before 1914. The first wave immigrated to the United States, the second to Canada and South America, and the third to Australia.

The offspring of kmieci and zagrodnicy were exempt from military service in limited circumstances. They had to prove that they were caring for parents or grandparents aged 70 or older who had no other means of support. (248) Otherwise, beginning in 1868, universal conscription laws required all male citizens to serve three years in active duty, plus a decade or more in the reserves. My grandfather leveraged his family connections to cross the German border. Women could leave whenever they had the means to go.

Getting Out

Chain migration occurs when one immigrant saves money to pay for the travel of other family members or

---

Society of Ontario. Page 12.

(247) Genealogical Research Society of Northeastern Pennsylvania website.

(248) "Military Recruitment in Galicia." Galicia Genealogy. https://www.galiciangenealogy.com/military-recruitment-in-galicia/.

friends. The resulting networks disseminated information about jobs, housing, and other resources to help immigrants settle into their new environment. Employers often relied on these networks to recruit new hires, especially in manufacturing, mining, and construction. Industry leaders and shipping magnates also collaborated to bring thousands of Eastern Europeans to work in U.S. mines, factories, and railroads, and even covered their transportation costs with the understanding that they would be reimbursed from their future earnings.

Approximately 95% of the new arrivals stayed with someone they knew. According to the ship's manifest, my grandfather's contact was his cousin, Alex Soroka, who had arrived in the U.S. in 1899. Alex moved to Plymouth, Pennsylvania, to work in the coal mines. His immigration records show that Alex was 32 years old when he arrived in Pennsylvania. The Family Search website said his wife and two children died from starvation or an epidemic shortly before he left. Another cousin, Andrew Soroka, immigrated in 1901. After working in the coal mines and steel mills near Pittsburgh, Andrew bought a farm north of Chisholm.

As a result, my grandfather had family ties in Pennsylvania's coal mining region and on Minnesota's Iron Range. He claimed he paid for his ticket, but some immigrants borrowed travel money from their village priest. My grandfather insisted he had no intention of going back— yet he didn't apply for American citizenship until there was no chance of his ever going home.

Form 548 — MANIFEST — U. S. DEPARTMENT OF LABOR — IMMIGRATION SERVICE — SERIAL No.

Family name		Given name		Port of
SOROKA		Mykoloj or Nick		
Age 39 yrs. 5 mos.	Sex M	Occupation Miner.		Date
Height 5 ft. 8 in.	Complexion med.	Hair bro.	Eyes gray	Nationality Poland	Race Ruth.
Place of birth Volo Michowa, Galicia, Poland.	Read Y	Language or reason for exemption Polish and English	Write Y	Money shown
Last permanent residence Poland.		Destination—Town		
Country Poland	Town Volo Michowa	Plymouth	State Penna.	
Ticket yes	Passage paid by self	Ever in U.S. no.	From	To	Where
Going to join relative or friend Cousin: Alex Soroka, Plymouth, Penna.		Address		
Time remaining in U.S. Permanent	Purpose in coming Reside	Intend to become U.S. citizen Yes.	Head tax status	
Accompanied by None.		Of what country a citizen before becoming citizen of Canada —		
Name and address of nearest relative or friend in country whence alien came	Name Michael Soroka, Volo Michowa, Poland.		Address	
Seaport of landing New York	Date of landing Oct. 25, 1906	Name of S. S. Batavia	Traveling by 3rd.	

Illustration 6.00: Nick Soroka Ship Manifest. In 1906, my grandfather received his work permit. Notice the spelling of his first name—and his age. He was 19, not 39. The transcribed version of the ship's manifest spelled his name as Nikolaj Yozoka, which is why I had so much difficulty finding it.

My grandmother arrived in New York Harbor with $12 in her pocket, the minimum needed to avoid suspicion—and likely the result of the coaching she received aboard her ship. She stayed with her sister, Ann, in Syracuse, New York, for several weeks to earn wages before taking a train to Minnesota in June 1912. Traveling alone, my grandmother faced many challenges. Although it was becoming a more common practice, it was still risky for women to travel without an escort, so she must have been desperate to leave. Female passengers were openly disrespected. Those without an escort were propositioned, harassed, and mistreated by other male passengers and crew members who treated "loose" women however they pleased. Her decision to travel alone proved she knew how to take care of herself. Single women were carefully examined at Ellis Island because officials questioned their motives. A woman traveling without a male escort might be detained until she proved she could support herself in the new country and wouldn't become a burden on society. If an unrelated male accompanied her, she would be detained on suspicion of prostitution. To address this concern, my grandmother identified her brother as her sponsor.

My grandfather arrived in New York City with $28, and like my grandmother, he traveled alone. Steerage tickets could be purchased without reservations and did not guarantee a specific departure date. This was done for a reason. Immigrants were often delayed on their way to ports of call. Some shipping agents inflated ticket prices or sold them expensive, inferior street clothes, claiming the US would reject anyone arriving in native attire. Before leaving Germany, the shipping staff also cheated immigrants out of fees that were already included in the price of their ticket.

There were other pre-departure challenges as well. According to one source (249)

> *The influx of immigrants created problems for the city of Bremen. Often, immigrants were left stranded without food and had to beg in the streets because they lacked money for lodging or passage. Unscrupulous agents lured them to Bremen with promises of shipping them to America and securing a plot of land. Instead, these agents took whatever money the immigrants had. Many other dishonest schemes also existed. Consequently, the city of Bremen had to provide financial assistance.*

In 1892, Russian migrants were blamed for a cholera outbreak in Hamburg that killed approximately 10,000

---

(249) (2010, October 23). *Immigration, The Trip to Port of Bremen.*
https://markprokosch.com/immigration-the-trip-to-port-of-bremen/

people in less than six weeks. (250) Cholera, however, is not a contagious disease that spreads from person to person; it is caused by contaminated water.

Immigrants from the Austro-Hungarian Empire usually left from Hamburg or Bremen on German ships. Single men typically departed from Hamburg, while those with families left from Bremen. My grandfather's journey began in Hamburg, arriving in New York Harbor on the steamship *Batavia* in late October 1906. His manifest said he was a miner/laborer. My grandmother left Bremen in December 1911 and reached New York City eighteen days later aboard the *Neckar*. Her manifest identified her as a servant.

Crossing the Atlantic Ocean was particularly difficult between November and March, when the North Atlantic experienced severe weather conditions, including fierce winds, high waves, and frequent storms. One immigrant described the winter crossing as *gruesome*. My father told me that my grandmother slept in a lifeboat. Given the general congestion of immigrant ships and the stormy weather, it's not surprising that she sought refuge on deck or in other areas of the ship. The third class was unsanitary, lacking privacy and ventilation, and was dark, damp, and foul-smelling. Immigrant ships did not provide adequate wash facilities for immigrants or their clothes. When immigrants became seasick during their journey, vomit permeated the air. Medical care was minimal, and outbreaks of measles, cholera, and typhus were common. The appalling conditions of immigrant ships were well-documented. They were dubbed *coffin ships* because they were generally overloaded and overinsured. Edward Steiner described steerage in the early 1900s aboard the SS Kaiser Wilhelm II:

---

(250) Nugent. *Crossings*. Page 33.

The nine hundred steerage passengers were packed like cattle, forced to walk on the deck when the weather was good, which was impossible, while breathing clean air below in rough weather was equally impossible. The stenches become unbearable. The gender division is not carefully considered, and young women are ranked among the married. The miserable food is dealt out of huge kettles into the dinner pails provided by the steamship company. . . Overall, we should condemn the modern ship's steerage as unsuitable for human transportation.

Another source described the journey, saying: (251)

For most, steerage felt like a nightmare. The conditions were cramped, dark, unsanitary, and so foul-smelling that they became the primary reason for America's early immigration laws. Unfortunately, enforcing these laws was almost impossible. Despite the dismal circumstances, the passengers held faith in the future. They played cards, sang, danced, and talked to pass the time. Rumors about life in America, mixed with stories of rejections and deportations at Ellis Island, circulated endlessly. They practiced answers to the immigration inspectors' questions and spent hours learning the new language.

Those who had never traveled outside their native village, been given time off from work, or were unaccustomed to getting regular meals were less likely to complain about the journey. By 1913, some steamships offered better sleeping arrangements, improved sanitation, and higher-quality food—though experiences varied. Immigrants were generally fed a monotonous diet of boiled herring or beef,

---

(251) "The Journey to America." The Devlin Family. http://devlin-family.com/Journey.htm.

bread, soup, and porridge. Some shipping companies required immigrants to prepare their own meals. Immigrants traveling after 1920 had a better experience. World War I devastated the German passenger ship industry. The British-owned Cunard and White Star Lines provided better accommodations and food. Immigrants typically brought few material belongings because they owned very little and had to carry everything themselves. Most brought a prayer book, which they cherished for the rest of their lives.

The Ships

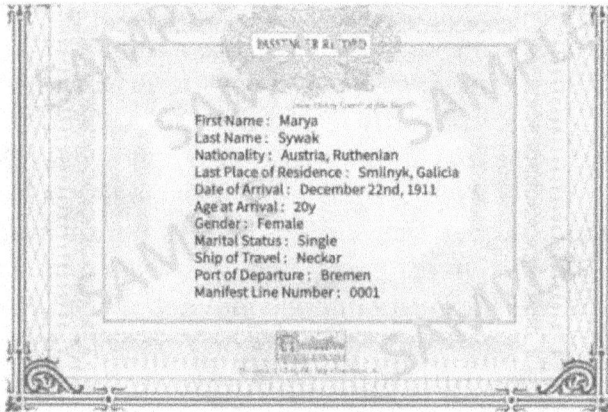

Illustration 6.01: Marya Syvak Ship Manifest. The original ship manifest identified my grandmother as Ruthenian and my grandfather as Polish and Austrian, so the manifests weren't always accurate.

Immigrants traveled in the space formerly used for cargo, known as "steerage." Steerage was highly profitable for steamship companies. While the average ticket cost was $30, a large ship could accommodate 1,500 to 2,000 immigrants, generating profits of $45,000 to $60,000 per voyage. The cost to feed an immigrant was just sixty cents per day! (252) The Batavia (built in 1899) and the Neckar (built in 1901) were similar in size and capacity. The Batavia could transport three hundred second-class and 2,400 steerage passengers. The Neckar could transport 370 second-class and 3,000 steerage passengers.

Illustration 6.02: The SS Batavia. Image from
https://cenaprintscom.blogspot.com/2012/11/ss-batavia.html

Steamship companies subsidized rail passage to German ports. At the time of my grandmother's departure, immigrant cars or *boat trains* (253) transported steamship passengers from Krakow to Bremen or Hamburg. The journey to the German ports was challenging and required careful planning and sufficient funds.

---

(252) "How They Arrived." Scarsdale Public Schools.
https://www.scarsdaleschools.k12.ny.us/cms/lib/NY01001205/Centricity/Domain/312/Immigrant_arrival.pdf.

(253) Immigrant trains were crowded and equipped with wooden benches that offered little comfort. Passengers had to bring their own food. Reaching ports of departure could take days or weeks, as cargo shipments often took priority over passenger travel.

Illustration 6.03: The S.S. Patricia was photographed on December 10, 1906. The photo offers some insight into how densely packed the steerage deck must have been. The Patricia was carrying nearly 2,600 passengers. Image from: https://www.loc.gov/resource/ds.11826/

Many immigrants relied on travel agents and community networks to navigate the process. Assuming no delays, the first leg of the journey took 30 hours; however, immigrants often traveled part of the way by wagon or on foot. No passenger transportation was available from my grandparents' villages.

Bremen became the preferred port of call and was eager to boost immigrant travel due to its underdeveloped export markets—the lack of cargo bound *for* the United States significantly increased shipping costs *from* the United States. Bremen quickly recognized the profitability of immigrant travel. In contrast, Hamburg had no regulations regarding the treatment of immigrants during their stay. Before departing Europe, the inflated cost of food and lodging drained the immigrants' savings. Conditions didn't improve until the shipping companies offered pre-departure services.

Bremen was the first port to establish minimum space requirements for each passenger and provisions for a ninety-day voyage at sea. A doctor accompanied every voyage, and passenger bathrooms and wash areas were regularly inspected and cleaned. Immigrants denied entry were sent back to Europe at the ship owner's expense. (Each person in steerage received an identification tag showing the company responsible for buying the return ticket and any costs incurred at Ellis Island.) As a result, shipping companies disinfected passengers and their baggage, conducted medical exams, and counseled immigrants on how to respond to questions at Ellis Island. Immigrants also had to provide evidence of smallpox immunization, with scars deemed adequate proof. Before leaving, passengers were quarantined in immigrant villages outside the city limits for 14 days.

In 1893, the United States required each passenger to answer thirty-one questions (recorded on the ship manifest) before journeying to its shores. These questions included name, age, sex, marital status, occupation, nationality, the ability to read or write, race, physical and mental health, last residence, and the name and address of the nearest relative or friend in the immigrant's country of origin. Officials also asked immigrants about their finances, such as whether they had at least $25 (recommended but not required), whether they had been in prison, an almshouse, or an institution, and whether they were polygamists or anarchists. Shipping companies advised immigrants to deny having a job upon arrival, as it was unlawful and could result in immediate expulsion.

Ships were divided by wealth and class. First- and second-class passengers traveled in staterooms and cabins. First-class passengers enjoyed private bathrooms, while second-class passengers had to share. Before entering New York Harbor, ships stopped at Staten Island, where doctors examined passengers for smallpox. Immigration officers processed first- and second-class passengers while still on board, as there were minimal concerns about them becoming a burden on society. They went to Ellis Island only if they failed one of the exams; otherwise, entry was guaranteed. Steerage passengers cleared immigration only after undergoing an additional medical examination. If steerage passengers were ill or considered a public safety risk, they were marked with chalk and pulled aside for further investigation. On average, such delays affected about 20% of immigrants.

One can only imagine the level of apprehension of those passing through Ellis Island, widely known as the *Golden Door*, but also called the *Island of Tears*. The facility was filled with uniformed officials, whose presence was always a cause for concern in Europe. The expulsion of family members meant losing what little kinship they had. Sick children aged 12 or older were sent back to Europe alone, while those under 12 had to be accompanied by a parent. Many witnessed heartbreaking scenes as families decided who would leave and who would stay. (254)

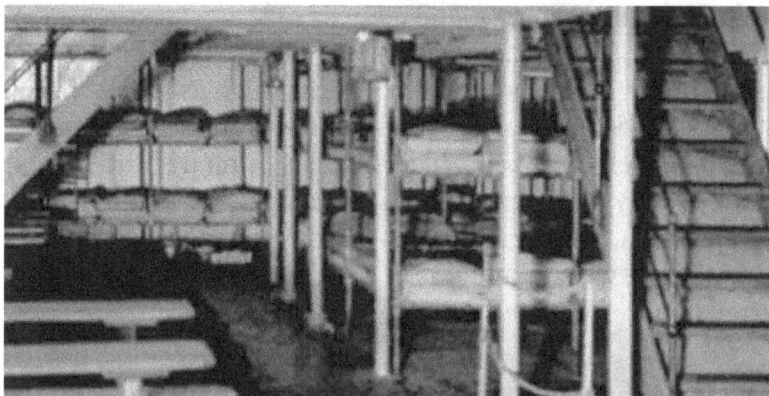

Illustration 6.04: Steerage Sleeping Quarters. (255)

---

(254) The Journey to America." The Devlin Family. http://devlin-family.com/Journey.htm.

(255) Parillo, Vince. "True Immigrant Stories." April 8, 2014. https://vinceparrillo.com/2014/04/08/true-immigrant-tales-traveling-in-steerage/.

A doctor, also in military attire, conducted the physical examinations, but medical *observation* began as immigrants carried their bags up a steep flight of stairs. Those needing time to rest were pulled aside and examined for heart and lung disorders. Physicians also observed the posture and gait of immigrants. According to the Ancestry website, physicians assessed cognitive abilities with a simple riddle: "A hat is to a head like a (blank) is to a hand." Doctors were particularly concerned about eye ailments, especially trachoma. The highly contagious infection, which today can be cured with a single dose of antibiotics, could cause blindness and even death. Ironically, doctors diagnosed the disease by lifting the eyelids of immigrants with a hook that they failed to sterilize after each examination. Doctors were only as thorough as time allowed. In 1905, 16 doctors examined 900,000 immigrants. Official sources referred to the examination as a *six-second physical*, during which medical personnel noticed only the most obvious problems. Yet, every immigrant knew someone who had been sent home.

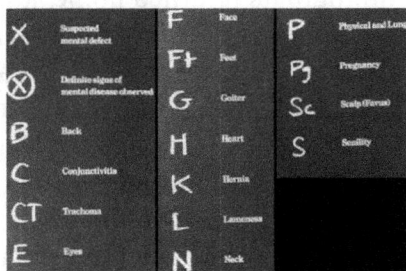

Illustration 6.05: Ellis Island Chalk Marks (Discovery Center)

After their medical evaluations, officials directed immigrants to the *stairs of separation*. Those traveling to other parts of the United States were sent to the right, while those remaining in New York were directed to the left. Those in the center were detained. Assuming there were no issues, the entire process took 3 to 4 hours.

Illustration 6.06: The Stairs of Separation at Ellis Island represents a symbolic and practical aspect of the immigration process. (256)

Returning Home

Immigrants who voluntarily returned home were called *birds of passage*. According to Walter Nugent, about 60% of all new immigrants returned home at least once, making the exact number of new immigrants impossible to determine because they were counted as new arrivals each time they re-entered the U.S.. Those who came to farm were less likely to return than those working for wages. Immigrants planning to return to Europe often lived in slums or boarding houses to save money to purchase land and livestock back home. My grandfather knew an Italian immigrant who lived in an uninsulated shack at a Chisholm mining site for ten years. He saved a tidy sum by denying himself every comfort and then returned to Italy, where he

---

(256) Landphair, Ted. "Ellis: Isle of Joy and Despair." Voice of America. August 17, 2012.
https://blogs.voanews.com/tedlandphairsamerica/2012/08/17/ellis-isle-of-joy-and-despair/.

bought an orchard. He wrote to the Sorokas, saying he was living like a king.

However, while many planned to return home, few actually did. Instead, they sent money, medicine, clothing, and other necessities to Europe. The impact of these remittances was significant. For the first time, many old-world communities had streetlights and clean drinking water. Even modest amounts could make a difference. At the turn of the twentieth century, saving $15 a month for a year could buy one hectare of land; six months could buy four cows, and nine months could pay for a brick farm building. Over time, however, this newfound wealth caused severe inflation.

Most Rusyns hadn't intended to become U.S. citizens, but World War I made them reconsider. The war made traveling to Europe uncertain, as men faced possible conscription. Women had more freedoms in the United States. Most decided it wasn't worth the risk, especially after the United States established immigration quotas in 1921. Around 80% of Rusyn immigrants applied for naturalization between 1922 and 1929, including my grandfather in 1926. Before 1922, a foreign-born woman automatically became a citizen when her husband was naturalized. But the *Cable Act of 1922* changed this, requiring women to apply for naturalization separately from their husbands. My grandmother needed to become a U.S. citizen to collect her portion of her husband's Social Security benefits.

Chapter 6 References

Cooper, Lisa (2013). A Forgotten Land: Growing Up in the Jewish Pale: Based on Pearl Unikow Cooper's Recollections. Jerusalem: Penina Press.

Duly, William (1993). The Rusins of Minnesota. United States: Rusin Association.

Genealogical Research Society of Northeastern Pennsylvania website.

"How They Arrived." Scarsdale Public Schools.
https://www.scarsdaleschools.k12.ny.us/cms/lib/NY01001205/Centricity/
Domain/312/Immigrant_arrival.pdf.

(2010, October 23). *Immigration, The Trip to Port of Bremen.*
https://markprokosch.com/immigration-the-trip-to-port-of-bremen/

Kotlarchik, Carl. "A Guide for Locating Austro-Hungarian Military
Records." https://ahmilitary.blogspot.com/2014/10/a-guide-for-locating-
austro-hungarian.html

Landphair, Ted. "Ellis: Isle of Joy and Despair." Voice of America.
August 17, 2012.
https://blogs.voanews.com/tedlandphairsamerica/2012/08/17/ellis-isle-of-
joy-and-despair/.

Magocsi, Paul R. 1984. *Our People: Carpatho-Rusyns and Their
Descendants in North America.* Magocsi, Paul R. (1984).The
Multicultural History Society of Ontario.

Markel, Howard. "Before Ebola, Ellis Island's Terrifying Medical
Inspections." PBS. October 14, 2015.
https://www.pbs.org/newshour/health/october-15-1965-remembering-
ellis-island.

Medical Exams on Ellis Island." WAMS: The New York Historical.
https://wams.nyhistory.org/modernizing-america/immigration-and-the-
great-migration/medical-exams-on-ellis-island/.

"Military Recruitment in Galicia." Galicia Genealogy.
https://www.galiciangenealogy.com/military-recruitment-in-galicia/.

Nugent, Walter. 1995. *Crossings: The Great Transatlantic Migrations,
1870-1914.* Indiana University Press.

Parillo, Vince. "True Immigrant Stories." April 8, 2014.
https://vinceparrillo.com/2014/04/08/true-immigrant-tales-traveling-in-
steerage/.

Polianski, Fr. Ioann (2012). Lemkovina: A History of the Lemko Region of the Carpathian Mountains in Central Europe.

(n.d.). *S.S. Batavia*. Cenaships and so on. https://cenaprintscom.blogspot.com/2012/11/ss-batavia.html

Rusinko, E. (2024). *Andy Warhol's Mother: The Woman Behind the Artist* (1st ed.). University of Pittsburgh Press.

Steiner, Edward A. 1923. *The Immigrant Tide: It's Ebb and Flow.* Republished by Ulan Press (August 31, 2012).

The Journey to America." The Devlin Family. http://devlin-family.com/Journey.htm

Wikipedia. 2024. "The Naturalization Act of 1906." Wikimedia Foundation. Last modified November 6, 2024. https://en.wikipedia.org/wiki/Naturalization_Act_of_1906.

"The Rush of Immigrants." US History. USHistory.Org, accessed July 31, 2024. https://www.ushistory.org/us/38c.asp.

(2012). *Titanic: The Shocking Truth* [Film].

Chapter 7
The Mines of Pennsylvania & Minnesota

After being processed through Ellis Island, my grandfather boarded a train to Plymouth, Pennsylvania, to work in the underground coal mines. He wasn't alone on this journey. Thousands of Eastern European men crossed the Atlantic in the late nineteenth and early twentieth centuries with similar intentions. Wilkes-Barre, located a few miles northeast of Plymouth, was nicknamed the *Diamond City,* a name that surely heightened the expectations of every new arrival. The term originated from the discovery of coal, however, not the riches a simple miner could accrue.

The immigrants were aware of the dangers. Due to inadequate workplace safety regulations, miners were three to four times more likely to die in accidents in the United States than in Europe. (257) Like all young men, they believed calamity would befall their peers. My grandfather arrived a few months before the 1907 Bankers Panic, which worsened the hardships for eastern coal miners by reducing the demand for coal.

---

(257) Rusinko, E. (2024). *Andy Warhol's Mother: The Woman Behind the Artist* (1st ed.). University of Pittsburgh Press. Page 83.

The Panic of 1907 had a significant impact on various sectors, including coal mining in eastern Pennsylvania. Some key effects include:

1. **Economic Hardship**: The financial instability caused by the panic led to a decrease in demand for coal as industries and households reduced their expenses. This resulted in lower coal prices and diminished income for coal miners.

2. **Job Losses and Wage Cuts**: Many coal mines had to reduce their workforce or cut wages to cope with decreased demand and financial strain. This exacerbated the economic hardship faced by coal miners and their families.

3. **Mining Disasters:** The year 1907 was especially tragic for coal miners in Pennsylvania, marked by numerous mining disasters. One of the most devastating was the Darr Mine explosion in Westmoreland County, which took the lives of 239 miners. These disasters highlighted the perilous working conditions and emphasized the urgent need for better safety regulations.

4. **Labor Unrest**: The economic challenges and inadequate safety regulations sparked heightened labor unrest and strikes among coal miners. They called for improved wages, safer working environments, and greater job security

Luzerne County, where Plymouth is located, experienced the deadliest mining disaster in Pennsylvania history, resulting in 371 fatalities. Mine explosions caused most disasters. Generally, state investigators cleared the mining companies of any liability for injury or death.

Source: Microsoft Co-pilot and <u>Historic Coal Mining Disasters in Pennsylvania</u> and <u>1907 — Dec 19, Darr Coal Mine Explosion, Jacob's Creek, Monessen, PA — 239 – Deadliest American Disasters and Large-Loss-of-Life Events</u>

Illustration 7.00: Bankers Panic of 1907

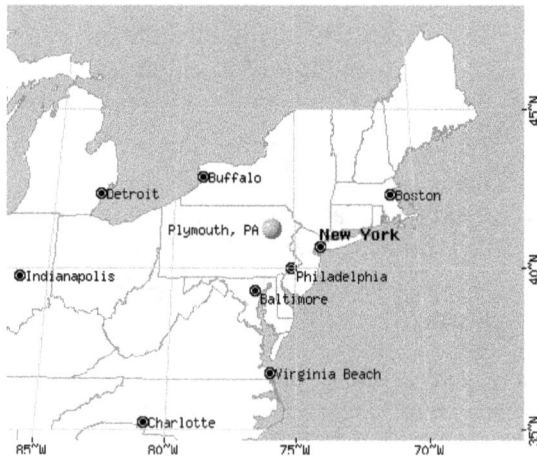

Illustration 7.01 Plymouth, PA.

Between 1850 and 1920, the population of Northeast Pennsylvania swelled from approximately 150,000 to over one million residents. (258) Originally a farming community, by the 1850s, coal mining had become Plymouth's principal occupation. (259) Most of the recruits were young men aged 18 to 25. Company agents visited old-world villages, promising peace and prosperity in the United States—a virtual Eden where they would earn a good wage and receive company housing, so they could save their earnings for whatever they desired. The agents even offered to advance them the money for steamship tickets to the United States and rail travel to and from each port. (260)

The mining companies preferred to hire experienced laborers from Ireland, Scotland, Cornwall, and Wales, or the graduates of German mining schools. However, within a few years, many English-speaking workers left for better-paying opportunities elsewhere. To reduce employee turnover and obtain greater control over their workforce, companies began hiring those who weren't sufficiently fluent in English to fully integrate into American society. Eastern Europeans were ideal because they were small in stature (due to years of malnutrition), could quickly adapt to low-ceiling working environments, and were accustomed to earning minimal pay. And so they labored, eleven hours a day, six days a week, for $1.50 a ton—the equivalent of four to five train cars filled

---

(258) Pennsylvania Anthracite Heritage Museum. Please note that some informational PDFs previously available on this site are no longer accessible on the website.

(259) Wikipedia. 2024. "Plymouth, Pennsylvania." Wikimedia Foundation. Last modified: April 30, 2024. https://en.wikipedia.org/wiki/Plymouth,_Pennsylvania.

(260) "Wartella Genealogy." https://wartella.com.

with coal (see Illustration 7.02). The miners worked in pairs, so their pay was half the promised sum. Just as industry executives had hoped, most Eastern European miners remained in Pennsylvania for the rest of their lives.

Illustration 7.02: Mining Coal Car. Image from
https://www.dreamstime.com/vemployer'ssty-ore-cart

Pennsylvania had soft or bituminous coal deposits in the west and hard or anthracite coal in the east. Hard coal required underground extraction but was especially valued for its slow-burning properties that generated immense heat. After the Civil War, demand for anthracite skyrocketed to support industrial expansion and heat American homes. Extracting anthracite was difficult because its veins lay unpredictably in solid rock far below the Earth's surface. So, men like my grandfather hammered away in near-total darkness six days a week. Railroad companies managed anthracite mines from a distance; executives from the industry's capital in Scranton had little contact with their immigrant workforce.

The labor hierarchy was based on ethnicity rather than skill. Immigrants from English-speaking countries worked as foremen and earned the highest wages, while

Eastern European immigrants held the most physically demanding, dangerous, and lowest-paying jobs. Language barriers, cultural differences, and workplace tensions hindered efforts to improve working and living conditions for everyone. Since miners were paid by the ton, mining superintendents often extorted bribes for the best excavation sites. Coal companies paid workers in scrip, forcing miners to rent company housing and get their supplies from company stores. After deducting amounts owed, including transportation costs to the U.S., miners often found themselves in worse financial shape than before they were paid.

There weren't any legal safeguards against workplace hazards or abuse. Immigrants in steel mills faced similar hardships. Ruthless industrialists like Andrew Carnegie did little to ensure workplace safety. Tired after 12-hour shifts, many new immigrants who didn't speak English and lacked proper training to operate heavy machinery often met tragic ends. Workers were blamed for injuries or deaths and could be easily replaced.

Coal mining was a labor-intensive industry, so companies were always finding ways to reduce costs. Managers cut scheduled work hours whenever possible and underreported production—using a technique called *short-weighing*—to cheat miners out of their pay. Families often took in single men as boarders to make ends meet. While their husbands worked in the mines, wives managed the domestic affairs of their boarders and their families. Boys left school early to work in mines and mills, and girls helped their mothers or worked as nannies for wealthy families who, due to ineffective methods of birth control, had many children. Every family member in an immigrant household had to work—survival was more important than following one's dreams or achieving one's goals.

Living conditions

Miners and their families lived in "coal patch" communities in the shadows of the industry's coal-breaking plants. Coal patch communities resembled small villages in Eastern Europe and were geographically isolated from the broader American society. In his novel **Out of This Furnace**, author Thomas Bell described Pennsylvania's industrial areas as black and dreary, suffocated by the soot emitted from their industrial stacks. Their remote location reduced employment, shopping, education, and social opportunities while heightening dependency on the mining companies. Miners' homes were overcrowded, unsanitary, cold, and lacked indoor plumbing. Nevertheless, many immigrants preferred living in company-provided housing because they thought it guaranteed future employment. However, company officials would quickly dismiss and evict anyone suspected of union activity. As one miner recollected:

> *The mine owners constructed and furnished two houses in a block, featuring one room on the first level and two upstairs. Each was equipped with a coal stove, a step stove, a bedstead made of square timber by the colliery carpenter, a deal table, and several benches. They paid $4 a month for the houses and received coal "thrown in" as a bonus. (261)*

(261) Wallace, Anthony F., and Paul A. Wallace. "Living Conditions-- Life in the Patches." Old Country in the New World.
https://www.amphilsoc.org/exhibits/wallace/patches.htm

Illustration 7.03: Coal Patch Homes. Houses were built as closely together as possible. (262)

Miners' wives baked in communal ovens, washed their laundry in communal tubs, and looked after each other's children. They also planted vegetable gardens to add variety to their otherwise monotonous diets and stretch their meager budgets.

Unions

Despite earning the lowest wages, including those of formerly enslaved individuals from the American South, most Eastern Europeans believed their opportunities for social mobility were better in the United States. (263)

---

(262) "Company Towns: 1880s to 1935." VCU Libraries Social Welfare History Project. https://socialwelfare.library.vcu.edu/programs/housing/company-towns-1890s-to-1935/.

(263) Wikipedia. 2024. "Plymouth, Pennsylvania." Wikimedia Foundation. Last modified: April 30, 2024. https://en.wikipedia.org/wiki/Plymouth,_Pennsylvania.

Eventually, however, even they would become dissatisfied with the status quo. Despite the risks associated with union participation, coal miners became the first industrial workers to form a union. (264) The first union was established in 1890 but did not gain full recognition until the coal strike of 1902, when President Theodore Roosevelt threatened to nationalize the coal industry. (265) The resulting settlement provided miners with higher pay for fewer hours, allowed owners to secure better prices for the coal they produced, and recognized the United Mine Workers of America (UMWA) as their collective bargaining representative. So what then persuaded my grandfather to move to Chisholm, Minnesota?

Gaylord Coal Breaker Between Cherry St. and Washington Ave. circa 1900
Plymouth Pa.   Plymouth Historical Society

Illustration 7.04: Plymouth Coal Mine. Image from Plymouth Historical Society.

(264) Gershon, Livia. "The Rise and Fall of Coal Miners' Unions." JSTOR Daily, September 25, 2015. https://daily.jstor.org/coal-miners-unions/.

(265) Berfield, Susan. "The Coal Strike That Defined Theodore Roosevelt's Presidency." July 15, 2020. https://www.smithsonianmag.com/history/when-roosevelt-and-jp-morgan-fixed-coal-mine(-strike-180975311/.

Moving On

Many immigrants remained in the United States only briefly before returning to Europe. But since my grandfather didn't plan to go back, he sought better-paying opportunities outside of Pennsylvania. He was painfully aware of the dangers and the long-term health effects of mining coal. (266) An estimated 1,200 Rusyn immigrants settled in Rusyn enclaves in Minnesota—some to work on the railroads, others to farm, and some to work in the iron mines in Northern Minnesota.

When Minnesota-based mining agents began canvassing eastern Pennsylvania to hire replacements for discharged ironworkers demanding union representation, my grandfather answered the call. At that time, Range cities were thriving, prompting a Hibbing journalist to report:

> *The Mesabi Range is unique because, unlike coal miners treated like serfs, workers are content because they receive good pay and enjoy many privileges.* (267)

According to a second journalist, Range miners could look for other work when an ore deposit was exhausted and the iron mines were temporarily shut down. While some workers harvested sugar beets in North Dakota, others were employed in mines in Arizona, Montana, and Colorado. Ironically, many of the same men who owned the coal companies also controlled the Mesabi Range.

---

(266) Duly, William (1993). *The Rusins of Minnesota.* Minnesota Rusin Association. Page 43.

(267) Alanen, Arnold R. "Early Labor Strife on Minnesota's Mining Frontier, 1882-1906." *Minnesota History 52*, no. 7 (1991): 246-263.

My grandfather also wanted to start a family, and there were few suitable, single women of marriageable age in coal mining communities. Multicultural marriages were viewed as unwise, causing significant loneliness in immigrant communities. Poverty and language barriers led to victimization and segregation from the rest of American society. Consequently, my grandfather moved to Chisholm in March 1910. He described the long train journey from Pennsylvania to Minneapolis, then to Duluth, and finally to Hibbing. When he finally arrived in Minnesota, it took twelve hours to get to the Iron Range, where he encountered muddy streets, wooden sidewalks, and saloons bustling in a half a dozen different languages. His time in coal country was just over three years.

Culturally, the Iron Range resembled Pennsylvania and his village home. The social hierarchy was ethnically based, and the region was multicultural, with thirty-five different languages spoken. Jewish families managed the commercial districts, and the mining companies held near-total control over their workforce. Those with large families sought other employment opportunities when the iron mines were idle. My maternal grandparents had eight children, so my grandfather worked in Arizona during the frigid winter months, a living arrangement that my maternal grandmother vehemently despised.

Chisholm

Archibald Chisholm, a Scottish investor, banker, and miner from Ontario, Canada, established Chisholm in 1901. Originally a lumber camp, Chisholm grew to a population of 6,000 in just seven years. In September 1908, a wildfire devastated the entire community. The flames did not claim any lives but drove residents into Longyear Lake. Within nine months, the town rebuilt its business district with brick and masonry construction to prevent a similar disaster from ever happening again.

Illustration 7.05: Chisholm Pre-1908 Fire (268)

In 1905, two-thirds of Chisholm's population was foreign-born--the highest percentage of any community on the Iron Range. (269) There was a particularly significant concentration of Austrians and Finns. Chisholm was "*located on a charming body of water known as Long Year Lake, its city hall described as the finest and largest on the Range, and its business district compactly built for a distance of five blocks.*" (270) Like many Range towns, the community also boasted a Finnish opera house that began as an entertainment venue but evolved into a political space as the Finns sought to unionize mine workers and promote their socialist agenda.

---

(268) Image from: https://www.angelfire.com/mn3/chisholm/bfire6.html

(269) Lamppa, Marvin G. 2004. *Minnesota's Iron Country, Rich Ore, Rich Lives.* 1st ed. Duluth, Minnesota: Lake Superior Port Cities Inc., page 167.

(270) Lamppa. *Minnesota's Iron Country.* Page 167.

Illustration 7.06: Mainstreet Chisholm 1911. Image from the Chisholm Pictorial Gallery.

Minnesota historian Marvin Lamppa said:

> *If there was ever a good place to profit from a townsite, it was Chisholm. Chisholm emerged as the business hub for eight nearby mining sites. Forty-eight ore-producing properties were identified near Chisholm, of which U.S Steel operated thirty-two.* (271)

Archibald Chisholm never lived in the community that bore his name. To honor his native Scottish homeland, he called his property the Glenn. It later became the site of the Glenn Mine and the Minnesota Discovery Center.

The Mesabi Iron Range

Charlemagne Tower and brothers Samuel and George Ely founded Northern Minnesota's first commercial hematite mining operation in 1882 near Lake Vermillion. (272)

---

(271) Lamppa. *Minnesota's Iron Country*. Page 167.

(272) Wikipedia. 2024. "Lake Vermilion-Soudan Underground Mine State Park." Wikimedia Foundation. Last modified September 20, 2024.

Traveling to and from the region was nearly impossible because everything had to be moved in horse-drawn wagons across muskeg swamps, which were only passable in winter when the swamps froze solid.

Illustration 7.07: Muskeg (peat) bogs in Minnesota (273)

In addition to the transportation challenges, Tower faced numerous obstacles in acquiring the land for his mining venture. Homestead laws limited private ownership to 160 acres. Title could only be obtained after the land had been surveyed and occupied for five consecutive years. The homestead law was so vague that fraudulent transactions were common, with most land being claimed by speculators, cattlemen, loggers, and railroad companies.

Tower recruited "*entry men*" to secure title to the land they wanted. Entry men distracted speculators looking for quick profits—an acquisition method that the region's lumber businesses had used for so many years it became more or

---

https://en.wikipedia.org/wiki/Lake_Vermilion-Soudan_Underground_Mine_State_Park.

(273) Minnesota Scientific and Natural Areas | Patterned Peatlands | Minnesota DNR

less publicly condoned. (274) In the late 19th and early 20th centuries, conflicts over land and resources emerged with the Native population, especially in areas abundant in timber and minerals. However, newcomers generally took whatever they wanted without fear of legal repercussions. During this time, the Mesabi Range became one of the country's most important iron ore mining regions.

Mining on the Mesabi Range began in 1856 when the Lewis Merritt family moved to Oneta, now known as Duluth, a name derived from an Ojibwa word meaning "*the rock from which the people sprang.*" The family ran a hotel while Lewis worked as a millwright. The patriarch also participated in the Vermillion Gold Rush of 1865, which, although brief, drew residents and miners to the area and helped set the stage for future mining activities. (275) No gold was ever found, but Lewis and other prospectors discovered rich iron deposits so abundant that Lewis told his sons the region would one day be "*covered with ore mines worth more than all the gold in California.*"

The brief gold rush provided additional proof of the region's isolation. Mining companies hired Civil War veterans to extend the Vermilion Trail, an Indian pathway that ran eighty-five miles from Duluth to Vermillion. (276) Initially, the trail was only accessible during the winter. Even after extensive clearing, the arduous journey could only be made on foot in other seasons of the year. Traveling to the

---

(274) Lamppa. *Minnesota's Iron Country.* Pages 54-55.

(275) DeCarlo, Peter J. "The Merritt Family and the Mesabi Iron Range." MNOpedia. February 11, 2014.
https://www.mnopedia.org/group/merritt-family-and-mesabi-iron-range.

(276) "The Old Vermilion Trail and Winston City." THE HISTORICAL MARKER DATABASE. HMdb.Org,
https://www.hmdb.org/m.asp?m=104381.

Vermillion mining site took three days, even on frozen ground. Mail service was so unreliable that the company's cash payroll was delivered in a sealed wooden box.

Despite the surveyor's warnings that prospecting for ore was a waste of time, Lewis's two sons, Leonidas and Alfred, followed their father's advice and began looking for ore. One, called hematite, was found on the southern end of the Mesabi Range, but its deposits were seen as "too thin" to be commercially viable. The other, magnetite, had a higher iron content but needed more processing and was, therefore, less profitable. After several years, the brothers discovered what they had been looking for. (277) Using unconventional methods, Captain J.A. Nichols and his crew discovered iron-rich blue ore in 1890.

The Merritts named the Mesabi region after an Ojibwa term that means "*giant mountain.*" Their discovery earned them the nickname *The Seven Iron Men.* (278) In 1890, the Merritts incorporated their mining enterprise and founded the community of Mountain Iron.

Merritt ore was different from the iron found in other regions of the world. (279) Mesabi ore was soft and powdery and could be skimmed from the surface. No drilling was required. At first, the ore was mistaken for garden soil, prompting experienced mining captains to retort, "*The*

---

(277) The Merritts used magnetic surveying techniques to locate ore deposits and drilled test pits, though experts reported that no viable deposits were found. They were also the first to employ steam shovels and open-pit mining techniques.

(278) DeCarlo, Peter J. "The Merritt Family and the Mesabi Iron Range." MNOpedia. February 11, 2014.
https://www.mnopedia.org/group/merritt-family-and-mesabi-iron-range.

(279) Lamppa. *Minnesota's Iron Country.* Page 113.

Merritts aren't miners; they're farmers." Samples, however, proved otherwise

*Illustration 7.08: The **Seven Iron Men**, also known as the Merritt Brothers, were pioneers of the Minnesota Mesabi Range. Photo of the Merritt family taken in 1871. (280)*

The Mesabi was called "*the poor man's iron range*" because, at least in its early days, the ore could be mined without expensive tools or machinery. Despite the ease of extraction, Merritt's ore presented other challenges. Because of its flour-like consistency, it clogged loading chutes and froze solid in the winter. Blast furnaces unsuited for Mesabi ore expelled it from their stacks, covering, in one instance, half of Cleveland, and causing hundreds of lawsuits. New technology was required to convert the unconventional ore into steel. (281)

The Merritts also needed the infrastructure to transport their ore to eastern steel mills. They initially considered laying track to connect to an existing railroad, but

(280) Image from Wikipedia. 2024. "Seven Iron Brothers." Wikimedia Foundation. Last modified: June 30, 2024.
https://en.wikipedia.org/wiki/Seven_Iron_Brothers.

(281) Lamppa. *Minnesota's Iron Country.* Page 115.

when that railroad experienced financial difficulties, they constructed the **Missabe and Northern Railway**. They also installed loading docks in West Duluth. The Merritt brothers offered company stock as collateral and borrowed the necessary capital from John D. Rockefeller.

The railway was completed in 1893, connecting to what was then the world's largest loading docks. That summer, Leonidas and Rockefeller merged their mining interests to establish the **Lake Superior Consolidated Mining Company**. Rockefeller invested over two million dollars in the Merritt enterprise to keep it afloat until the stockpiled ore could be transported and sold. When the nation experienced an economic downturn in 1893, Rockefeller called in his loans. In February 1894, unable to repay their debts, the Merritts surrendered their entire enterprise to Rockefeller.

The resulting shock was blamed for Cassius Merritt's premature death. Lewis Jr. profited from Rockefeller's hostile takeover and became a family outcast. He and his family relocated to California, where his son later became the largest shareholder of U.S. Steel. A third brother decided to file a lawsuit. Although never convicted of wrongdoing, Rockefeller settled for half a million dollars because he was sure he would not get a fair trial in Minnesota. In less than five years, the Merritt brothers lost their entire mining, railroad, and shipping enterprise. From that point forward, members of the eastern elite, who had no connections to the Iron Range, would garner most of the profits from Mesabi ore.

Clash of the Robber Barons (282)

The Mesabi drama was not over just yet. In 1893, Henry Oliver agreed to mine the Merritt ore and traveled to Duluth to secure legal representation from Chester Congdon. This meeting resulted in a partnership between Congdon and Oliver, which they called the **Oliver Mining Company**. Rockefeller then increased the price to transport Oliver's ore to Carnegie's mills in Pennsylvania—prompting Congdon, Oliver, and Carnegie to resist Rockefeller's takeover of the region. Although Carnegie disliked Oliver, his savvy business manager, Henry Frick, suggested that Carnegie and Rockefeller negotiate a deal. Rockefeller agreed to stay out of the steel manufacturing business, while Carnegie agreed to stay out of mining. When J.P. Morgan saw how the monopolistic practices of Rockefeller and Carnegie were impacting his investments—and threatening his vision of a consolidated U.S. economy—he decided to merge all competing interests into one company he called U.S. Steel. Morgan bought out Carnegie (for a large sum that even surprised Carnegie) and then acquired Oliver's, Rockefeller's, and any remaining mining interests on the Vermillion Range.

In 1901, Morgan curiously named his Mesabi mining venture the Oliver Iron Mining Company (283), a subsidiary of the United States Steel Corporation--the world's largest corporation at that time. Morgan's company controlled 60 percent of the steel industry and employed 168,000 people.

---

(286) Robber barons were affluent industrialists in the 19th century who employed unethical business practices to dominate major industries.

(283) It is unclear why he named the company the Oliver Mining Company when Oliver no longer had anything to do with the enterprise.

(284) The colossus included Andrew Carnegie's former steelworks and John D. Rockefeller's iron ore and shipping interests in Minnesota. By 1903, U.S. Steel controlled the entire Mesabi Range, accounted for two-thirds of the region's ore production, and three-quarters of its workforce. Locals called the company "the Oliver." Along with other dubious tactics to stifle union demands and guarantee that operations continued unhindered despite high turnover and injury rates, U.S. Steel gained notoriety for its severe anti-labor policies. **Slavery by Another Name** author Douglas Blackmon said that to maintain low wages, U.S. Steel's southern subsidiaries employed convicts and the formerly enslaved. By 1907, only eleven iron mines worldwide produced over a million tons of ore; nine of them were on the Mesabi Range. (285)

Mining Challenges

As the surface ore of the Mesabi Range neared depletion, the Oliver Mining Company was forced to adopt more advanced and costly extraction methods. Despite the high cost and workplace hazards, the company favored underground mining because it provided a consistent supply of high-quality ore, and thus a higher return on investment. While open-pit mines were cheaper and potentially safer, accidents and deaths were common due to their reliance on unskilled workers, and from cave-ins, falling rocks, machinery failures, and poorly executed mining blasts.

---

(284) Chernow, Ron. "The Deal Of The Century." AmericanHeritage.Com. https://www.americanheritage.com/deal-century.

(285) "Mesabi Range, Minnesota, USA." Earth Shots. https://eros.usgs.gov/earthshots/mesabi-range-minnesota-usa.

Illustration 7.09: Early Tower Pit 1890. Observe how the miners lowered themselves on ropes and notice the significant differences between them and modern open-pit mines. Some pits were quite deep and dangerous. (286)

The Mesabi Range's underground mines extracted ore by drilling a vertical or nearly vertical shaft deep into the earth's surface. The *headframe*, also known as the *winding tower* or *pit head*, stood over the shaft and hoisted men, machinery, and materials in and out of the mine. Most headframes were dismantled after the mining industry shifted to open-pit extraction. However, the former Bruce Mine headframe still stands near the northernmost exit to Chisholm off Highway 53. Built in 1926, the headframe continued to operate until the mine closed in the early 1940s. It was listed on the National Register of Historic Places in 1978 because it is the only underground headframe remaining on the Iron Range. (287)

---

(286) Alanen, Arnold R. "Early Labor Strife on Minnesota's Mining Frontier, 1882-1906." *Minnesota History 52*, no. 7 (1991). Minnesota Historical Society.

(287) "Bruce Mine Headframe." Discover the Range. https://ironrange.org/listings/bruce-mine-headframe/.

Illustration 7.10: Bruce Mine Headframe Near Chisholm

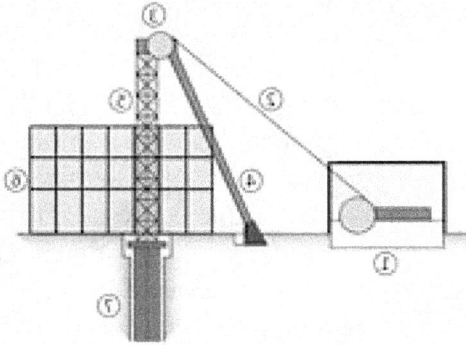

Illustration 7.11: Miners in the Godfrey Mine. The photo is misleading because it was lit for the photograph, whereas the men generally worked in total darkness. (288)

     Communication breakdowns posed the greatest hazard in the underground mines. Corrupt mining superintendents preferred that miners channel their communications through them because it minimized their accountability. Underground mining also raised serious health and safety concerns. Miners described their work environment as *perpetual night*. The continual moan of the timber supports heightened concerns of being buried alive. Natural gases released into the subterranean environment caused asphyxiation and unanticipated explosions. After electricity was introduced into the damp atmosphere, electrocution became a common cause of death.

     The speed at which a miner could escape workplace hazards often spelled the difference between life and death. But these were the harsh realities of the miners' daily lives. In 1894, the Minnesota State Legislature first introduced legislation requiring the Oliver to report occupational

---

(288) Image from "Underground Mining Methods."
MN Underground Mining

injuries and fatalities. Lobbyists opposed the bill for nearly a decade. When it finally became law, the Oliver found it more challenging to deny its responsibility for injuries and death. Still, miners were reluctant to testify in mining disasters, for fear of retaliation and loss of employment. As a result, state investigators often wrongly concluded that accidents were unavoidable and absolved the company of guilt.

Illustration 7.12: Miners in the Godfrey Mine Lighting a Fuse (289)

To attract and retain an increasingly specialized workforce, the Oliver worked to improve the living conditions of workers and their families by building company *locations* near the mines where they toiled. My grandfather spent his entire career working in the underground mines. He retired at age 65 on November 30, 1951, after 37 years of service. Before purchasing a Monroe Location home and moving it to Chisholm, he and his wife, Mary, lived at two separate mining locations for over twenty years.

---

(289) Image from "Underground Mining Methods."
MN Underground Mining

Chapter 7 References

Alanen, Arnold R. "Early Labor Strife on Minnesota's Mining Frontier, 1882-1906." *Minnesota History 52*, no. 7 (1991): 246-263.

Bell, Thomas. 1941. *Out of This Furnace*. Little, Brown, and Company.

Berfield, Susan. "The Coal Strike That Defined Theodore Roosevelt's Presidency." July 15, 2020. https://www.smithsonianmag.com/history/when-roosevelt-and-jp-morgan-fixed-coal-mine(-strike-180975311/.

"Bruce Mine Headframe." Discover the Range. https://ironrange.org/listings/bruce-mine-headframe/.

Chernow, Ron. "The Deal Of The Century." AmericanHeritage.Com. https://www.americanheritage.com/deal-century.

Wikipedia. 2024. "Chisholm, Minnesota." Wikimedia Foundation. Last modified: June 30, 2024. https://en.wikipedia.org/wiki/Chisholm,_Minnesota.

"Company Towns: 1880s to 1935." VCU Libraries Social Welfare History Project. https://socialwelfare.library.vcu.edu/programs/housing/company-towns-1890s-to-1935/.

Duly, William. The Rusins of Minnesota. United States: Rusin Association, 1993.

DeCarlo, Peter J. "The Merritt Family and the Mesabi Iron Range." MNOpedia. February 11, 2014. https://www.mnopedia.org/group/merritt-family-and-mesabi-iron-range.

"Eckley Miners Village Museum." http://eckleyminersvillage.com/the-village/.Pennsylvania Anthracite Heritage Museum

Gershon, Livia. "The Rise and Fall of Coal Miners' Unions." JSTOR Daily, September 25, 2015. https://daily.jstor.org/coal-miners-unions/. Wikipedia. 2024. "History of Coal Miners." Wikimedia Foundation. Last modified: June 18, 2024. https://en.wikipedia.org/wiki/History_of_coal_miners.

Wikipedia. 2024. "Lake Vermilion-Soudan Underground Mine State Park." Wikimedia Foundation. Last modified September 20, 2024. https://en.wikipedia.org/wiki/Lake_Vermilion-Soudan_Underground_Mine_State_Park.

Lamppa, Marvin G. 2004. *Minnesota's Iron Country, Rich Ore, Rich Lives*. 1st ed. Duluth, Minnesota: Lake Superior Port Cities Inc.

Morawska, Ewa, and others. Johnstown's Immigration History. JAHA, https://www.jaha.org/attractions/heritage-discovery-center/johnstown-history/johnstowns-immigration-history/.

"Mesabi Range, Minnesota, USA." Earth Shots. https://eros.usgs.gov/earthshots/mesabi-range-minnesota-usa.

"The Old Vermilion Trail and Winston City." THE HISTORICAL MARKER DATABASE, HMdb.org, https://www.hmdb.org/m.asp?m=104381.

Wikipedia. 2024. "Plymouth, Pennsylvania." Wikimedia Foundation. Last modified: April 30, 2024. https://en.wikipedia.org/wiki/Plymouth,_Pennsylvania.

Rusinko, E. (2024). *Andy Warhol's Mother: The Woman Behind the Artist* (1st ed.). University of Pittsburgh Press.

Wikipedia 2024. "Seven Iron Brothers." Wikimedia Foundation. Last modified: June 30, 2024. https://en.wikipedia.org/wiki/Seven_Iron_Brothers.

Underground Mining Methods." http://www.miningartifacts.org/MNUndergroundMining.html. Wikipedia. 2024. "U.S. Steel." Wikimedia Foundation. Last modified: June 27, 2024. https://en.wikipedia.org/wiki/U.S._Steel.

Wallace, Anthony F., and Paul A. Wallace. "Living Conditions--Life in the Patches." Old Country in the New World. https://www.amphilsoc.org/exhibits/wallace/patches.htm.
"Wartella Genealogy." https://wartella.com

"What Was the Homestead Act?" History. https://www.history.com/topics/american-civil-war/homestead-act.

Chapter 8
The Iron Range & Life in the Glenn Location

Self-sufficiency was the survival tool; everybody in the family worked hard to maintain a delicate status quo. (290)

My grandparents were married in Chisholm on November 25, 1912, at St. Joseph's Roman Catholic Church. Back then, the community didn't have Greek Catholic clergy, so the Roman Catholic priest stepped in to address the spiritual needs of any new arrivals, hoping they might convert. Unlike other ethnic immigrant groups, the Rusyns arrived before their spiritual advisors. Roman Catholicism was already well-established in the United States, thanks to missionaries like Father Frederic Baraga (291) who came years before to convert the indigenous people and advance the interests of the church. However, due to widespread fear that papal authority might overrun democratically elected governments, the general perception of Roman Catholicism in the United States was mostly negative.

---

(290) Duly, William (1993). *The Rusins of Minnesota*. Minnesota Rusin Association. Page 41.

(291) Father Frederic Baraga, a Slovenian missionary, arrived in the United States in 1830. He came to serve the Native American communities, particularly the Ojibwe people, in the Lake Superior region. His dedication and work with the Ojibwe earned him the nickname "The Snowshoe Priest" due to his extensive travels on snowshoes to reach those in need. (Father Baraga's History | Father Baraga And The Ojibwe Natives)

Illustration 8.00: A bishop is shown trying to control Uncle Sam. (292)

St. Joseph's was built by Slovenian and Croatian immigrants who followed their religious leaders from Michigan's copper-rich Upper Peninsula to the Mesabi Iron Range. (293) Immigrant communities were often organized around their churches and spiritual leaders, who helped them maintain connections to cherished cultural traditions and to family members in Europe. (294) Due to the persecution of Rusyns by the Roman Catholic majority overseas, my grandparents' religious community quickly established its own parish. Rusyns are religiously tolerant and open to alternative forms of worship because their beliefs have been shaped by both Eastern (Greek) and Western (Catholic)

---

(292) Tikkanen, Amy. "Uncle Sam." Britannica. https://www.britannica.com/topic/Uncle-Sam.

(293) "Keweenaw Ethnic Groups--The Slovenes." Michigan Tech. https://ethnicity.lib.mtu.edu/groups_Slovenes.html.

(294) Lubotina, Paul.2018. "Michigan to Minnesota: The Early Development of the Mesabi Range." *Upper Country: A Journal of the Lake Superior Region*: Vol 6, Article 6.

traditions. However, the dogma and stoic nature of the Roman Catholic liturgy were incompatible with the participatory traditions of the Greek Catholic Church. (295) Like Protestants, Eastern Christians believe that a direct relationship with God is possible; no intermediary is required.

Traditional Rusyn weddings were three-day events that were celebrated in months that didn't conflict with agricultural and religious calendars. As a result, my grandparents exchanged vows on a Monday in late November. In a traditional Rusyn wedding ceremony, the priest wraps a red scarf around the hands of the bride and groom to symbolize life and fertility. They are also crowned with floral wreaths, representing the couple's commitment to each other and their promise to uphold the values and traditions of their faith.

(295) Duly. *The Rusins of Minnesota.* Page 73.

Illustration 8.01: My grandparents' wedding. Rusyn peasants typically married in traditional, embroidered costumes, while nobles wore white. (296) Perhaps the couple was saying that things were better in the U.S. The best man was from Smolnik and related to the Soroka family by marriage. The maid of honor came from nearby Maniow, where my great-grandmother was born. (Personal Photo)

At the time of their wedding, my grandfather had been living in the United States for six years, while my grandmother had arrived only a year before. This was typical of most immigrant couples. Courtship was necessarily brief due to economic, emotional, and cultural constraints, which encouraged them to seek the comfort, financial security, and emotional intimacy that only a marital partner could provide. Mary and Nicholas spoke the same Rusyn dialect, shared the same religious faith, and hailed from neighboring villages. Immigrants rarely married outside their faith for fear of being rejected by their families and shunned by their communities, a fate often experienced by mixed-faith

(296) Wikipedia. 2024. "Ukrainian Nobility of Galicia." Wikimedia Foundation. Last modified: April 8, 2024. https://en.wikipedia./wiki/Ukrainian_nobility_of_Galicia.

couples. My grandfather's sister, Sophia, knew Mary, but it's unlikely they courted in Europe. At the time of Nicholas's departure, Mary was only 13 years old.

Rusyns typically married for convenience. (297) The groom's parents arranged the marriage. Economic factors mainly influenced marital choices, but a bride's character, health, and moral temperament were also considered. (298) Marriage required the approval of both families, with the couple playing largely a passive role. As a result, U.S. civil authorities had to inquire if immigrant brides were acting under duress. (299) The shortage of unmarried women in Range communities, combined with immigrants' preference for marrying partners from the same or nearby village, reduced Nicholas's chances of finding a suitable partner on his own. Nearly 75% of Rusyn immigrants arriving in the United States between 1870 and 1914 were men. (300) Shared dialects and cultural traditions were important because, as one Rusyn immigrant explained, *"Over every hill, a different tongue is spoken."* (301) Most Europeans did not think Rusyn was a language because of its variations and the fact that it was so rarely spoken outside of Rusyn communities.

---

(297) Gall, Emily, ed. 6AD. Review of Rusyn DNA Myths and Ethnic Erasure: A Symbiotic Relationship. 6AD. rusynsociety.com

(298) Gall." Rusyn DNA Myths and Ethnic Erasure: A Symbiotic Relationship.

(299) Oberly, James W. "Love at First Sight and Arrangement for Life: Investigating and Interpreting a 1910 Hungarian Migrant Marriage." *East European Genealogist 29*, no. 1 (1990): 7-23.

(300) Ancestry.com

(301) Duly. *Rusins of Minnesota*. Page 81.

According to his 1914 World War I draft card, my grandfather worked for the Arthur Mining Company (later acquired by the Oliver Mining Company) as an "underground mine motor operator." At about this time, he and his new wife established their first home in Glenn Location, first at 51 and later at 141 Glenn Location. The location began as a lumber camp but transitioned into a residential site after all the timber had been cleared. According to the Minnesota Discovery Center, in 1923, Glenn Location had 50 homes, a boarding house, a school, a park and playground, an ice rink, and a rubbish dump. Boardwalks connected it to other nearby locations and townsites, including Chisholm. It closed in 1935 due to encroaching mining activity.

The year my grandparents welcomed their first child, the Range experienced a severe economic downturn (1914-15). The following year, demand for iron ore intensified along with the country's growing involvement in World War I. The Mesabi Range has always had a boom-or-bust economy, compelling families to adopt an "all-for-one, one-for-all" mentality.

Illustration 8.02: Underground Motor Operator. Image from Minnesota Digital Library.

Before being outlawed in Minnesota in 1909, mining companies employed child laborers aged 10 to 14 to work alongside their fathers or other family members. A child's small stature and agility made them well-suited for specific tasks, and their contributions helped alleviate family poverty, even though mining companies paid juvenile laborers significantly less than adults.

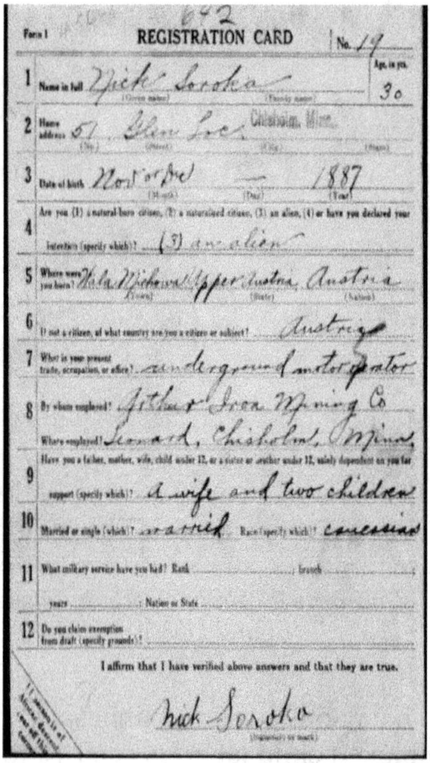
642

Form 1 REGISTRATION CARD No. 19

1 Name in full Nick Soroka (Given name) (Family name) Age, in yrs. 30

2 Home address 51 Glen Loc. Chisholm, Minn. (No.) (Street) (City) (State)

3 Date of birth Nov or Dec — 1887 (Month) (Day) (Year)

4 Are you (1) a natural-born citizen, (2) a naturalized citizen, (3) an alien, (4) or have you declared your intention (specify which)? (3) an alien

5 Where were you born? Wola Michowa Upper Austria Austria (Town) (State) (Nation)

6 If not a citizen, of what country are you a citizen or subject? Austria

7 What is your present trade, occupation, or office? underground motor operator

8 By whom employed? Arthur Iron Mining Co
Where employed? Leonard, Chisholm, Minn.

9 Have you a father, mother, wife, child under 12, or a sister or brother under 12, solely dependent on you for support (specify which)? A wife and two children

10 Married or single (which)? married Race (specify which)? Caucasian

11 What military service have you had? Rank ; branch ; years ; Nation or State

12 Do you claim exemption from draft (specify grounds)?

I affirm that I have verified above answers and that they are true.

Nick Soroka (Signature or mark)

Illustration 8.03: Nick Soroka Draft Card. My grandfather only said—It is not my war to fight."

Families also alleviated poverty by more creative means, such as poaching, bartering, producing moonshine, and gambling. Immigrants like my grandparents were self-sufficient and accustomed to a modest lifestyle. However, alongside significant economic challenges, working-class Europeans also experienced racism and discrimination. Slavic people were viewed as mentally inferior and not entirely white. All immigrants were seen as a threat to the American way of life.

Location Living

　　Mining locations played a vital role in the settlement of Minnesota's Iron Range. Communities sprang up near mine entrances, offering men temporary shelters that initially were little more than tarpaper shacks. Living close to the mines was essential due to the harsh climate and primitive conditions that forced miners to walk to work.

Illustration 8.04 A Company Location. Image from Pinterest.

Ethnic & Religious Tensions

The Mesabi Range has a long-standing cultural tradition of ethnic and religious divisiveness. Mining officials thwarted collective bargaining efforts by inciting anger and distrust among ethnic communities. Andrew Carnegie and William Frick, for instance, capitalized on ethnic tensions to quell labor disturbances in their Pennsylvania ironworks and Colorado coal mines. This strategy also unfolded in the mining communities of the Mesabi Range, especially after the company hired Southern and Eastern Europeans to replace American and Western European mine workers. During the early 20th century, U.S. Steel and its subsidiary, the Oliver Mining Company, fueled ethnic-based suspicions to maintain total control over their workers and keep wages low, thereby maximizing profits.

The transition from underground to open-pit mining made experienced hard-rock miners obsolete. English-speaking or highly skilled mine workers earned more than twice as much as unskilled laborers. Some men left the region to pursue better opportunities or start their own businesses. However, as the number of underground mines decreased, the availability of skilled positions diminished, resulting in increased job competition and bitter disputes among the competing immigrants.

By 1907, the more established European immigrants conformed to American ideals and sought to protect the mining companies and their financial interests. As a result, the Mesabi Range split into two types of communities, with the towns of Hibbing and Virginia forming "white towns" because of their large Nordic populations, while neighboring Chisholm and Eveleth became "black towns" due to the significant numbers of Italians and Slavs who resided there. Tensions between the two communities remained high but often turned deadly when miners received their monthly paychecks and consumed too much alcohol. Nordic miners expressed their racist and nativist prejudices through physical attacks and other exploitative behaviors.

Swedish, Finnish Swedes, and Northern Italian immigrants held supervisory positions, giving them the power to act on their prejudices against working-class newcomers. These prejudices included unfounded beliefs that the new immigrants were lazy, intellectually inferior, or worked only when verbally abused. The Klan also gained influence among the populations of Hibbing and Virginia, calling for "white" unity based on middle-class values, Protestantism, temperance, anti-Catholicism, anti-socialism, and the Republican Party. They shared a desire to suppress the growing political power of all Catholics and Socialists on the Mesabi Range.

Miners also faced terrible working conditions. Mining captains failed to promote Eastern and Southern European miners to authoritative positions, resulting in limited effective communication with their staff, and training for itinerant miners remained basic. Miners worked ten-hour shifts, using only hammers, picks, and shovels to remove hundreds of tons of ore each day.

The long hours and heavy manual labor often caused the average miner's health to decline after just five years. Immigrants frequently turned to farming to survive after their work in the mines left them incapacitated. The combination of strenuous work, long hours, indifferent supervisors, a lack of communication, and a large number of unskilled workers resulted in at least 583 injuries or deaths between 1905 and 1915 in the Mesabi mines.

Sources:

Lubotina, Paul. 2015 "Corporate Supported Ethnic Conflict on the Mesabi Range, 1890-1930," *Upper Country: A Journal of the Lake Superior Region*: Vol. 3, Article 2.

Syrjamaki, John. "Iron Range Communities." Yale University, Minnesota Historical Society, 1940, pp. 195–270."

"Pay Day Celebration: Finlanders and Italians Fight with Rocks and Revolvers." *Mesabi Ore & Hibbing Tribune* (Hibbing, Minnesota), February 25, 1905.

Illustration 8.05: Ethnic and Religious Tensions

Early motorized vehicles were no match for the rocky and muddy terrain. Swedish immigrant Eric Wickman, who later founded the *Greyhound Bus Company,* nearly abandoned his fledgling transportation business because of the treacherous driving conditions around Hibbing. (302) A failed car salesman, he transformed a factory-model vehicle to shuttle miners from Alice Location to Hibbing in under 20 minutes for just 15 cents a ride

Over time, three types of locations emerged on the Iron Range: squatter, company, and model locations. Unlike nearby town sites, locations didn't have a commercial district. Some locations, near Hibbing, Eveleth, Chisholm, and Mountain Iron, evolved into larger communities, but most faded into obscurity. Abandoned pits now serve as the only reminders of former location communities, providing Range towns with their municipal water supply.

Life in location settlements was difficult and fraught with danger. As the miners worked deep underground to extract iron ore, their families often lived in constant fear of accidents and mining blasts. One miner vividly described the terror of hearing a mighty roar followed by debris crashing through the roof of his home, threatening the lives of everyone inside.

(302) Wikipedia. 2024. "Greyhound Lines." Wikimedia Foundation. Last modified: July 1, 2024. https://en.wikipedia.org/wiki/Greyhound_Lines.

You sit with your family around the table, partaking in the humble repast your daily pittance allows. Suddenly, a mighty roar and blast shake everything in view, and a few seconds later, there comes crashing through your roof... rocks and debris endangering your life and those of your loved ones.
(303)

Location life revolved around the mine whistle that signaled the start and end of shifts. Occasionally, the whistle wailed in a single, unbroken blast, widely understood as the harbinger of bad news. Families would gather at the entrance to the mine, anxious to learn what had happened. Did the mine cave in? Did it flood with water? Was anyone hurt or killed? One of the worst mining disasters occurred in February 1924, when the Milford Mine on the Cuyuna Range was flooded by a nearby lake, resulting in the deaths of 41 miners. Thirty-eight of the miners who drowned were married, leaving their widows and 80 children in desperate circumstances.

---

(303) Lamppa, Marvin G. 2004. *Minnesota's Iron Country, Rich Ore, Rich Lives*. 1st ed. Duluth, Minnesota: Lake Superior Port Cities Inc. Page 204.

Illustration 8.06: Clearing a Cave-in. Image from Minnesota Digital Library.

Locations were never intended to offer any permanency. When ore deposits were depleted or a location itself was to be mined, entire communities were relocated to nearby sites. Hibbing was relocated to its current site between 1919 and 1921. In total, 188 buildings were relocated for 16 million dollars. (304) The Oliver Mining Company supplied horses, logs, tractors, and labor. Buildings that were too large to move were cut in two. Relocating Hibbing proved to be a smart use of company resources, however. The Hull Rust Mine became one of the nation's leading iron producers, accounting for one-quarter of the United States' production between the two world wars. The mine is still in operation today. (305) Eveleth was also moved when a rich ore vein was found beneath the original

(304) Weber, Eric W. "Relocation of Hibbing, 1919–1921." MNOpedia. August 27, 2012. https://www.mnopedia.org/event/relocation-hibbing-1919-1921.

(305) Wikipedia. 2023. "Hull Rust Open Pit Mine." Wikimedia Foundation. Last modified: December 1, 2023. https://en.wikipedia.org/wiki/Hull%E2%80%93Rust%E2%80%93Mahoning_Open_Pit_Iron_Mine.

village. The Thunderbird Mine has been operating since the 1850s. (306)

Illustration 8.07: The Colonial Hotel Move in 1920. (307)

Between 1892 and 1920, over 175 locations dotted the Mesabi Range, many of which were named after a nearby mine. The Mesabi iron formation, spanning 100 miles from Biwabik to Grand Rapids, necessitated the construction of more sites than its population might have otherwise required. While living conditions varied, squatter locations were notably worse than those maintained by the mining company. Residents often joked about the squalid conditions to make their lives a bit more bearable. James Corrigan, the editor of a Hibbing newspaper, described one such location as *a huddle of 20 unpainted, weather-beaten shacks, 95% of which look like they are ready to collapse* (308).

---

(306) Wikipedia. 2024. "Eveleth, Mn." Wikimedia Foundation. Last modified: June 1, 2024.
https://en.wikipedia.org/wiki/Eveleth,_Minnesota.

(307) Weber. Relocation of Hibbing, 1919–1921.

(308) Alanen, Alan R. "The Locations: Company Communities on Minnesota's Iron Ranges." Hibbing Historical Society. Accessed

Squatter Locations

Squatters established their homes wherever they could find adequate space, paying the company $1 per month for the privilege. Dwellings were constructed before the installation of roads, so when they were later introduced, they ran in all directions and lacked proper streetlights, grading, and regular maintenance. Farm animals roamed freely, creating an unsanitary and unpleasant environment. Poole, a squatter community near Chisholm, lacked a reliable source of clean water. The poor conditions discouraged residents from improving their properties. It closed after Hibbing Taconite began excavating the site in the late 1970s. The dwellings were in such bad shape that many residents left without even closing their front doors. My parents felt sorry for anyone who lived there.

Illustration 8.08: Poole Location Near Chisholm (Personal Photo)

December 11, 2023. hibbinghistory.org/files/the-locations-by-arnold-alanen-2/.

Company Locations

The mining establishment also designed, constructed, and maintained *"company"* locations where mining personnel supervised everything from house painting to garbage disposal. (309) Historian Marvin Lamppa described company locations as:

> *Simple frame cottages and two-story boarding houses were painted gray, featuring fenced-in yards and dirt streets. At night, the town was dark except for a few street corners where a dim light glowed, powered by electricity from the mine. Houses were heated with box stoves, and rooms were illuminated by kerosene lamps. Every home had its outhouse. A boardwalk wound through town and connected to a wooden stairway to the mine.* (310)

Company locations were leased to employees with wives and families because married men were considered more dependable and less likely to abuse alcohol or demand union representation. Due to limited capacity, the company could accommodate only a small percentage of its workforce. In 1908, management of company locations was transferred to its corporate welfare division to improve the company's reputation, increase worker satisfaction, and boost the bottom line. (311) The company also invested significant resources in constructing high-quality homes in attractively landscaped settings known as *"model locations."* Model locations were designated for valued employees,

---

(309) Lamppa. *Minnesota's Iron Country.* Page 82.

(310) Lamppa. *Minnesota's Iron Country.* Page 83.

(311) Alanen. The Locations.

particularly supervisory personnel, and served as proof of their *corporate benevolence*. (312). Model locations accounted for 6% of the Range locations. The Monroe Location was the only model location by Chisholm.

Illustration 8.09: Monroe "Model" Location, Image from Chisholm Pictorial Gallery 1912

In 1913, a newspaper reported that company locations had improved the miners' standard of living.

> *Years ago, mining locations were cesspools for the collection of dirt and all kinds of filth, as well as hotbeds for the propagation of vice and crime. Today, this has all changed.* (313)

Most of the locations near Chisholm were company sites. Despite the Glenn's proximity to work, my grandfather walked a mile before and after his 10-hour shift, six days a

(312) <u>Minnesota's Lost Mining Towns. PBS</u> documentary.

(313) Alanen. The Locations.

week. In company locations, employees rented their homes from the mining company. The monthly rent was $1 for every $100 of company investment. In the early twentieth century, the average monthly rent was $12.50—one-third to one-half of what a miner would pay for comparable living arrangements in town. The cost of living on the Iron Range was higher than in the Twin Cities metropolitan area because nearly every human need had to be supplied from somewhere else. As a result, many families, including the Sorokas, depended on company-subsidized housing. Miners earned $2 a day—about the same as my grandfather did in Pennsylvania—but they were paid in cash, not company scrip. (Scrip was not outlawed until the Fair Labor Standards Act was enacted in 1938.)

Rent consumed a week's wages, or about 26% of a miner's annual pay. Many of the first arrivals left their mining jobs to start small businesses in nearby towns. Even as a teenager, I remember all the grocery stores, bakeries, cobblers, and meat shops established by immigrant families. I watched each of them close as the mines gradually reduced their workforce, and their descendants moved to other parts of the State. The most recent boom in mining operations occurred in the 1960s and 1970s, when the Mesabi's mining workforce reached 9,000; however, that number declined sharply over the next 20 years. Today, the mines employ less than half that number, though interest in reclaiming century-old mining waste is sparking a modest rebirth. According to the Discovery Center, the Iron Range still produces 85% of the country's domestic iron.

By the 1930s, public transit and roadways made company locations obsolete. However, as early as the 1920s, the company started closing sites because they had become an unnecessary expense. By the 1950s, nearly all the locations had either been demolished or moved to nearby communities. Miners could buy location homes, as long as they agreed to move the structure within 90 days. Some of the better-built houses were moved to Chisholm and Hibbing. The cost to purchase and relocate a structure was approximately $1,700 (roughly $34,000 in 2024), mostly to cover the cost of the move itself. My grandparents purchased a Monroe Location property and relocated it to Chisholm. Their Glenn Location home was sold for $75 and moved north of Chisholm, where it served as a hunting shack until the Roy Marino family donated it to the Minnesota Discovery Center in 2015.

Illustration 8.10: Glenn Location 1920-29. Image from the Iron Range Research Center. John Syrjamaki described locations as dismal, forsaken groupings of residences huddled near a mining operation." (314)

In contrast to the chaotic organization of squatter communities, mining engineers laid out company housing on a pre-planned grid. The size of the housing units varied, yet they all shared the same design, color, and dimensions, resulting in a nearly identical appearance. Company painters typically selected exterior paint colors, such as white or gray,

---

(314) Syrjamaki quote from Alan Alanen's article, The Locations

but tenants were free to paint the interiors however they wished.

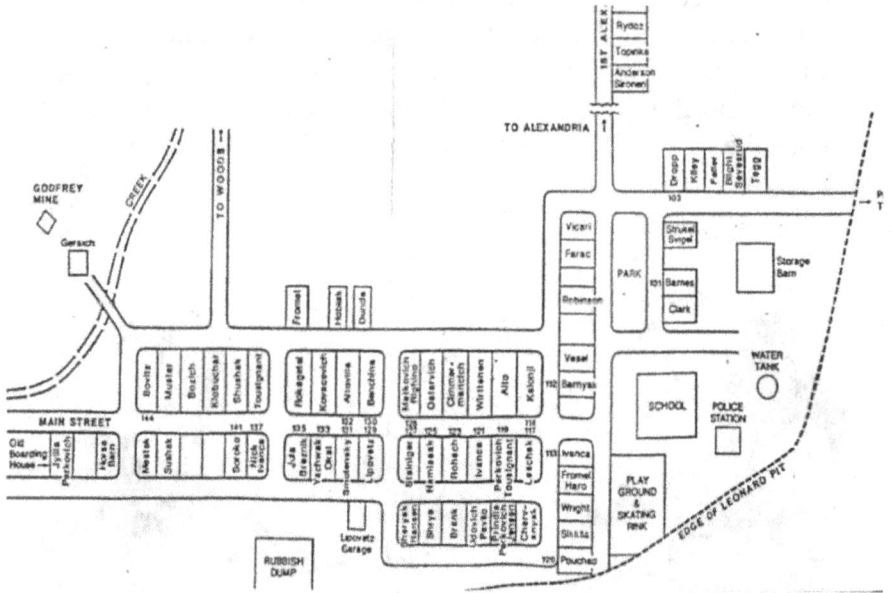

Illustration 8.11: Map of Glenn Location. Image from the Iron Range Research Center. The Soroka residence is number 141.

Although shockingly small by today's living standards, location homes marked a significant improvement over an old-country cottage. The company assigned workers to single-story, slab-on-grade homes with wood floors and outdoor toilets. The Soroka home was 552 square feet and featured three small rooms: a kitchen, a bedroom, and a living room, accommodating two adults and their five children. My grandparents and their two youngest children slept in the bedroom, while the other boys shared a sofa bed. Due to a lack of modern conveniences, mining families preferred having daughters over sons because daughters could help with household chores. My grandmother, who had no daughters and could not afford outside help, had to manage everything herself. As my uncle recalled:

> *My mother's tasks seemed endless. She took care of us kids, cooked, planted a large garden, and hand-washed all the clothes and bedding. She was also responsible for milking and feeding a cow. My brother, John, delivered extra milk to neighbors for some additional income. Canning and storing potatoes for the winter were necessities. She made bread, butter, and cottage cheese; she also sewed and mended all our clothes. My brother Mike cut and stacked the firewood.*

Another reason families preferred daughters was that, with extra domestic help, they could rent part of their living space to boarders and thus establish a reliable source of income. Boarders were often friends or relatives from the same old country village, whose families encouraged them to emigrate. Boarders paid $12 to $15 a month for room and board. A miner's wages fluctuated throughout the year, depending on the intensity and scale of operations, and were influenced by factors such as market demand and weather conditions. Surface mining was seasonal, so there was no guarantee of year-round employment. Therefore, even a single lodger could add some stability to a family's monthly income. (315) Best of all, boarding houses required a minimal investment. According to one miner, *"A woman was the first and most essential requirement. One needed a strong and capable wife to manage a boarding house."*

---

(315) Duly. *The Rusins of Minnesota.* Page 62.

Women thus became the Range's first entrepreneurs, but it came at a cost. Comparing the old country to the United States, one immigrant woman said, "*In the old country, in summer, we work. In winter, rest a little. Here we work all the time.*" (316) However, immigrant women were accustomed to demanding work, and boarding arrangements enabled both parties to accumulate sufficient capital to return home, bring other family members to the United States, or purchase a place of their own. Boarders could also assist with chores that women were unable to handle themselves.

Glenn Location had a company-run boarding house. One miner described it as "*Hot in the summer, cold in the winter, and full of cockroaches year-round*" (317). The boarding house utilized a "hotbed" system, meaning that someone was always occupying a bed. The mines operated 24 hours a day, allowing several men to share the same living quarters. While two miners went to work, two more were ready for bed. When the mines closed, men slept widthwise, resting their feet on nearby chairs. As a teenager, I knew several women who managed boarding houses, and despite their small stature and advanced age, they remained a formidable presence. Like the madams of Western brothels and saloons, these women were tough and capable because they had no choice.

(316) Holmquist, et al. *They Chose Minnesota*. Page 390.

(317) Eleff, Robert M. "The 1916 Minnesota Miners' Strike Against U.S. Steel." *Minnesota History* 51, no. 2 (Summer 1988): 63–74. http://collections.mnhs.org/MNHistoryMagazine/articles/51/v51i02p063-074.pdf

Illustration 8.12: Hill-Fin boarding house in Buhl, 1905-1910. Image from the Minnesota Digital Library.

The mining superintendent's residence was located on a separate block, just a short distance from his employees. The superintendent's homes were nicer and more spacious—two-story structures with indoor plumbing. The company's housing policy was based on its corporate hierarchy rather than on individual need.

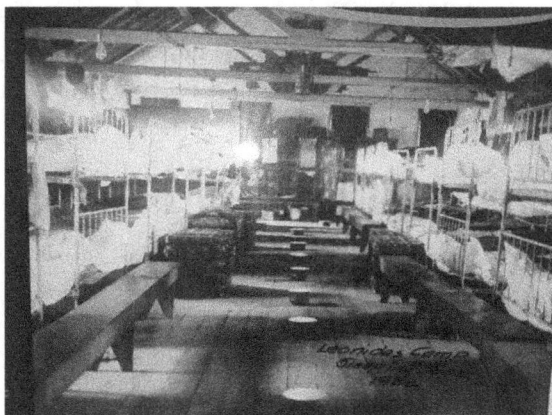

Illustration 8.13: Interior of an Early Company Boarding House. Image from the Iron Range Research Center.

The superintendent was responsible for securing homes for his crew, giving him an uncomfortable level of control over his workers' personal lives. A boss's primary objective was to produce as much iron ore in as short a time as possible, even at the risk of human life. With new workers steadily arriving from Europe, replacements were always available. Fluctuating ore prices made timing crucial. An employee's performance determined his boss's annual bonus, so underperformers risked losing their homes and their jobs.

Mining companies encouraged residents to plant gardens and shrubs to beautify their surroundings and create a natural barrier against the harsh Minnesota climate. Prizes were awarded for the nicest gardens. Growing vegetables helped mining families make ends meet, kept wages low, and the men preoccupied so they wouldn't have time for union activities. Out of necessity, my grandmother planted root vegetables—such as rutabagas, turnips, carrots, beets, and potatoes—because they could be easily preserved in a cellar. Cabbage was a staple of the immigrant diet. My father's earliest memory of Glenn Location was the enormous cabbages around the miners' homes (see Illustration 8.14). He also recalled the abundance of mosquitoes, gnats, ticks, and black flies; standing pools of water and human activity encouraged a variety of pests to breed on location grounds.

Illustration 8.14: Location Cabbage Patch, Circa 1917 in Ely, Minnesota. Image from the Iron Range Research Center.

Education

The Oliver operated elementary schools in some mining locations to introduce American values into immigrant homes. The Glenn Location school provided education up to the fourth grade, after which students were transported to Hibbing for grades 5 through 12. Many different languages were spoken in the immigrant homes, so one of the goals of the company-run schools was to "Americanize" young children by breaking down ethnic distinctions. Most children were fluent in their parents' native tongue by kindergarten or first grade. My parents told me that their teachers administered corporal punishment to anyone who dared to speak a foreign language at school, and there was zero tolerance for those who disobeyed the rules. As a result, children were eager to learn the English language. Even as an adult, my mother spoke Slovenian only when visiting family members. The push for assimilation intensified around the time my father started school.

> *Americanization efforts reached their peak during the patriotic fervor of World War I, when many governments believed that the only remedy was education. St. Louis County school authorities embraced the then-popular idea that foreigners must be familiar with English before they could appreciate American ideals. In 1924, they launched a "Speak English" program. They distributed "We Speak English" buttons and certificates that read, "We, the undersigned, believe that to be true Americans, we must speak the language of America. Therefore, we pledge to speak English as much as possible at school and home, and to encourage and teach others to do the same.* (318)

Unfortunately, the history of the Iron Range was never part of the curriculum of Chisholm schools. Despite the crucial role that mining and immigration played in supporting the local economy, its history was sadly forgotten. I recall how our 4-H club raised funds for the Iron Man statue on Highway 73, which wasn't completed until after I had graduated from college. It wasn't until I started working at the Iron Range Interpretive Center, now the Minnesota Discovery Center, that I began learning about the region's history and its inhabitants.

Range Development

The Oliver constructed several notable buildings in downtown Hibbing, including the Androy Hotel and City Hall. It also built Hibbing High School, once described as a

---

(318) Riippa. *They Chose Minnesota.* Page 312.

"castle in the woods" for its lavish features, including gold leaf embellishments and Tiffany-stained glass windows--all at a cost of nearly $4 million dollars.

However, corporate generosity had its limits. In 1909, Joseph Austin from Chisholm introduced legislation that allowed Range communities to tax ore reserves within their city limits. As a result, tax revenues flowed into schools and other public facilities. Towns competed to see which community could make the best improvements. In 1921, company lobbyists persuaded the legislature to reduce their tax burden. Nevertheless, after a decade of public works, many crude mining towns had transformed into modern urban centers. (319) Many of these buildings remain in use today.

Quality of Life

Early settlements started as rough lumber or mining camps, offering work and shelter for workers and their families. Over time, mining companies hired social workers to improve living standards and provide vital services. They organized picnics, holiday parties, and social gatherings to foster workplace camaraderie. They also built parks and sports fields—though my father often mused that few had the time to enjoy them.

The Oliver installed electrical and sewage systems, made repairs, and pumped untreated spring water into miners' homes, while carefully monitoring water quality to curb epidemics. Ministers were sometimes recruited to assist because locations were filled with a *"staggering array of complicated human problems."* (320) The company hired nurses to serve as midwives, care for the sick, promote hygienic living practices, and counsel those with marital and

---

(319) Lamppa. *Minnesota's Iron Country*. Page 188.

(320) Alanen. The Locations.

financial difficulties. Their duties included mediating disputes among the various ethnic groups. Nurses described immigrant living practices as "*barbaric*" because they employed old country survival strategies, such as bringing farm animals into their homes during the birthing season to prevent newborns from freezing to death. One nurse said that their work required "*infinite patience*" because they had to teach the immigrants how to do nearly everything. Immigrant customs and traditions frustrated support personnel, whether it was mothers giving babies coffee or not living up to American cleaning standards. (321) Unsurprisingly, nurses complained that the needs of the poor, non-English speaking, quarrelsome immigrants were overwhelming. Despite their good intentions, those assisting the immigrants, along with the rest of American society, failed to grasp the difficulties of their lives.

The immigrants lived in stressful environments where they couldn't trust their neighbors and were legally exploited by English-speaking opportunists, all while being thousands of miles away from any support system they had ever known. Lacking education and the ability to speak English, they were unable to advocate for themselves, get work promotions, or share their perspectives with the American public, who, in turn, blamed them for their suffering. Birth control was largely ineffective or discouraged by religious authorities because infertility was perceived as a punishment from God. Cleanliness in the muddy, dusty, and sooty environment was almost impossible. Those who had a choice didn't live near the mines.

Despite having access to a wide range of social services, many objected to corporate policies that prohibited the sale and consumption of alcohol. "Demon rum" measures

---

(321) Alanen. The Locations.

aimed at eliminating overindulgence led to a proliferation of drinking establishments in nearby towns. Taverns provided miners with their only outlet outside their homes to socialize, build friendships, and catch up on the latest gossip, away from the watchful gaze of company officials. As in the old country, taverns served as vital community centers. Alcohol offered a brief respite from their relentless lives.

> *Saloons were much more than just drinking
> establishments. They served as convenient social
> clubs for newcomers, where vital information about
> wages, job opportunities, and housing could be easily
> shared and exchanged. Letters could be translated,
> written, or read, and money orders could be sent
> home. Many of these establishments featured card
> rooms and dance halls. The saloonkeeper often acted
> as a labor agent, banker, and general advisor. (322)*

In 1909, over 350 licensed bars operated on the Mesabi Range. Many of these establishments served men from similar ethnic backgrounds. Chisholm had forty-eight taverns, with around sixty in Hibbing, and these figures did not include all the illegal drinking establishments known as *blind pigs.* Saloons were a primary source of tax revenue for Range communities, generating more than twice as much as general taxes. Any criminal activity happening on the premises was considered outside the reach of local law enforcement. Unsurprisingly, many "suicides" occurred on saloon grounds. Because saloons brought in most of the city's tax money, they were open 24 hours a day. Men took the streetcar to Virginia or Buhl for more immoral forms of entertainment (prostitution and gambling) because police officers were generously bribed to look the other way.

_____

(322) Holmquist, et al., *They Chose Minnesota.* Page 391.

My father was very bitter about his early life. Most he chose to forget. What he remembered, he preferred not to discuss. He marveled at my daughter's amusements, recalling that he didn't have toys, bikes, roller skates, or pets. One of his fondest memories was meeting my mother in Glenn Location when she was four years old. After professing his plans to marry her, her father, John Breznik, chased him from the yard! Despite their initial objections, my father eventually married the girl next door. But aside from meeting my mother, he mostly remembered how hard he worked, how cold it was during the winter, how hot it was in the summer, how little they had, and how hungry he was nearly every day of his young life. There was no childhood back then. The family had beef or pork once or twice a year. My father hunted partridges and other small game to add meat and variety to their otherwise monotonous diet.

The family lived on potatoes and cabbage. My grandmother baked "dark" bread and made pirohy and pasta. Eggs, cottage cheese, and potato skins offered an affordable way to add protein to their diet. The family canned bushels of wild berries in the summer and mushrooms in the fall. My uncle remembered having pancakes for breakfast and cabbage soup for dinner. Desserts often featured canned berries. As an adult, my mother couldn't bear the sight of blueberries. For similar reasons, my father refused to eat pasta. When they were young, they had no choice. My grandmothers only said, "*If food doesn't taste good, it's because you're not hungry.*" Others reminded them that "*Hunger is the best seasoning.*"

The family drank green tea and brewed other herbal varieties for medicinal purposes. My grandfather made wine by fermenting grapes he purchased from an immigrant-run grocery store. He shared some with his friends, while my grandmother used whatever remained for cooking and cleaning after it soured. Nothing was wasted.

John, the oldest of the Soroka brothers, described location homes as "shacks" because they were icy cold in the winter, unbearably hot in the summer, and had outdoor plumbing. Their dwellings lacked insulation to handle the extreme temperature fluctuations. Because all the trees had been harvested, there was nothing to block the wind. During winter, any standing water froze by morning. The stove served as both the home's water heater and furnace. The interiors were especially miserable on wash days during the winter because of the cold and damp conditions.

Drinking water was pumped from the Glenn pit and tasted like ore. So, whenever possible, the family transported spring water from Buhl. By 1921, 33% of the Oliver Mining Company homes had outdoor toilets, while two-thirds had piped-in water. (323) In the early 1920s, electricity was redirected from the mines. Before that, the family relied on kerosene lamps.

Illustration 8.15: Interior of Soroka Home (Personal Photos)

---

(323) The Locations, Alanen.

Families purchased coal and chopped firewood to heat their homes. Chimney fires destroyed many location properties. However, some residents, including my maternal grandfather, privately admitted to setting fires to collect insurance money to put towards better housing in town.

The Sorokas owned a Jersey cow, so they had to cut and gather hay, an arduous task for which they made clothespin rakes. When they ran out of hay, they had to pay $2 per bale, which was equivalent to an entire day's wage. During the Great Depression, they sold milk for five cents a quart. The family also raised a pig, but couldn't afford to keep it, so they sold it for an impressive $60. During the Depression, the company paid miners with scrip to buy essentials from a company-run warehouse.

The family walked to town for most activities, such as shopping, banking, and healthcare. Before bus transportation became available, elevated boardwalks connected locations to nearby towns. The Soroka boys cut through the Glenn pit. My grandmother ordered groceries from Chisholm for next-day delivery. When miners were laid off, local businesses extended credit to mining families until they earned wages again, although at inflated prices.

Illustration 8.16: General Store, Chisholm 1911. Image from Chisholm Pictorial Gallery.

Impacts

Company paternalism and the established mining hierarchy greatly affected everyone's lives. In the mines, disobeying an order resulted in immediate dismissal, so authority figures were obeyed without question. Whether just or fair, their actions and decisions remained unquestioned by the immigrant population. This ideology found its way into Iron Range culture, where questioning authority figures for any reason was simply not tolerated. Needless to say, this lack of accountability created endless opportunities for abuse.

John was expelled from school after being labeled a "troublemaker" for publicly challenging one of his teachers. Bill had an eighth-grade education, but that was not by choice. Steve graduated from high school, an honor denied to my father after he rebuffed a teacher's sexual advances. My mother was the first in her family of eight to graduate from high school, but only because her English teacher recognized her talent and hired her to grade student papers. Typical of most Rusyn households, only the youngest child received an advanced education, while the older siblings followed in their fathers' footsteps and did the same work. Thus, Frank, the youngest member of the Soroka family, earned an engineering degree from the University of Minnesota, partly due to the support he received from my father and grandmother, who sent him food, money, and clean clothes by post.

My grandparents sacrificed everything they could to help their children succeed. My grandfather never owned a car, and my grandmother didn't have a modern stove until shortly before her passing in 1959. After being denied many of life's necessities, my father joined the CCC (Civilian Conservation Corps, Company 717, established on June 10, 1933) before enlisting in the army. The CCC allowed him to earn money, support his family, access dental care, and finally have enough to eat.

Illustration 8.17: Civil Conservation Corps (CCC) Recruits (324)

Illustration 8.18: CCC Camp at Side Lake, Minnesota Discovery Center

---

(324) Image from <u>Conservation Corps Minnesota & Iowa – Restoring Resources. Changing Lives.</u>

Established during the Great Depression by the Roosevelt administration, the CCC provided unemployed men ages 18 to 25 with up to 12 months of full-time employment. The program focused on soil and water conservation, but the men also constructed picnic shelters, retaining walls, roads, and bridges in many state parks, earning $30 a month for their labor. Most of their wages were sent to their families, but they were allowed to keep $5 each month for personal use. Each camp had barracks that could accommodate up to 200 men. My father's company was stationed at McCarthy State Beach, just north of Chisholm. The park was named Camp 717 to honor the men who built it. (325)

Life Challenges

Many miners passed away prematurely from electrocution, accidents, and heart and lung conditions brought on by breathing in carbon dioxide, methane, and particulate matter. In the early years, no disability benefits were available, leaving widows and families completely on their own. Widows often lacked marketable skills, spoke little English, and had young children, which made it challenging for them to work outside the home. If a family's breadwinner left the company for any reason, they lost their company home as well. Complaining did no good because they were constantly reminded of how easily they could be replaced.

---

(325) Cameron, Linda A. "Civilian Conservation Corps in Minnesota, 1933–1942." MNOpedia. July 25, 2016. https://www.mnopedia.org/civilian-conservation-corps-minnesota-1933-1942.

In response, immigrants formed fraternal organizations to provide insurance and worker compensation benefits that Wall Street was unwilling to provide. Some of these fraternal organizations are still in operation today. Women also died prematurely from childbirth or a high-fat diet. Lard and bacon fat were key ingredients in old-world recipes as they were an inexpensive way to enhance flavor and add calories; however, they also contributed to heart disease. The stress of immigration and the challenges of raising large families in an uncertain environment also compromised their mental health.

Residents entertained themselves by gossiping about their neighbors. They shared stories of their past-life experiences and letters from overseas. Social activities centered on ethnic foods, religious holidays, and the consumption of alcohol. Sadly, societal norms condoning alcoholism and domestic abuse were among the traditions the immigrants brought from Europe. One of the characters in **Out of This Furnace** *bragged* that he only assaulted his wife a couple of times a week and got drunk on payday. Piety in immigrant communities was more loosely defined than in mainstream sentiment. Resentments ran deep, and forgiveness was often hard to come by.

Thus, there were countless stories of women who abandoned their husbands and stole their life savings; husbands who regularly abused their wives and children and spent their entire paycheck on alcohol; cohabiting couples who never married but were nonetheless accepted as family; men imprisoned for bootlegging, gambling, robbery, and violent crimes; sons and daughters who stole their parents' assets behind their siblings' backs; wives who physically attacked their inebriated husbands to protect their children; men who were blacklisted or fired for participating in union activity and could no longer support their families; and family members who left the Iron Range and were never heard from again. True stories that remained hidden or were common knowledge but went unspoken due to shame, embarrassment, or perhaps simple gratitude that God had spared them the same fate. Life was tough, but for most, divorce was unthinkable. Old country marriages bound couples and their families. As families grew, so did their dysfunction. Poverty exacted an immeasurable toll.

My father had more leisure time during the CCC and his military service than he ever did in civilian life. He learned to dance while training in California and treasured those memories for the rest of his life. As a child, I don't remember my parents doing anything but work. They let us have fun only after we finished our day's work. If something needed to be done, my parents figured out how to do it themselves.

The Soroka family lived in the Glenn Location for over fifteen years. After it closed, they moved to the Pillsbury Location, where they stayed for another two years. Their home in Pillsbury was an upgrade from their previous residence, featuring four rooms, a bathroom, and indoor plumbing. Despite these improvements, my grandparents were hesitant to leave the Glenn Location because they were worried about proximity to work.

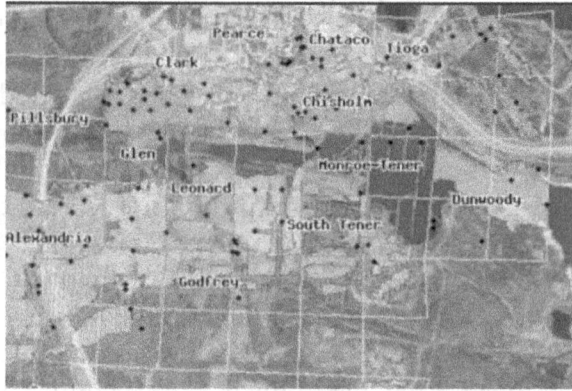

Illustration **8.19**: *Underground Mines by Chisholm. Image from Minnesota DNR.*

Illustration 8.20: This picture was taken at the Godfrey Mine. Slightly visible on the left is the Glenn location. Image from Iron Range Research Center.

My grandfather concluded his career at the Godfrey Mine. He worked underground because it offered higher pay than open-pit operations. In 1907, one in every three mines was underground. Even 40 years later, six of the largest mines—Agnew, Bennett, Fraser, Godfrey, Fayla, and

Sargent—were underground. (326) Some mines had both open-pit and underground operations.. My grandfather was involved in five memorable cave-ins. As a safety precaution, the men were instructed to raise their arms above their heads for easier identification. After the last cave-in nearly killed him, he retired in 1952. Underground mining ceased entirely in 1960.

Of Mules and Men

On-site company management had little concern for the safety of those risking their lives to mine the ore from which they profited. According to my uncle:

> *My father worked ten-hour days for a pittance. I remember him saying the company took better care of the mules than the miners.*

My grandfather wasn't the only miner to complain that the mining companies cared more about their mules than their workers. After all, mules could haul more ore than a man ever could. Leo Lampton, a retired underground miner, echoed these sentiments:

> *They had mules when I went down there in 1927. After they got their first battery-operated motor underground, they only used the mules on the upper levels. They took good care of the mules, telling everyone to be diligent because if one got hurt or killed, they would have to buy a new one. But a man's life didn't mean much. They could pick another man up off the street the next day.* (327)

---

(326) Lamppa. *Minnesota's Iron Country*. Page 154.
(327) Rosemore, Lisa. "The Range Was Built on the Work of the Underground Mines." *Hibbing Tribune* (Hibbing, MN), June 25, 2014.

State investigators concurred, saying:

> *The foremen, notably the Swedish, developed a reputation for cruelty and indifference towards Southern European laborers. A common perspective was that mules were more valuable than laborers because animals required investment for training, while miners supported themselves and could easily be replaced.* (328)

Retiree Herb Noren described the mules as both belligerent and highly intelligent. They pushed miners against log supports to express their displeasure, sometimes causing cave-ins or crushing men when the cars overturned. When startled, a frightened animal would charge down the narrow tunnels, risking injury or death to anyone in its path. A mule's kick could also be deadly. Some miners believed that the mules could count the number of cars being hitched to their load because they refused to pull the additional weight. Despite their high cost, the company preferred mules over horses because they demonstrated greater strength and stamina, and with a lower center of gravity, were more sure-footed on uneven terrain. Unlike horses, mules wouldn't work themselves to death. The company hired veterinarians to give the animals the best possible care. Miners who mistreated their mules were severely reprimanded. If a mule succumbed to neglect or abuse, the responsible parties were fired. The company even secured life and accident insurance for its mules. Mining families were on their own.

---

(328) Lubotina, Paul. 2015 "Corporate Supported Ethnic Conflict on the Mesabi Range, 1890-1930," *Upper Country: A Journal of the Lake Superior Region*: Vol. 3, Article 2. Page 39.

Illustration 8.21: Mining Mule. Image from www.repository.mines.edu

In the early days, miners were required to buy candles for their hard hats and explosives to break up the ore. Gradually, open-pit mining replaced underground operations. According to historian John Syrjamaki:

> *As open-pit mining and stripping activities increased in significance, immigrants found employment in surface operations. This type of work attracted Carpatho-Russians, Montenegrins, Serbs, Bulgarians, Romanians, South Italians, Galician Poles, Lithuanians, and Greeks who arrived during that time. They primarily worked on track gangs in the open pits.* (329)

---

(329) Syrjamaki. The People of the Mesabi Range. Page 210.

Illustration 8.22: Early open-pit mine near Ely. Image from the Iron Range Historical Society.

By the mid-1940s, Mesabi ore reserves were nearly depleted. Consequently, the company restructured and redirected its efforts to produce taconite instead. Taconite, first discovered by the University of Minnesota in the 1920s but considered too expensive to be profitable at the time, replaced iron production in the 1950s. But even open-pit mining had its hazards. My father repaired train cars during the winter when temperatures plummeted to 40 or 50 degrees below zero. As a result, arthritis crippled his entire body, particularly his legs, hands, and feet. The crushed rock produced dust that caused heart and lung disorders, including mesothelioma. Some miners were crushed by the rail cars or died in other machinery mishaps. Most of my father's peers passed away in their sixties, often within months of retirement.

Labor Unrest

Despite corporate welfare programs, disputes between employees and management were a frequent occurrence. Before 1907, there were fifty small-scale strikes, largely protesting unsafe working conditions and low wages. Strikes were often triggered by mining accidents, particularly if they resulted in death. Workers protested unfair labor practices, unreasonable work expectations—such as being required to work on significant religious holidays-- substandard food in company boarding houses, and delays in receiving their pay.

The first strike occurred in 1893, less than a year after the first ore was shipped from the Mesabi Range. Slavic miners resisted calls for eight-hour shifts because they wanted to maximize their earnings. They endured workplace abuse and low pay in exchange for job security. However, they too joined the struggle for union representation after U.S. Steel became the world's first billion-dollar corporation.

Illustration 8.23: Chisholm Iron Miners 1912. Image. From http://www.miningartifacts.org/TheMiners.html.

The first *organized* strike, involving several mines, occurred in 1907. However, all of the men returned to their jobs after just two months. Most were not yet American citizens and were not fluent in English. The company hired strikebreakers, armed guards, and invited the state militia. It also pressured local businesses to deny credit to its striking workforce. The strike resulted in at least one miner's death. Anyone connected to or suspected of union activity was dismissed without due process or pay.

A second organized strike occurred in 1916. The IWW coordinated the protest, demanding higher wages and an 8-hour workday. About 8,000 miners walked off the job, seeking $3.50 per day for work in wet areas, $3 per day for dry tasks, and $2.75 per day for surface assignments. They also protested unreasonable production standards and corrupt management practices. Before the 1916 strike, miners were paid as contract laborers or by the ton, rather than receiving a guaranteed hourly wage. This was standard practice to ensure that the men remained productive during their entire shift. Fluctuating ore prices meant that the miners didn't know what their pay would be until the end of the month. Contract laborers were paid the same regardless of the difficulty in extracting the ore. (330)

As a result, miners bribed their supervisors for prime mining sites—those that were easiest to mine and had the highest mineral content. Single miners bought whiskey and cigars for mining bosses—a practice that severely strained the finances of married men with family responsibilities. (331) Thus, bribery began to encompass offers of the miners'

---

(330) Peck, Lauren. 2016. Review of *Murder and Mayhem*. Mn Good Age. June 28, 2016. https://www.mngoodage.com/voices/mn-history/2016/06/murder-and-mayhem/.

(331) Eleff, Robert M. "The 1916 Minnesota Miners' Strike Against U.S. Steel."

wives or daughters for sex. Some resourceful married couples ensnared mining bosses in adulterous relationships so that the mining supervisor could be blackmailed instead of the other way around. (332) The practice was so pervasive that even my mother knew women who were forced into sexual liaisons with a mining captain. State investigators found:

> *Foremen became adept at manipulating laborers by arbitrarily changing wages and replacing anybody who slipped below expected output levels. Additionally, laborers had to submit to a system of gifts and kickbacks, which included forced sexual favors from miners' wives to keep their jobs or gain employment in lucrative positions.* (333)

Strikers also objected to policies that required them to spend their entire 12-hour shift underground. My grandfathers gazed at the sky on Sundays because they had not seen daylight all week.

Management's response to the 1916 strike was both swift and brutal. Mining supervisors dug trenches around the mine entrances and topped them with barbed-wire fences. They hired armed guards to fend off pro-union men, whom they labeled as radicals. One manager compared the atmosphere to the battlefields of World War I. (334) Minnesota Governor Joseph A.A. Burnquist urged U.S. Steel to hire a private army to end the strike, resulting in hundreds of arrests, layoffs, and the deaths of at least three men. The

---

(332) Lamppa. *Minnesota's Iron Country*. Page 211
.
(333) Syrjamaki, John. "Iron Range Communities." Pages 185-186.

(334) Kaunonen, Gary. The Minnesota Miners' Strike that Brought Immigrant Workers Together.

strike lasted from June through September. Although unsuccessful, the mining company offered the workers a 10% pay increase and dismissed mining captains known for exploitation. These concessions were primarily due to the company's inability to recruit strike-breakers from overseas during World War I.

Despite the violence and exploitation, the governor continued to urge the Minnesota Legislature to impose significant restrictions on individuals and organizations he deemed "anti-American." Minnesota courts even denied Finnish immigrants' citizenship, saying they were descendants of eastern barbarian tribes (Mongols) and were not entirely Caucasian. (335) Fortunately, this decision was later overturned.

The repercussions for anyone involved in union activities were severe. U.S. Steel owned or controlled nearly every commercial enterprise on the Iron Range. The company boycotted businesses that extended credit to its striking workforce. U.S. Steel effectively dominated the Iron Range economy and almost every aspect of the miners' lives, similar to the large landowners in Europe.

> *In the early days, mining companies were not only sources of livelihood but also protectors of health and safety, community promoters, and dispensers of law and justice. In a rapidly evolving America, companies could not long maintain these roles. The company's attempts to maintain order and control led to repression, conflict, strikes, and violence. (336)*

---

(335) Alanen. *The Finns in Minnesota*. St. Paul: Page 55.

(336) Blog. Marvin Lamppa: The Making of an Iron Ranger: The Impact of Mining Environment on a People.

Anyone accused of disrupting mining operations, whether acting alone or in a group, was terminated. Finnish immigrants were among the most militant, owing to their literacy and experience protesting against the Russian Empire. (337) Many Finns identified as *Red Finns* or socialists who believed that workers should own the mines. Blacklisted miners often had no choice but to leave the Range or turn to hard-scrabble farming on the outskirts of mining communities. Initially, Finns constituted 18% of the Range's workforce, but this percentage dropped to less than half after 1907. Because Finnish leaders supported the International Workers of the World, or the I.W.W. (also known as the Wobblies), U.S. Steel terminated or refused to hire anyone with a Finnish-sounding name. Some Finns, however, decided that mining was not worth the risks. They couldn't tolerate working in total darkness deep beneath the Earth's surface, or the idea that their injury or death would leave their widows and children destitute. After a cave-in left him buried for fifty-eight hours, Elias Pekkala said,

> *The solitude of that cold chamber was terrible, and I cannot begin to tell you one-half of the horrors I endured. Only those who had death, long drawn out, staring them in the face, can realize what I suffered.*
> (338)

---

(337)Wikipedia. 2024. "The Russification of Finland." Wikimedia Foundation. Last modified: June 16, 2024. https://en.wikipedia.org/wiki/Russification_of_Finland. Finns were mostly literate because they had to prove they could read and write before they were allowed to marry, as noted by Sevander, Mayme, and Laurie Hertzel. 1992. *They Took My Father*—University of Minnesota Press.

(338) Alanen. *The Finns*. Page 35.

Many Finns founded farming enclaves or ran saloons. Out of the 350 taverns on the Mesabi Range, 59, or nearly 20%, were owned by Finns. (339) Other confirmed socialists immigrated to the USSR in the 1930s, where, due to Stalinist policies, many unfortunately died.

After the 1916 strike, U.S. Steel adopted more subtle methods to discourage pro-union activities. Company spies known as "*dollar-a-day men*" were paid to report any anti-company sentiments they might overhear. They infiltrated community organizations, even churches, which had previously been off-limits. (340) Miners grew increasingly suspicious of English-speaking union organizers (341), and labor unrest and union activity effectively ceased until the passage of the Wagner Act in 1935. (342) Even then, the Oliver refused to sign a formal agreement with the Congress of Industrial Organizations or recognize the miners' union until 1943.

In the meantime, those fluent in English took unfair advantage of those who were not. Managers pitted ethnic groups against each other to maintain control. And abusive practices remained as before. During the Great Depression, corrupt mining officials *sold* items meant for distribution to mining families. When my father complained, company officials told him to keep his mouth shut. At that time, my father was twelve years old. To combat this and other forms of exploitation, the Oliver began offering adult English

---

(339) *They Chose Minnesota.* Page 307.

(340) Selinkski, T., dir.1999. Spies in Steel: The Dollar-a-Day Man. Duluth: T. Selinski Productions.

(341) Lamppa. *Minnesota's Iron Country.* Page 207.

(342) Lamppa. *Minnesota's Iron Country.* Page 218.

literacy classes to address unethical management practices, promote workplace safety, and enhance worker productivity. In 1907, fewer than 3% of the miners spoke English. (343) My grandfather attended night school during the winter of 1926 to become a U.S. citizen, when the mines were closed.

Mining and Its Impact

Just as the mining industry scarred the landscape of Northern Minnesota, the Iron Range had a deep and lasting impact on everyone's lives. The climate, the economy, the poverty and ethnic diversity, and the often desperate circumstances of immigrant families challenged human endurance in countless ways. It made us strong, but it wasn't without consequences.

Many Range immigrants, including some of my aunts and uncles, became dependent on pills and alcohol, which negatively affected everyone's lives. Both of my grandmothers had nervous breakdowns. One underwent electroshock therapy, while the other remained in bed for months at a time. Lacking anyone else to vent their frustrations, family members often directed their anger at their parents and siblings because, if for no other reason, they had no one else to blame. It's tempting to look back and romanticize the past. But the reality simply wasn't.

However, in their suffering, they also found a rare sort of determination that refused to accept no for an answer. A determination to make something of their lives. Despite the trials and hardships, my grandparents built on what little they had to do something more. Eight of Soroka's grandchildren graduated from college, and four earned advanced degrees, ending the family's dependence on mining. I believe this would have made them very proud. Like them, we too had been forged in iron.

---

(343) Lamppa. *Minnesota's Iron Country*. Page 205.

Chapter 8 References

Alanen, Arnold R. (2012). *The Finns in Minnesota*. St. Paul: Minnesota Historical Society Press.

Alanen, Arnold R. "Early Labor Strife." *Minnesota History*, no. Fall 1991 (1991): 247-263.

The_Locations_by_Arnold_Alanen_1982_Carson_Lake_pg_96_99_103. pdf.

Alanen, Alan R. "The Locations: Company Communities on Minnesota's Iron Ranges." Hibbing Historical Society. Accessed December 11, 2023. hibbinghistory.org/files/the-locations-by-arnold-alanen-2/.

Cameron, Linda A. 2021. Review of Civilian Conservation Corps in Minnesota, 1933–1942. Minnesota Historical Society, July 15, 2021. Civilian Conservation Corps in Minnesota, 1933–1942 | MnOpedia

Duly, William (1993). The Rusins of Minnesota. United States: Rusin Association.

Eleff, Robert M. "The 1916 Minnesota Miners' Strike Against U.S. Steel." Minnesota History 51, no. 2 (Summer 1988): 63–74.http://collections.mnhs.org/MNHistoryMagazine/articles/51/v51i02p0 63-074.pdf

Wikipedia. 2024. "Eveleth, MN." Wikimedia Foundation. Last modified: June 1, 2024. https://en.wikipedia.org/wiki/Eveleth,_Minnesota.

"Father Baraga and the Ojibwa Natives." FatherBaraga.Org. https://www.fatherbaraga.org/fatherbaragashistory.

Gall, Emily, ed. 6AD. Review of Rusyn DNA Myths and Ethnic Erasure: A Symbiotic Relationship. 6AD. rusynsociety.com

Wikipedia. 2024. "Greyhound Lines." Wikimedia Foundation. Last modified: April 18, 2024. https://en.wikipedia.org/wiki/Greyhound_Lines.

Goman, John D. 1990. *Galician Rusyns on the Iron Range.* Rohart Services Desktop Publishing.

Hibbing." https://hibbingmn.gov/283/Facts-History

Holmquist, June D. (Editor), et al., 1981. *"They Chose Minnesota: A Survey of the State's Ethnic Groups,"* St. Paul: Minnesota Historical Society Press.

Wikipedia. 2023. "Hull–Rust–Mahoning Open Pit Iron Mine." Wikimedia Foundation. Last modified: December 12, 2023. https://en.wikipedia.org/wiki/Hull%E2%80%93Rust%E2%80%93Mahoning_Open_Pit_Iron_Mine.

Iron Range Miners at Chisholm, 1912. Photograph. http://www.Miningartifacts.Org/TheMiners.Html.

Kaunonen, Gary. The Minnesota Miners' Strike that Brought Immigrant Workers Together. May 10, 2018. https://www.whatitmeanstobeamerican.org/places/the-minnesota-miners-strike-that-brought-immigrant-workers-together/.

"Keweenaw Ethnic Groups--The Slovenes." Michigan Tech. https://ethnicity.lib.mtu.edu/groups_Slovenes.html.

Lamppa, Marvin G. 2004. *Minnesota's Iron Country, Rich Ore, Rich Lives.* 1st ed. Duluth, Minnesota: Lake Superior Port Cities Inc.

Lamppa, Marvin G., contributor. *Minnesota Lost Mining Towns.* PBS North, 2019. Fifty-six hr., 47 minutes. https://www.pbs.org/show/minnesotas-lost-mining-towns/.

Lavigne, David. "Immigration to the Iron Range, 1880–1930." MNOpedia, Minnesota Historical Society, August 26, 2015. www.mnopedia.org/immigration-iron-range-1880-1930.

Lubotina, Paul. 2015 "Corporate Supported Ethnic Conflict on the Mesabi Range, 1890-1930," *Upper Country: A Journal of the Lake Superior Region*: Vol. 3, Article 2.

Lubotina, Paul 2018. "Michigan to Minnesota: The Early Development of the Mesabi Range." *Upper Country: A Journal of the Lake Superior Region*: Vol 6, Article 6.

Minnesota Lost Mining Towns (2019), PBS North Documentary. Minnesota's Lost Mining Towns | PBS

Oberly, James W. "Love at First Sight and Arrangement for Life: Investigating and Interpreting a 1910 Hungarian Migrant Marriage." *East European Genealogist 29*, no. 1 (1990): 7-23.

"Pay Day Celebration: Finlanders and Italians Fight with Rocks and Revolvers." *Mesabi Ore & Hibbing Tribune* (Hibbing, Minnesota), February 25, 1905.

Peck, Lauren. 2016. Review of Murder and Mayhem. Mn Good Age. June 28, 2016. https://www.mngoodage.com/voices/mn-history/2016/06/murder-and-mayhem/.

Rosemore, Lisa. "The Range Was Built on the Work of the Underground Mines." *Hibbing Tribune* (Hibbing, MN), June 25, 2014.

Selinkski, T., dir.1999. Spies in Steel: The Dollar-a-Day Man. Duluth: T. Selinski Productions.

Sevander, Mayme, and Laurie Hertzel. 1992. *They Took My Father—* University of Minnesota Press.

Syrjamaki, John. "The People of the Iron Range." Https://Storage.Googleapis.Com/Mnhs-Org-Support/Mn_history_articles/27/V27i03p203-215.Pdf, Minnesota Historical Society, storage.googleapis.com.

Syrjamaki, John. "Iron Range Communities." Yale University, Minnesota Historical Society, 1940, pp. 195–270
.

Tikkanen, Amy. "Uncle Sam." Britannica.
https://www.britannica.com/topic/Uncle-Sam.

Weber, Eric W. "Relocation of Hibbing 1919-1920," MNOpedia.
Minnesota Historical Society, July 23, 2021. Relocation of Hibbing,
1919–1921 | MNOpedia.

Relocation of Hibbing." https://hibbingmn.gov/283/Facts-History.

Wikipedia. 2024. "Russification of Finland." Wikimedia Foundation.
Last modified: March 24, 2024.
https://en.wikipedia.org/wiki/Russification_of_Finland.

Wikipedia. 2024. "Ukrainian Nobility of Galicia." Wikimedia
Foundation. Last modified: April 8, 2024.
https://en.wikipedia./wiki/Ukrainian_nobility_of_Galicia.

Chapter 9
Concluding Remarks

My investigation into my family's ancestry began when the Minnesota Discovery Center asked for information about the Soroka family for their Glenn Location exhibit. At first, I only planned to reply to their inquiry. But what started as notes on the back of a recycled envelope evolved into years of research and a published book. Unlike an academic's structured work plan, my methodology was mostly informal. Rather than working from a clear set of research questions, I let my discoveries guide me as I connected the remnants of Central and Eastern European history to whatever family information I could find. I took solace in knowing that even respected historians rarely have more than a few pages of concrete evidence for their biographical works, and therefore complete their accounts with numerous "could haves" and "must haves" to fill in the gaps. I'm not the first historian to expand a few pieces of evidence into a 300-page book.

My second purpose in authoring this book was to help others who might benefit from my experience. While genealogical research can be immensely rewarding, it can also lead to considerable frustration. Inaccuracies for subjects who lacked *historical significance* were of trivial importance. As borders and lexicons changed, so too did official documents. My experience has shown that databases are sporadically updated, so it pays to look again. And the way a question is framed matters just as much as the question itself.

I am deeply indebted to many individuals, organizations, and groups, including Brian Lenius, Maciej Orzechowski, Wojciech Makowiecki, Genealogic Polinica, the Minnesota Rusyn Association, and the Eastern European Genealogical Society. Fellow Rusyns, like John Righetti, John Senick, and Marie Margitan, made important suggestions to ensure accuracy and flow. Individuals whom I've never met, including Paul Magocsi, Arnold Alanen, John Syrjamaki, and Marvin Lamppa, conducted extensive research on Rusyns, immigrants, the mining industry, and life in the mining locations. Facebook groups shared photos and personal stories, while family members contributed memories, letters, and even a recorded interview. My family endured countless hours supporting my authorship. After ten years of research, I talked to many people, read lots of books, and spent countless hours online.

However, in my quest to learn about my ancestors, I gained a deeper understanding of myself. As John D. Acton said, *"History is an illumination of the soul."* Like the villagers in the old country, my parents made church and family the center of our lives. My maternal grandmother emancipated her children at the shocking age of 14. My dad and his siblings stayed loyal to each other until the very end. In both families, modest beginnings fostered resilience rarely seen today. Quitting was never an option; you found another way. Given my ancestry, it is little wonder that I have always challenged the status quo and refused to let anything stop me from achieving my goals.

Until very late in this process, I remained skeptical of my Rusyn ancestry. Relinquishing my Ukrainian identity was difficult after believing it for most of my life. I finally accepted my true identity when I discovered that my second great-grandfather's name was unmistakably Rusyn.

With that discovery, I finally embraced the words of the notable Rusyn Alexander Duchnovich: "I was, I am, and will always be, Rusyn."

Appendix A
Christmas

According to the old Julian calendar, Christmas started on January 6, on Christmas Eve. The children would go outside to look for the Christmas star. Father would dress in his best clothes and lead the family to the shed to gather fresh wheat, while the children collected armloads of straw. When the procession reached the front door of the house, Father would say "Chrystos Razdaketska" (Christ is Born).

The women and children would spread hay on the dining room table and place straw on the floor. Father would put the bundle of wheat in the dining room to symbolize God's abundance, who feeds, clothes, and protects His people. Mother would cover the hay on the table with her finest embroidered tablecloth to symbolize the manger. Then, Mother would serve the Christmas Eve dinner with twelve courses, representing the twelve apostles. Traditional Christmas dishes include kutia, kolache, meatless borscht, fried fish, pickled herring, meatless stuffed cabbage rolls, pirohy, mashed beans, popinky (mushrooms with gravy), fruit compote, and pampushky (fried donuts). The meal would begin with a prayer, and then Father would taste the kutia with a big wooden spoon—a dish made from wheat berries, poppy seeds, and honey. Sometimes, they added walnuts, dried fruit, and raisins. Afterward, each family member would taste the dish to symbolize solidarity, unity, and togetherness. There were other small ceremonies during the dinner. Father would throw a spoonful of kutia against the ceiling to see if any seeds stuck. If many seeds stuck, it was a good sign of a fruitful harvest in the coming year. After preparing the twelve dishes, the children would look for nuts, and candies would be scattered in the hay under the table. After dinner, the unmarried girls would go outside to listen to the sound of barking dogs, which would tell them from which direction their sweetheart would come. The children would dress up as shepherds and angels and go caroling, traveling from house to house and collecting hazelnuts. While singing, the women would dance. At midnight, the family would attend the liturgy and celebrate the birth of Christ. The traditional greeting is "Khrystos Razdayetsia" (Christ is Born), with the response "Slavite Yoho" (Let us glorify him).

Although Rusyn families did not exchange gifts, my great-grandfather lived in Germany for many years, where gift-giving was customary. The Christmas holy days ended on January 20th, the feast of John the Baptist.

Appendix B
Easter

Easter, known as the *Great Day* in Lemko, is the most significant religious holiday for Greek Catholics. It commemorates the forty days following the final days of Christ.

On Palm Sunday, we received blessed pussywillows. As we entered the church, we gently tapped each other on the shoulder to emulate Christ's scourging while wishing family and friends health, wealth, and happiness. We would also say, "Be as big as the willow, healthy as water, and rich as the earth," and placed our blessed willows behind sacred images and icons in our home. The following year, we burned the willows and scattered their ashes in the family garden. We commemorated Christ's passion on Holy Thursday by cleaning the entire house and preparing the Easter dinner. We were not allowed to work for the rest of Holy Week. While making the Easter bread (paska), we had to keep our minds pure.

A shroud of Christ's body was placed on the altar during noon services on Good Friday. On Easter Sunday, parishioners would carry the shroud around the church to symbolize Christ's journey from the crucifixion to the tomb. Parishioners sang "Khrystos Voskres" (Christ has risen) and responded with "Voistynu Voskres" (he has indeed risen).

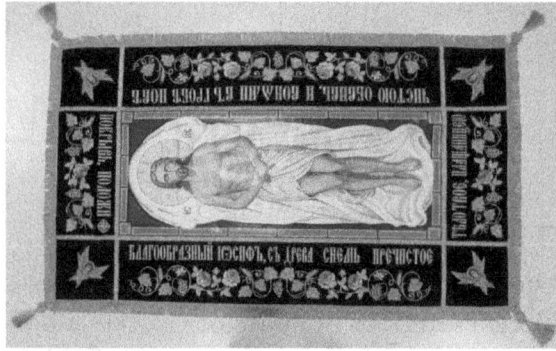

Easter Altar Linen. At Mass, we kissed Christ's wounds.

Easter baskets were blessed on Holy Saturday. Each basket was filled with bread, butter, eggs, and other items believed to represent Christ's crucifixion and resurrection.

A Traditional Easter Basket

Paska (Bread)	Christ as the bread of life
Hard-Boiled Eggs	Christ's resurrection
Hren (beets & horseradish)	Christ's crucifixion
Cheese	Moderation in all things
Ham	Abundance of Easter
Butter	Christ's goodness
Sausage	God's generosity

Symbolic meaning of Easter foods

Appendix C
Life as a Russian Cossack (344)

Cossack communities were built on principles of political and social equality. The village collectively owned land and selected its leaders democratically. Their egalitarian communities were mainly Christian but also included Jews and Muslim Tatars. The Cossacks prioritized family and loyalty to their village more than anything else. In return for their loyalty, villages established social welfare systems to support their members. The Cossacks believed that teaching all children to read and write was essential, considering illiteracy the greatest shame. They also valued cleanliness, clear thinking, honesty, hospitality, military skill, physical strength, and loyalty to the Tsar.

Public assemblies governed village life. During the 16th and 17th centuries, village assemblies approved marriages, provided dowries, and reviewed divorce requests. If a Cossack died in battle, the village supported his family. The Cossacks would never stop trying to rescue their women and children if they were taken into slavery. If the rescued women ended up having children of mixed heritage, the Cossacks would adopt them as their own.

Cossack women were known for their strong character and striking beauty. They were skilled with horses,

(344) Cossack Family Values." Nicholas Kotar. February 11, 2016. https://nicholaskotar.com/2016/02/11/cossack-family-values/.

boats, and weapons, and defended their homes while maintaining respected domestic roles within the paternalistic Cossack society.

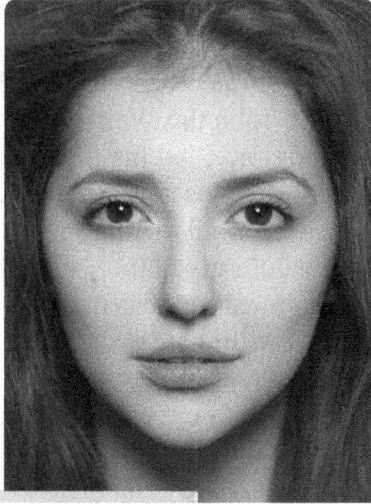

Cossack Woman (Model Photo)

      Throughout the 18th century, Cossack men wielded complete authority over their wives. Male bonding was highly valued, and people looked down on men who spent too much time with their wives or families. However, a wife was also regarded as a Cossack's most valuable asset. She managed the farm during her husband's absence and prepared the family for winter. Cossack communities showed more respect to women than those in Western Europe, allowing them to vote and own property. The groom's family provided a dowry, also known as the *bride price*, and no one could access these resources without the bride's explicit consent. Unlike Western Christianity, which adopted the Roman Empire's views on women's inferiority to ease its conversion, Eastern Christians viewed the different genders more as equals.

Cossack justice was severe. Thieves were publicly whipped, and one Cossack could sentence another to death. The Cossacks' military sentences frequently resulted in execution.

Parents strictly adhered to old traditions because Cossack life was dangerous. Boys were raised differently from girls. When a boy turned one year old, his parents held a prayer service for St. John the Warrior. He was taught to ride at age three. A boy received his first haircut on his first birthday and his second on his seventh, marking the end of childhood. After that, he would learn how to shoot and wield a saber. The village would give him his first pair of Cossack pants to celebrate his transition into manhood. Boys spent their days in the fields with their grandfathers, flocks, and horses, learning to fight and engage in warfare. By age fourteen, a Cossack boy was expected to demonstrate his skill by knocking down a flying bird with a stone.

A girl's first steps were celebrated grandly. From age five, she helped care for her siblings. For a Cossack girl, being able to sing and dance was essential. When it was time for her to start a family, her grandfather would give her a silver ring, symbolizing that she was no longer a child.

Cossack Family Image from: https://larastock.com/photo-23436-group-portrait-of-a-cossack-with-family/

When young girls reached marriageable age and young men had to prepare for military service, families often faced financial difficulties. This transition marked the costliest period in the Cossack family's life.

Appendix D
Family Recipes

Cabbage Rolls (Holubtsi)

One medium cabbage, cored and brined
½ cup apple cider vinegar
1 Tbsp salt
1 pound ground beef, 85% lean
One package of rice pilaf
One egg
1 tsp onion powder
1 tsp garlic powder
1 or 2 cans of tomato soup
2 Tbsp seasoned rice vinegar
½ cup sauerkraut

To brine the cabbage, after removing the core, place it in a Dutch oven and add water until it floats to the top. Add ½ cup of apple cider vinegar and a pinch of salt. Bring to a boil and simmer for 45 minutes. Cover and let the cabbage sit overnight. Remove the cabbage from the water bath the next day and let it drain. For the sauce, reserve 1 cup of cabbage water to mix with the tomato soup and rice vinegar.

Prepare the rice pilaf according to the package instructions. After it cools, combine it with ground beef, onion powder, garlic, and eggs and mix it like meatballs. Then, roll the cabbage leaves with the meat mixture and place one layer in a cake pan. Cover the rolls with sauerkraut and sauce, then cover the pan with aluminum foil.

You can freeze them or bake them in a 350-degree oven for 90 minutes to 2 hours.

Dumplings (Pirohy)

4 cups flour
One egg
4 Tbsp olive oil
1 cup of carbonated water

Make a well in the flour. Add the egg and olive oil. Cut into the flour, then add the water. Knead the dough for a few minutes until it is smooth. Cover with more oil and wrap tightly with plastic wrap. Rest for 1 hour or overnight in the fridge.

Potato Cheese Filling

One good-sized baking potato (or you can cheat and use instant potatoes)
One package of extra-sharp cheddar cheese
Cook the potato until very soft, then mash it with the cheese.

Sauerkraut Filling

2 cups drained sauerkraut
2 tsp of pepper

Put the kraut in a food processor and cut it fine. Fry the sauerkraut in a bit of oil, then add the pepper. Combine with four tablespoons of cottage cheese to form a binder.

Beet Relish (Hrin)

Served at Easter to symbolize what Christ received on the cross. It pairs well with ham or sausage.

One can beets
1-pound horseradish
1 tsp salt
1 Tbsp. sugar
2 ounces of vinegar

Combine in a food processor. Store it in a jar in the refrigerator.

Paska (Easter Bread)

Two pkgs. yeast
4 Tbsp warm water
1 ½ cups milk (1 cup evaporated, ½ cup water)
½ cup butter
½ cup sugar
2 tsp salt
6 cups of bread or all-purpose flour
Three eggs
1 cup of raisins (plump in water with orange extract)
2 Tbsp lemon zest

Combine the water and yeast in a bowl with one teaspoon of sugar. When it gets frothy, add 2 cups of flour and let the sponge rest for 20 minutes. Scald the milk with the sugar and butter. Let it cool. In a bowl, combine the milk mixture with 3 cups of flour, 1 cup at a time. Add the yeast mixture.

The dough will be soft and a little sticky. Do not add more flour than needed. Drain the raisins and add them to the dough along with the lemon zest. Knead well (3 minutes or so). Then, place the dough in a bowl, lightly butter the top, and cover with a damp cloth. Let it rise until it has doubled in size.

Form the dough into loaves. Before baking, mix a small amount of water with an egg yolk to create a glaze for the bread. Bake at 350°F until the internal temperature reaches 200°F. If not eaten immediately, wrap the paska in plastic wrap and freeze it, as it dries out quickly.

Infused Vodka (Nalevkas)

1-pound sour cherries
1 cup sugar
2 cups good vodka

In a quart jar, pour sugar over the cherries without shaking them, and let them ferment for at least two weeks. Stir daily. After fermentation, strain the cherries and add a bottle of good-quality vodka. Cover tightly and let it sit at room temperature for three months in a dark place. Rebottle it, allow it to age further, or drink it immediately.

Christmas Porridge (Kutia)

https://natashaskitchen.com/kutia-recipe-sweet-wheat-berry-pudding/

1 1/2 cups wheat berries (we used Hard White Winter Wheat Berries)
4 1/2 cups of milk (or water, but milk tastes better)
3/4 cups poppy seeds
1/2 cup honey
1/2 cup of raisins
2/3 cup dried apricots, chopped
2/3 cup slivered almonds (or chopped walnuts)
1/8 tsp salt

Rinse the wheat berries in cold water until the water runs clear. Then transfer them to a bowl and soak overnight in lukewarm water, adding enough water to cover them by 2 inches. The following day, drain the wheat berries, place them in a medium-sized heavy pot, and cover them with 4 1/2 cups of milk. Bring the mixture to a boil over high heat. When the milk starts to boil, reduce the heat to low, cover with a lid, and simmer until the wheat berries are very tender, 3 1/2 to 4 hours, depending on the quality of the wheat. Stir occasionally to prevent sticking and add more milk if needed to keep the wheat berries fully submerged (if you simmer over low heat, you will not have to add any more milk).

While the wheat berries are cooking, rinse 3/4 cup of poppy seeds thoroughly in a fine mesh sieve, drain them well, and transfer the seeds to a medium saucepan. Add 3 cups of water and return to a simmer (do not boil). Then cover it and let it sit for 30 minutes. You can either drain the poppy seeds thoroughly using a colander or keep the lid on and place several layers of cheesecloth over it to catch stray seeds. Pass the poppy seeds through a food processor or grinder.

Preheat the oven to 350°F. Spread 2/3 cup of slivered almonds on a baking sheet and toast for 5 minutes. Set the almonds aside and lower the temperature to 325°F. Once the wheat berries are tender, drain the milk into a glass measuring cup. Keep 1/2 cup of the cooked milk and discard the rest. Mix 1/2 cup of honey with the retained milk and stir until combined. Place the cooked wheat berries in a mixing bowl. Add the ground poppy seeds, 1/2 cup of raisins, 2/3 cup of dried, chopped apricots, 2/3 cup of toasted, slivered almonds, the honey-milk mixture, and 1/8 tsp of salt. Combine all the ingredients and transfer them to a casserole or pie dish. Bake your kutia uncovered for 20 minutes at 325°F. Remove the kutia from the oven, cover it with aluminum foil, and let it rest for 15 minutes. Serve it warm or cold. The longer it rests, the more flavor it develops. Kutia will stay fresh in the fridge for two weeks.

Nut Roll (Potica)

Thought to represent Christ's crown of thorns.

Ingredients for Dough:
1 Cup Whole Milk
½ Cup Sugar
2 Tsp Salt
½ cup butter
One package of dry yeast (2 ½ tsp)
4 Eggs
4 to 5 Cups Flour

Ingredients for Filling:
1/2 cup of butter
1 Cup Honey
1 Cup Sugar
1 Cup Milk
2 Pounds Ground Walnuts
2 eggs, well beaten
1 Cup Whipping Cream
1 Tbsp. lemon juice

Scald the milk, then add sugar, salt, and butter. Set it aside to cool. Dissolve the yeast in ½ cup of warm water with 2 tsp of sugar and set aside until it becomes foamy. Next, incorporate the yeast into the milk. Add well-beaten eggs, followed by flour, one cup at a time, mixing by hand or with an electric mixer. Continue adding flour until the dough can be handled without sticking to your hands. Knead the dough for about 20 minutes. Cover the dough in a greased bowl and let it rest for 2 hours. Spread the dough on a table covered with a fitted sheet. Roll the dough to the edge of the table and stretch it until it's paper-thin. Spread the filling over the dough, then roll it up like a jelly roll. Cut the roll into pieces that fit into greased bread pans. Let it sit for 30 minutes, then bake in a preheated oven at 325 degrees for approximately 1 hour.

Filling: Melt butter, add honey, sugar, and milk, and bring to a rolling boil. Cool. Mix in nuts, beaten eggs, whipping cream, and lemon juice.

Appendix E
Ancestral Records

My great-grandfather, Michal's parents were Hryce (also known as Gregory or Harry) Soroka and Anna Kowalsky. Hryce was the son of Lukasz Soroka and Maria Dunda. Maria was the daughter of Jakub and Anna Dunda, peasants from Wola Michowa. Despite being incredibly young, Anna Kowalsky was a widow when she married Hryce. She married her first husband at the age of fourteen; he was fifteen years old. Her first husband died from a disease or possibly during an epidemic.

Anna and Hryce married in 1829 when she was seventeen and he was nineteen. Based on her surname, I assume Anna was of Polish descent. In Polish, Kowal means blacksmith. Marrying someone of Polish descent may have been economically advantageous because, during the mid-19th century, Poles generally held a higher social status than Ruthenians. Fluency in Polish expanded one's career options beyond agriculture.

Together, Anna and Hryce had eight children: Timothy (1831), Maks (1834), Maria (1838), Stefanus (1841), Michal (1843), Joannes (1846), and Josephus (1851). All survived to adulthood except for a daughter, Anna, who died as an infant in 1849. This was an incredible achievement, given the region's poverty. Michal's family did not fare as well, which may indicate increasingly difficult circumstances. Anna and Hryce's children were born in the same residence (house number 42).

My paternal great-great-great-grandfather, Lukasz Soroka, was born sometime between 1757 and 1763. He married at nineteen and died at approximately age 90 in 1847. Maria was born in 1771, married at the age of 17, and died in 1838 at the age of 67. They had five children together: Maria (born in 1806, died as an infant), Basilus (born in 1808), Hryce (born in 1811), Theodorus (born in 1813), and Parascevia (born in 1815). Only Parascevia was born in house number 42, the same home where both Lukasz and Maria died. Before moving to Wola Michowa, the family may have lived in Radoszyce.

My grandmother's brother, Stefan Syvak (later known as Steve Savak), immigrated to the United States in 1904 at the age of 21. He purchased a farm and worked at the Monroe Mine outside Chisholm. He had a wife in the old country who presumably died, so in 1927, Stefan married Ewa (Eva) Sawaczka, a widow with three children. He was 42 at the time. Ewa immigrated from Poland in 1910. Following their marriage in Ohio, they bought a farm in Oneida, New York. Steve died in 1963, and Eva passed away in 1972. New York census data reported that Steve and Eva's son, John, was born in New York in 1927. John served in the US Navy and married Rose Washeleski in October 1957. Rose was born in 1930 in Fell, Pennsylvania; her father, Joseph, was a coal miner. Rose's parents were born in Poland, and the family had ten children, with Rose being the youngest.

My grandmother's older sister, Ann Syvak, immigrated to the United States sometime before 1908. In 1909, at age 20, she married a bartender named Matthew Valliskey in Syracuse, New York. According to 1920 census data, Matthew was born in Oslawica, Austria, a village about seven miles from Wola Michowa. He emigrated from Bremen in 1898. Ann and Matthew had a son, Stephen, born in 1911, and a daughter, Julia, born in 1916. Matthew became a naturalized citizen in 1913 but reported being a widower in the 1920 census. Ann may have died in

childbirth or from a heart ailment, common in my
grandmother's family. After Ann passed away, Matthew
lived with his sister and brother-in-law, but later married a
Ukrainian woman named Lena, who was 14 years his junior.
He worked as a railroad supervisor, and his final resting
place is in the St. John the Baptist Ukrainian Catholic
Cemetery in Rome, New York. He died the year I was born.

Appendix F
Documents

Nicholas's Birth Certificate

Cadastral Maps—Soroka Parcels

Soroka Land Records (Plot 49 is the residence)

The 40th Infantry Regiment in Galicia was part of the Austrian Empire's military forces during the early 19th century. This regiment primarily recruited soldiers from various regions within Galicia, including Wola Michowa.

The soldiers in the 40th Infantry Regiment were typically trained for traditional battlefield roles such as forming battle lines, engaging in close combat, and executing coordinated maneuvers. The regiment included:

4.   **Infantrymen**: The main force, equipped with muskets and bayonets.

5.   **Grenadiers**: Elite troops known for their strength and bravery, often leading assaults.

6.   **Light Infantry**: Specialized in skirmishing and reconnaissance, operating in more flexible formations

These well-disciplined soldiers played crucial roles in the regiment's military campaigns throughout the 19th century.

Source: "An Overview of Galician Military Records between 1781-1865." April 7, 2022. https://galicia-gen.com/galician-military-records-between-1781-1865/.

Certificate of Marriage

STATE OF MINNESOTA, } ss
COUNTY OF ST. LOUIS

I Hereby Certify, that on the 25th day of November in the year of our Lord one thousand nine hundred and twelve at Chisholm in said County, I the undersigned, a Catholic Priest did join in the holy bonds of Matrimony, according to the laws of this State,

Nick Saroka

of the County of St. Louis State of Minnesota and

Mary Sovak (Savok)

of the County of St. Louis State of Minnesota in presence of

Juan Kostio

Katherine Fromli
Witness:

Rev. J. E. Schiffrer
Officiating

I hereby certify that the above is a true and correct copy of the Certificate of Marriage

of Nick Saroka (Soroka)

and Mary Sovak (Savok)

on file and of record in this office on page 141 of Volume I-1 of Marriage Records

under date of December 15th 19 12

WITNESS MY HAND AND SEAL of office at Duluth, Minn.

this 11th day of December 1957

FRED ASH, Clerk of District Court,

By _[signature]_
Deputy Clerk.

64

U. S. DEPARTMENT OF LABOR
NATURALIZATION SERVICE

No. 1564

UNITED STATES OF AMERICA

PETITION FOR NATURALIZATION

To the Honorable the .... District .... Court of .... St. Louis County .... at Hibbing, Minnesota

The petition of .... Nick Soroka .... hereby filed, respectfully showeth:

First. My place of residence is .... 1st .... Glen Location, Chisholm, Minnesota
(Give number, street, city or town, and State.)

Second. My occupation is .... Miner

Third. I was born on the 19th day of .... November .... anno Domini 1887, at .... Wila Mickzow, Poland

Fourth. I emigrated to the United States from .... Hamburg, Germany .... on or about the 1st day of .... October
anno Domini 19.. and arrived in the United States, at the port of .... New York, N.Y. .... on the 16 day of October .... anno Domini 1919
on the vessel .... Batavia
(If the alien arrived otherwise than by vessel, the character of conveyance or name of transportation company should be given.)

Fifth. I declared my intention to become a citizen of the United States on the .... day of .... October .... anno Domini 919
at .... Hibbing .... in the District .... Court of .... St. Louis County Minnesota

Sixth. I am married. My wife's name is .... Mary .... she was born on the 7th day of .... March, anno Domini 1893
Sprotuck, Poland .... and now resides at .... Chisholm, Minnesota
(Give number, street, city or town, and State.)

I have five children, and the names, dates, and places of birth, and places of residence of each of said children are as follows:

William, born July 7th, 1914; Steve, born January 16th, 1916;
John, born April 18th, 1918; Mike, born September 7(?);
Richard, Frank, born February 13th, 1923, all born at
Chisholm, Minnesota and all reside with parents.

Seventh. I am not a disbeliever in or opposed to organized government or a member of or affiliated with any organization or body of persons teaching disbelief in or opposed to organized government. I am not a polygamist nor a believer in the practice of polygamy. I am attached to the principles of the Constitution of the United States, and it is my intention to become a citizen of the United States and to renounce absolutely and forever all allegiance and fidelity to any foreign prince, potentate, state, or sovereignty, and particularly to .... the Republic of Poland .... of whom at this time I am a subject, and it is my intention to reside permanently in the United States.

Grandpa Nick

www.ingramcontent.com/pod-product-compliance
Lightning Source LLC
Chambersburg PA
CBHW071834270326
41929CB00013B/1992